This book is for
Anne Caitlin Robinson Marsh
Siobhan Eleanor Wise Marsh
Andrew David Whitcomb Marsh
and forever in our hearts
David Scott Marsh

The ABCs of Autism in the Classroom

SETTING THE STAGE FOR SUCCESS

Wendela Whitcomb Marsh, MA, BCBA, RSD

The ABCs of Autism in the Classroom:
Setting the Stage for Success

All marketing and publishing rights guaranteed to and reserved by:

FUTURE HORIZONS INC.

721 W. Abram Street
Arlington, TX 76013
(800) 489-0727
(817) 277-0727
(817) 277-2270 (fax)
E-mail: info@fhautism.com
www.fhautism.com

Cover & interior design by John Yacio III

ISBN: 9781941765685

Acknowledgements

This book would not have been written without the encouragement and support of many.

My parents: David and Susanne Whitcomb, who instilled and nurtured a deep desire to learn, and who served as loving and discerning mentors throughout their lifetimes.

My siblings, writers all: Jonathan David Whitcomb, Cynthia Whitcomb, Laura Louise Whitcomb. You have inspired me to follow in your footsteps.

My readers: Cynthia Susanne Whitcomb, Cherie Walters, Laura Whitcomb, and Diane Hagood, for never complaining when I sent you chapter after chapter to review for me, and for making this a better book.

Writers Support Group: Linda Leslie, Kristi Negri, Cherie Walters, Cynthia Whitcomb, Laura Whitcomb. Thank you for encouraging me, listening to my dreams, and believing they could come true.

"Chez" Writers who Lunch: Pamela Smith Hill, Cynthia Whitcomb, Laura Whitcomb, for celebrating this book with me.

My Managing Editor, Rose Heredia-Bechtel, for taking a chance on a new author and guiding me on the path to publication.

Jennifer Gilpin-Yacio, Future Horizon's president, for giving me the opportunity to publish this book.

Authors who have inspired me and from whom I continue to learn: Ellen Notbohm. Tony Attwood. Temple Grandin. Raymond Miltenberger.

Dear friends: Diane Cords Hagood. Richard Scaffidi. You always believed I could do this, and apparently you were right.

Contributors for *In Their Own Words*: Aidan Mondo, Anne Marsh, CD, Cat, DW, Elliot Cook, Joseph Walker, MJS, Sean Robinson. Thank you for sharing your stories so that teachers might learn from your experiences. You are awesome!

I am incredibly grateful for my children, Anne, Siobhan, Dave, whose unwavering love, support, and patience carried me through the writing and rewriting of this book. You continue to teach me every day.

Finally, David Scott Marsh, source of inspiration and love in this life and beyond.

CONTENTS

CONTENTS

CONTENTS

CONTENTS

Prologue

What's the biggest challenge facing teachers today? Behavior. And which students present the most baffling and unique behavior problems? Our awesome kids on the autism spectrum. We love them, but it can be difficult to understand and deal with their challenging behaviors.

Behavior analysts understand behaviors of those with autism and the science behind behavior change. There is an overwhelming amount of research supporting strategies which have been proven to be effective in improving classroom behavior. We know which techniques will work successfully in the classroom, because the evidence supports it.

But behavior analysts aren't in the classroom; teachers are. And most teachers can't call a behavior analyst every time a behavior problem crops up. Even when they do call in a behavior analyst, they might not understand all that talk about the "discriminative stimulus" and the "conditioned reinforcer." It's all so dry and confusing. Teachers don't have time to wade through all that jargon, they're too busy teaching. So what's a teacher to do when a student throws a chair, or bites her hand, or refuses to work? It's up to teachers to figure out solutions before the behavior gets worse. They need help.

That's why this book was written. *The ABCs of Autism in the Classroom: Setting the Stage for Success* was written by a Board Certified Behavior Analyst® who was also a teacher for many years, as well as an autism mom. Here you will find evidence-based, research-supported behavioral tools presented in teacher-friendly language. You'll meet a virtual village of students with problem behaviors you might find in your own classroom. You'll also read stories shared by kids and adults on the autism spectrum in their own words.

How can you use this book? Chapters (scenes) could provide topics for discussion at staff meetings at your school. If you have a study group or teachers' book club, I hope the discussion topics and questions will spark some in-depth conversations about autism and behavior. If you don't have a support network, start one. As teachers, you have an awesome responsibility toward the next generation. It can be as stressful as it is fulfilling, so don't try to do it alone.

Finally, thank you for the amazing work you do every day. The difference you make in your students' lives spreads in ripples beyond what you may ever know.

ACT I
Learning the Basics

The thing about being autistic is that you gradually get less and less autistic, because you keep learning, you keep learning how to behave. It's like being in a play; I'm always in a play.

~ *Temple Grandin*

Knowledge is the wing wherewith we fly ...

~ *William Shakespeare*

Scene One

Autism: Studying the Script

I f you are a teacher, you probably already know something about *autism spectrum disorder (ASD)*. By now, pretty much everyone has heard of autism, and a lot of us think we know something about it.

People may picture *Rain Man*, or *Temple Grandin*, or they may imagine a quirky billionaire computer genius, or a silent child rocking in a corner, flapping his hands and staring at the wall. Some may think of a nephew or niece, a neighbor, a student, a stranger seen in a supermarket, or a son or daughter. But how much do we really understand about the autism spectrum, and the wide range of people whose lives it touches? Let's pick up the script and get started, so we can set the stage for our students' success.

What Autism Isn't, and What It Is

Autism is not a disease. It cannot be diagnosed with a blood test or brain scan. It cannot be "caught" like a cold, and it cannot be prevented. (This doesn't mean we can't work with a child to learn the skills needed to cope and succeed in a *neurotypical* world. We can, and we do.)

Autism is not a parenting problem. It is not learned, it is no one's fault, and there is no one to blame.

It's not true that all children with autism avoid eye contact, or that anyone who makes eye contact must not have autism. There is no one single behavior whose presence or absence confirms or rules out autism.

As a teacher, don't dismiss ASD behaviors as being somehow a product of the home environment. Autism is not caused by poor parenting skills. It's not caused by poor teaching skills, either, but there are skills that both parents and teachers can practice to help students with autism learn and achieve.

Autism is not a discipline or behavior problem. Taking away his recess, sending him to the office, or suspending him from school will not cure autism, either. This does not mean that challenging behaviors cannot be changed. Many strategies and interventions based on the science of applied behavior analysis (ABA) are effective in making important behavior changes; but not withholding recess.

There are a lot of things that autism isn't, but what exactly is autism?

Autism is a *neurobiological developmental* condition. It is a combination of characteristics or behaviors. It's called autism spectrum disorder because of the wide range, or spectrum of characteristics, levels of severity, and manifestations.

Each person on the autism spectrum is unique. There are many traits or characteristics associated with the spectrum, and your student may have any number of them, in many different combinations, at varying levels of intensity.

Symptoms may significantly interfere with learning one day, but not at all the next day. This doesn't mean the student was faking the symptoms, only that symptom severity, and ability to cope, can change from day to day.

Some students are only minimally affected by autism. These students may require some level of support at times in their lives, but they may have the potential for complete independence. This includes those who, in the past, have been identified with *Asperger's disorder*, also called *Asperger's syndrome*, which is no longer a separate diagnosis in the USA.

Other students are more significantly affected or exhibit a greater number of autism behaviors and characteristics, often combined with *intellectual disability (ID)*. They may need substantial lifelong support.

There is a lot we don't know yet about autism. We don't know enough about the causes, but we do know it is not caused by vaccines or immunizations. Unfortunately, this rumor lives on despite many, many research studies that show zero correlation. The fact that some children with autism do not show symptoms until they are toddlers, around the time they receive vaccinations, helps fuel the fire, but there is no evidence supporting a link between autism and immunizations.

We know there is no cure.

But scientists are studying, doing research, and learning more and more every day about this complex and fascinating condition called autism.

We know our students did not choose to have autism, and they cannot choose to become *neurotypical* (or *NT*—not on the spectrum). While they may learn to control unwanted behaviors associated with autism (and we hope they do, with our help), they will not "grow out of it." Autism is, and will continue to be, a big part of their lives. It's a big part of the lives of the people who love them, care for them, and teach them, too.

But autism is not the only thing that makes them who they are. As Stephen Shore has said (and many have quoted), "If you've met one person with autism, you've met one person with autism."

Our students on the spectrum deserve the same educational opportunities that their neurotypical peers have, but sometimes their behaviors get in the way of their own success. We can help them master their own behaviors so they can perform at their best in our classrooms. Then we can help them take their show on the road: into their homes, other classrooms, communities, and the world after school.

But first, we need to learn more about autism.

Characteristics of Autism

The presence or absence of a number of symptoms of autism give us the diagnosis. There are two ways of identifying autism. A child may have a clinical or medical diagnosis from a clinical psychologist, psychiatrist, neurologist, or other qualified, licensed professional. In the USA, the *Diagnostic and Statistical Manual of Mental Disorders, Fifth Edition (DSM-5)* is used to help professionals identify or rule out a range of disorders, including autism spectrum disorder. Within the school system in the United States, a student may be identified as meeting eligibility criteria as a student with autism under the *Code of Federal Regulations (CFR)* for special education, usually after evaluation by a school psychologist.

Clinical Diagnosis Using DSM-5

The DSM-5 identifies two major areas of deficit associated with autism spectrum disorder (ASD):

- social communication and interaction
- restricted, repetitive patterns of behavior, interests or activities

There are only two, but these two characteristics affect a person's life in many significant ways.

Communication, for example, includes both verbal communication—talking—and nonverbal communication such as gestures, signs, facial expressions, or eye contact. It includes *expressive* communication, such as speaking, writing, or using signs, gestures, or other nonverbal communication so that other people can understand them. It also includes *receptive* communication, such as listening, reading, or understanding and interpreting other's speech, signs, gestures, facial expressions, and tone.

Not only are all of these communication challenges part of the autism spectrum, but *social interaction* is also included in this single major characteristic.

Social communication is not just being able to respond when someone makes a social approach ("Do you want to play with us?"), but it is also being able to initiate socially ("Can I play with you?"). It is not only the ability to carry on a back-and-forth conversation, but being able to relate to someone else's topic of conversation rather than changing the subject and lecturing on their own favorite topic. Interaction is not just making eye contact and smiling on one's own terms, but responding to other's attempts to make contact, demonstrating *social-emotional reciprocity*. When your students engage in conversation, share their excitement when something good happens to a friend, commiserate and comfort a friend who is hurt or upset, or cooperate to play a game or work on a group project, they are using social-emotional reciprocity. Your students on the spectrum may not engage in the typical social chat about their weekends, or show their empathy when a friend is hurt or upset. This doesn't mean they don't feel empathy—they often feel very deeply for others, but are at a loss as to what to do or how to express their feelings.

Social communication is also noticing and paying attention to what other people are noticing and paying attention to, or *joint attention*. When a preschooler points to a picture of his favorite TV character and looks back and forth between your eyes and the picture to make sure you see what he's pointing at, he is initiating joint attention. When your students follow along in group discussions or look at the illustrations of the book you are showing to the class, they are engaging in joint attention. Your students with autism may not look at what their classmates are pointing at, or they may not follow along in back-and-forth conversations.

Another aspect of social communication is *sharing enjoyment*. At school, students share enjoyment when they tell a friend about their weekend or show them a new game or book. Another way of sharing enjoyment is showing interest in their friend's weekend or the book or toy their friend shows them. Any time you say something like "what a beautiful sunset!", you are sharing your enjoyment with the people around you. In contrast, your student with autism may never show their classmates a picture they drew, or call others over to see when they have found an unusual leaf or insect on the playground.

Then there's the *restricted*, repetitive patterns of behavior, interests, or activities. For some, restricted interests can get in the way of learning. Perhaps a student only wants to read books about astronomy, draw pictures of stars and moons, and lecture her classmates at length on her rationale for keeping Pluto as a planet. The only math problems she will do are word problems that include astronomy-related themes. (If solar system "A" has nine planets, and solar system "B" has five planets, how many planets are there in both solar systems?) If she won't listen to stories on other topics or participate in classroom activities that are astronomy-free, her education may suffer. The same is true for the boy who loves only trains, or the one who is constantly replaying his favorite movie in his head, line for line, and doesn't notice what is going on in the classroom.

Repetitive actions, *mannerisms*, or unusual behaviors can set a child apart from other children. One child walks around the perimeter of the playground staring at her feet throughout every recess. Another flaps his hands and bounces up and down when he is excited, such as when the answer to a math problem is a palindrome ("494! It's the same frontwards and backwards!"). These behaviors are different, or unexpected. Their classmates may think they act "weird" or "crazy." When our ASD students display unusual behaviors in addition to weakness in social interaction, they are often left isolated and alone in class, on the playground, or in the cafeteria.

Educational Eligibility Using CFR Criteria

While similar to the DSM-5, the special education Code of Federal Regulations (CFR) defines autism as it relates to a school setting to determine if a student may be eligible for special education services. According to the *Individuals with Disabilities Education Act (IDEA)*:

> Autism means a developmental disability significantly affecting verbal and nonverbal communication and social interaction, generally evident before age three, that adversely affects a child's

educational performance. Other characteristics often associated with autism are engagement in repetitive activities and stereotyped movements, resistance to environmental change or change in daily routines, and unusual responses to sensory experiences.

These are the characteristics that are evaluated by a school psychologist and documented in order for your student to be eligible for an *Individualized Education Program (IEP)* as a student with autism. In addition to the communication and repetitive activities and movements also noted in the DSM-5, the CFR also notes two other characteristics: resistance to change in daily routines, and unusual responses to sensory experiences.

Resistance to Change

Resistance to change in environment or routines can affect behavior. If the class goes to the auditorium or to another classroom for a lesson, it may be difficult for our student on the spectrum to handle the change. If your classroom routine is different one day, or if there is a substitute teacher, this also is challenging for our students with autism.

Sensory Responses

Unusual responses to sensory experiences may lead to behavior problems. One child may get dizzy and have to shut her eyes or look away every time you wear that striped shirt. Another may get a severe headache when he hears the lawnmower across campus. You may have a student unable to enter the restroom within several hours of it being cleaned because the lingering chemical smell makes him nauseated, or a student who cannot touch his carpet square at circle time because of the texture. Lunch and snack time are difficult for students with aversions to food tastes or textures. You may need to put on your detective hat to figure out what is going on when behavior has its roots in sensory experiences.

Theories

Experts in the field of autism have developed theories about some of the unusual behaviors and characteristics associated with autism, including theories related to delayed *theory of mind (ToM), weak central coherence*, impaired *executive function*, and challenges of *sensory processing.*

Delayed Theory of Mind

Delayed *theory of mind (ToM)* has been studied by Simon Baron-Cohen, Alan M. Leslie, and Uta Frith. They concluded that children with autism have a specific deficit in ToM, which is the ability to think about what another person is thinking, and to realize that their thoughts may differ from one's own thoughts.

Your ASD student may say, "What was that food I had when I stayed with Grandma and Grandpa? You know, it was in the blue dish. What was that?" He expects you to remember something he experienced, even though you weren't there at the time. This shows a lack of ToM.

A first grader may assume that because he knows all about the ancient Aztecs, then everyone knows about them. When he finds out his classmates have no idea what he is talking about, he believes they must be stupid. When you don't have theory of mind, anything that you know is thought to be common knowledge.

A student who can't put himself in someone else's shoes may not offer sympathy or show he cares when a friend's grandfather dies. It looks like he lacks empathy, but in fact he may not have the ToM to figure out how his friend is feeling. If he is told that his friend feels the same way he felt when his dog died, then he can understand and empathize, even if he doesn't know what to say or do to help his friend feel better.

ToM is unrelated to intellectual disability (ID). Children with ID who have a mental age of about four years old demonstrate ToM, but even highly intelligent students with autism may have trouble understanding what someone else may be thinking. They often assume that everyone sees the world exactly as they do. It could explain why so many children with autism seem to lack flexible, imaginative pretend play and social understanding.

The Sally-Ann Test is Baron-Cohen, Leslie, and Frith's test of ToM: the ability to realize that others have a different perspective or understand things differently than you do. In this test, the child is introduced to two dolls: Sally and Ann. Sally has a basket, and Ann has a box. Sally also has a marble. She puts her marble in her basket so she can play with it later, and then she goes outside. After she leaves, Ann takes the marble out of Sally's basket and puts it into her own box, and then she goes away. Sally comes back and wants to play with her marble. The question is, where will she look for the marble? Typical children who are four years old or older, and children with intellectual disability who have a mental age of four or older, correctly predict that Sally will look in her basket. They realize that Sally was not here when Ann moved the marble, so she doesn't know what we know: that the marble is not where she left it.

Children with a mental age of three or younger, and many people with autism who are much older than four (even many intelligent adults) will predict that Sally will look in the box for the marble. Why? Because the marble is in the box, of course. If the student with autism knows where the marble is, then everyone must know.

Weak Central Coherence Theory

Weak central coherence has been described by Francesca Happe and Uta Frith as a "detail-focused processing style." Some people on the spectrum focus so intensely on details, even insignificant ones, that they completely miss the main idea. They can't see the forest for the trees. In school and in much of life this is considered a weakness.

One of Uta Frith's research studies involved jigsaw puzzles. She found that children with autism did just as well, or better, when the puzzle pieces were placed on the table upside down, cardboard-side up, so they couldn't look at the picture to put the puzzle together. They weren't using the information from the "big picture" at all, but were focusing on the small details, the shapes of the pieces.

Imagine you have just finished teaching a unit on Paul Bunyan and you ask your students to write a paragraph about what they learned. One student on the spectrum may write a single sentence stating that Paul Bunyan has a beard. Another may write a lengthy dissertation on the various colors of oxen in the animal world, to support the position that Babe could not possibly have been a blue ox. Each of these students completely overlooked the main ideas of the folk hero's story. That's weak central coherence.

Some tasks require strong attention to detail. Many of our students on the spectrum excel at activities that require hyper-focused attention and concentration, especially within their areas of strong interest. They often carry the weight of a group project themselves, taking care of every detail perfectly, even though this may not carry over into other academic assignments.

Impaired Executive Function Theory

Executive function (EF) is a set of mental processes that connect experience with action; we need EF to plan, organize, evaluate options, and predict potential outcomes. When EF is impaired, students are more likely to be disorganized and unsystematic, to miss assignment deadlines, and to have difficulty solving problems and making decisions. This deficit leads to significant challenges in daily school life, such as completing and turning in long-term assignments as well as daily homework. You may notice that your students with other learning disabilities or attention deficit-hyperactive disorder also struggle with EF.

Sensory Processing Theory

Much has been written about *sensory processing* or *sensory integration*, in which the brain has trouble receiving, understanding, integrating, processing, or responding to information brought in through the senses. Currently, neither sensory processing disorder nor sensory integration disorder are recognized in the DSM-5 or the CFR as stand-alone disabilities. However, many people, including many on the autism spectrum, experience unusual sensory responses and sensory-based behaviors, and this is part of the CFR eligibility for autism.

The senses that may be affected include *visual*, (sight) *auditory* (hearing), *gustatory* (taste), *olfactory* (smell), *tactile* (touch), *proprioceptive* (pressure), and *vestibular* (balance).

Some sensory responses are *sensory-seeking behaviors*.

Students who seek visual stimulation may give close visual inspection to tiny things and can get distracted from the lesson by staring at the venetian blinds or the ceiling fan. Visual supports and visual schedules will be appreciated by these visual learners.

Students who seek auditory stimulation may make noises, tap, or hum throughout the day, and may have super hearing. They are often distracted by the sound of a distant train or the murmur of conversation across the room. They may enjoy listening to classical music while working, at top volume.

Students who seek gustatory sensation may put pencils or their fingers in their mouths, and younger children may lick, bite, or chew on inedible objects. In extreme cases they may be prescribed a food-grade firm plastic "chew" fidget that they can safely bite or chew on.

Those who seek olfactory stimulation may become fascinated by the scent of markers or play dough, or may sniff all food before tasting it. They might even sniff other people. They would enjoy a free-time station that included categorizing smells by sorting bottles with cotton balls soaked in vanilla, lavender, or other oils or extracts.

Students who seek tactile stimulation can't seem to keep their hands to themselves. They want to touch everything around them, and they work well with hands-on *manipulatives*.

A proprioceptive-seeking student may crave long, strong hugs, and may bump into walls, furniture, and people. Some try to press themselves into a small, tight space such as behind furniture. Others stomp their feet to feel that deep pressure up through their legs. When under stress, some drop to the ground, needing to feel their full body pressed to the hard surface. They may be provided with a pressure vest, which should only be used as prescribed by the professional making the recommendation. If you have a trampoline available at your school, allowing a short period of bouncing before a challenging academic subject may help focus. Jumping rope or doing jumping jacks can have the same kind of positive effect.

Vestibular-seeking students may twirl around for long periods of time. You wonder how they can keep it up without getting dizzy. You might see them on the playground turning around and around on a swing so that the chain is twisted, and then letting go to let it spin them. Younger children enjoy sit-and-spin equipment, and older students might hold onto a pole with one hand and walk around it. Some may be risk-takers, trying to climb up onto the highest point or balance on the tops of walls, fences, or furniture. A balance beam may be just the kind of P.E. activity that will help them meet their sensory need.

Other responses are sensory-avoiding behaviors, such as overreacting to typical sensory experiences.

Students who avoid visual input may squint or cover their eyes and complain about the sun when they go outside. They may become dizzy or get a headache when they see certain patterns, like stripes of a particular width or plaids. Bright colors and crowded bulletin boards and walls can be overwhelming for them. Consider providing a plain, unadorned study carrel they can choose if overwhelmed. These students may also benefit from being allowed to wear a hat, sunshade, or dark glasses outside.

Those who avoid auditory input are the ones covering their ears and shouting for everyone to be quiet. They may become completely overwhelmed by people cheering at a game or applauding after a performance. In gym they cringe at the echoes of bouncing balls, or the sound of tennis shoes squeaking on the floor. Consider providing noise-cancelling headphones in the classroom and earbuds or earplugs in other settings.

Students who avoid gustatory input are probably picky eaters and may not eat lunch at school. Be aware if they have difficulty coping during the afternoon and check to see if they have eaten.

Olfactory-avoiding students are put off by normal smells in the environment. Your favorite perfume or cologne, your coffee breath, the popcorn you popped in the room yesterday, or the smell of the chemical cleaners the custodian uses may be overpowering for these students. If the problem is extreme, consider allowing a cloth handkerchief which has been soaked in an extract or oil the student finds pleasant or calming, such as lavender, vanilla, or lemon extract. The handkerchief could be held to the nose to block out unpleasant odors.

Your tactile-avoiding students should not be touched, especially unexpectedly, as they may be overly startled. Touch can escalate a problem behavior for these students.

Students who avoid proprioceptive or deep pressure may have a weak pencil grasp and may walk softly or tiptoe. They will not want to be bumped, and may interpret unintentional jostling in line as an attack.

Those who avoid vestibular input are likely to have poor balance, and may avoid physical activities which require their feet to leave the ground, such as running or jumping.

Autism and Learning

Any of these core characteristics of autism could get in the way of our students on the spectrum mastering their challenging behaviors so they can learn. Students who have more than one of the characteristics will experience greater challenges; and let's face it, most students on the spectrum have far more than one spectrum-disorder behavior. You'll even find that many of your students who are not on the spectrum have at least one of the characteristics. Behavioral strategies that work for your students with autism can work for your other challenging students as well.

Five Students with Autism

Throughout this book, we will be getting to know five example students with autism and examining their problem behaviors more closely. These students are Anthony, who acts out, disruptive Destiny, defiant Daniel, Sophia, who engages in self-injurious behaviors, and aggressive Aiden. Let's meet them.

Example One: Introducing Anthony, Who Acts Out

Anthony is a seven-year-old boy with a diagnosis of autism, being served in a *special day class (SDC)* at his local elementary school. His classroom contains twelve students ranging from first grade through third grade, who are identified as having either *specific learning disability (SLD)* or mild-to-moderate *intellectual disability (ID)*. This is his teacher's second year, and Anthony is the first ASD student she has taught. Anthony lives with his mother, who is a receptionist in a medical building. He is the only child. The custodial agreement stipulates that he sees his father, a grocery store manager, on weekends and some holidays. Record review of assessments reveals that he is verbal, although he learned to speak late; his first words were spoken at age four, and his use of language continues to be delayed and simplistic. His nonverbal cognitive ability is estimated to be within the average to low average range. His interests include dinosaurs and water play; he often stays at the sink running the water through his fingers long after he has finished washing his hands.

Example Two: Introducing Disruptive Destiny

Destiny is a ten-year-old girl identified as being on the autism spectrum, and is considered "high functioning." She is in a general education fourth grade classroom and has above-average academic skills. She frequently comments that her classmates are "idiots." Destiny's teacher, an experienced teacher near retirement, has expressed that she does not believe Destiny has autism because she is so smart and she makes eye contact. Destiny lives with both parents, who are professors at the local university. She is the only child, and also the only grandchild on both sides of the family. Her parents are strong advocates for her rights as a disabled child; her grandparents do not believe that she has a disability. Parents and grandparents attend every IEP meeting. Assessment revealed that Destiny talked early, speaking her first meaningful words before her first birthday. Her ability to engage in reciprocal, back-and-forth social conversations, especially on topics that are not of her choosing, is an area of significant weakness. She learned to read with comprehension at age four years. Her verbal cognitive ability is estimated to be within the superior to very superior range, and her nonverbal ability is high average to superior. Her interests are reading and *Harry Potter*.

Example Three: Introducing Defiant Daniel

Daniel is twelve years old and has been identified as a student with autism and an unspecified learning disability. He is in a special day class (SDC) at his local middle school with classmates in grades fifth through eigth who have mild-to-moderate ID. His teacher is experienced in teaching mild-to-moderate disabilities as well as moderate to severe; she has not had a student with autism yet, but is confident that her teaching strategies will be as successful with Daniel as they have been with his classmates. Daniel is the middle of three children; his parents are busy entrepreneurs in the computer industry. His nonverbal cognitive ability is estimated in the average range, and his verbal ability is in the extremely low range; he was late to develop speech. He has an intensely strong interest in all things technical, and loves to spend hours on the computer or with an electronic tablet or smart phone.

Example Four: Introducing Sophia, and her Self-Injurious Behavior (SIB)

Sophia is six years old and has a diagnosis of autism spectrum disorder and a history of *self-injurious behavior (SIB)*. She is being served in a specialized classroom for students with moderate to severe disabilities operated by her County Office of Education (COE) because her local school district did not have an appropriate program for her. Her teacher is an experienced special educator with a long career working with severely disabled students. Sophia's mother is retired from a career as an elementary school librarian, and her father is CEO of a local accounting firm. Sophia has two older siblings who have been out of the home since she was an infant; they are each married, and one has a toddler. Assessment information is limited. Sophia does not yet speak more than a few whispered words, mostly numbers. She has not been observed to attempt to initiate contact with other people. She does not participate in assessment tasks or look at the materials unless there are numbers involved, and it is difficult to estimate her cognitive ability because of her unusual scatter of strengths and weaknesses. Although she has only recently achieved toileting independence, Sophia is able to complete mathematical addition and subtraction problems that are several years above her grade level. When given the opportunity she will choose a math paper over other free-time activities every time. She tends to ignore written letters or words, and if given a book she focuses on the page numbers, putting her face close to them and whispering the numbers as she flips through the pages. She loves playing with a deck of cards, and examines them closely, sifting through them and sorting them by numbers; she discards the face cards.

Example Five: Introducing Aggressive Aiden

Aiden is a fourteen-year-old with autism. He attends his local high school, where he takes core classes in the SDC with classmates who have SLD or mild ID, and electives and P.E. in mainstream general education classes. His core SDC teacher is new this year. Aiden is the oldest of four children and was homeschooled until he was twelve. His mother still homeschools his younger siblings, but reports that she is unable to provide Aiden with the education he needs now that he is older. His father is a mechanic and owns and operates a successful local garage. Aiden is verbal, and his cognitive ability is within the average to low-average range when measured both verbally and nonverbally. He has a strong interest in vehicles; when he was young he was reported to be fascinated with trains, and now he is interested in cars, trucks, and motorcycles.

ACT I, Scene One Summary

In Scene One, we learned that autism is a neurobiological developmental disorder affecting communication and social interaction. It is present from birth even if it is not recognized until later. Each person on the autism spectrum is unique, but many share common characteristics, such as repetitive movements, restricted interests or behaviors, resistance to change, and unusual responses to sensory experiences. Autism may be clinically diagnosed using the DSM-5, or it may be identified using CFR educational eligibility criteria for special services in school. There are several theories about autism, such as the theory of mind: difficulty understanding someone else's point of view or realizing that everyone does not share the same knowledge. Another theory is weak central coherence, or an inability to see the big picture; when this is weak, our students focus on tiny details and miss the main idea. Impaired executive function (EF) theory explains why many students on the spectrum have problems with organizing, planning, decision making, and time management. We learned sensory integration theory posits that our ASD students' sensory-seeking or sensory-avoiding behaviors play a large part in their challenges. Finally, we met the five students we'll be following throughout this book: Anthony, who acts out, disruptive Destiny, Sophia, who engages in self-injurious behaviors, defiant Daniel, and aggressive Aiden. We'll learn more about these students, the functions of their behaviors, and various interventions and strategies to use with them later on.

In Their Own Words

"To me, autism is a part of who I am. It's woven into my brain and it means the way I think is different from the norm. It's a very fundamental difference, it can't be separated out from the rest of me. There are parts of me that I consider important, like interests and hobbies, likes and dislikes, and if you removed that one aspect of my personality, the rest of me wouldn't change much. If I preferred green beans to broccoli, I would still be the same me, essentially. I would still have the same thoughts and emotions, I would still interact with the world the same way. If I was less depressed or anxious, or if I didn't have one particular obsessive-compulsive quirk, if you removed one of those things from me, it would be a change to my daily life and my brain, but it wouldn't make me a different person.

"Autism is different. You can't separate it out from the rest of me. It would require a whole new brain—a different ratio of grey to white brain matter! I wouldn't be the same person on any level if I did not have autism. I wouldn't process emotions the same way, I wouldn't engage with my hobbies and interests on the same level, I would not think the way that I think, I wouldn't remember information the way that I remember! I would be a completely different person, and this would erase not only the difficulties that come with autism, but all the things that I do like about myself. This is something that I think people who talk about 'curing' autism don't understand—you can't separate out the good from the bad. A brain has autism or it doesn't, and if you had the ability to wave a magic wand and make an autism brain not, you would be changing everything, not just the parts that 'look like autism.'

"I am a lot of things. I use different labels when I interact with different groups, and those labels carry different levels of importance. To some people, it's important that I am a writer, but not that I am a *Star Trek* fan. To others, it's important to know that I love *Star Trek*, but it's not important to know that I bake, or what kind of people I date. But there is no group where my autism ceases to be a part of my identity. As a writer with autism, I process and plan and connect things a certain way. I write ASD characters, and I describe sensory details based on my experiences. As a *Star Trek* fan with autism, I engage with the material in certain ways. I relate to certain characters (Spock, Data, Bashir) more than others. I read and memorize bits of trivia, and I find comfort in having a special interest that I can turn to. As a baker with autism, I crave or dislike certain sensory aspects of the process. I like to know the science behind how everything works in the kitchen, and if I am used to doing things a certain way, I don't like change. Having to use a different oven might stop me in my tracks, even if it's not that different from the oven I learned to bake using. And as an ASD person in general, it's very important to me that the people I befriend or date understand how autism impacts my life.

"You might think 'Well, a lot of neurotypical passionate *Star Trek* fans obsess over trivia, and a lot of neurotypical writers draw from experience when writing sensory details, and a lot of neurotypical bakers enjoy the feel of dough or prefer a routine,' and that's all true. (I mean, except for the part where you thought there were 'a lot' of neurotypical passionate *Star Trek* fans.) Having autism doesn't mean I'm an alien species, or a robot. People with autism still have a lot in common with neurotypical people, and there are things we can all understand. But there are also ways in which our experience is, even in quiet ways, fundamentally different.

"Because it isn't just the one thing. It's the way that every aspect of the experience connects."

~ Anne, diagnosed with autism spectrum disorder as an adult

What Can We Learn from Anne's Story?

While we all share things in common, autism is complex and intrinsic to each person. To say, "Well, we're all a little bit ASD, aren't we?" is to oversimplify a complicated diagnosis and minimize their experience.

 ACT I, Scene One Vocabulary

Asperger's disorder	auditory
autism spectrum disorder (ASD)	developmental
DSM-5	executive function (EF)
expressive	code of federal regulations (CFR)
gustatory	individualized education program (IEP)
Individuals with Disabilities Education Act (IDEA)	
intellectual disability (ID)	joint attention
manipulatives	mannerisms
neurobiological	neurotypical (NT)

olfactory	proprioceptive
receptive	restricted
sensory-avoiding behaviors	sensory integration
sensory processing	sensory-seeking behaviors
sharing enjoyment	social-emotional reciprocity
spectrum	tactile
theory of mind (ToM)	vestibular
visual	weak central coherence

ACT I, Scene One Discussion Topic

Think about a child you know who has autism, or who shows characteristics of autism, then answer these questions in discussion with your small group.

- What do people notice first upon meeting this child?
- What behaviors might get in the way of their education?
- Are there some behaviors that don't interfere with learning, but seem to bother other people?
- To what extent do you believe others should learn to tolerate unusual but non-interfering behaviors, rather than seeking to change every ASD behavior?

ACT I, Scene One Questions

1. The two main characteristics of autism cited in the DSM-5 are:
   A. Weak central coherence and delayed theory of mind.
   B. Social communication and interaction; restricted, repetitive patterns of behavior, interests, or activities.
   C. Unusual responses to sensory experiences and resistance to change.
   D. None of the above.

2. Two other characteristics associated with autism noted in the CFR are:

    A. Weak central coherence and delayed theory of mind.

    B. Social communication and interaction; restricted, repetitive patterns of behavior, interests, or activities.

    C. Unusual responses to sensory experiences and resistance to change.

    D. None of the above.

3. We do not yet know the causes of autism, but we know it is not caused by:

    A. Immunizations or vaccinations.

    B. Poor parenting skills.

    C. Poor teaching skills.

    D. Autism is not caused by any of the above.

    E. Autism is caused by A, B, and C, combined.

4. Autism can be cured by:

    A. Taking away recess.

    B. Improving teaching skills.

    C. Improving parenting skills.

    D. Autism is cured by A, B, and C, combined.

    E. Autism cannot be cured.

5. All people with autism share the same characteristics of autism; if you've met one person with autism, you've met them all. TRUE or FALSE?

Scene Two

Behavior: Action!

What is *behavior*? It's what we do. It is acting. Many people hear the word "behavior" and immediately think of "bad behavior" or "behavior problems." Actually, behavior isn't bad or good, it just *is*. As Shakespeare's Hamlet said, "There is nothing either good or bad, but thinking makes it so."

Even though behavior itself is neither good nor bad, we all know our students' behaviors can get them into trouble. So, what can we learn about behavior that will help our students stay out of trouble and keep on learning?

First, let's take a look at the characteristics of behavior.

Behavior is Observable

Behavior is something that can be seen (usually; more on that later.) Walking is an *observable* behavior; we can see someone doing it. Talking is an observable behavior, and also a *verbal* behavior.

Think about verbs: running, jumping, skipping, dancing, smiling, and laughing. They are all observable, and they are all behavior.

Is everything we see behavior, then? Well, no. Falling off a log is not behavior; it is a thing that happened to a person, not what the person did. Walking on a slippery log with untied shoes is a behavior, at least the walking part is behavior. Having untied shoes is the effect of the lack of a specific behavior: the person failed to perform the behavior of tying the shoes before walking on the log. The actual falling off of the log is not behavior.

How do we know? I like to use the *rock test*. Ask yourself: Can a rock do it? Can a rock fall off a log? Yes, it could. I could set a rock on a slippery log, and if I'm not careful about how I place it, it could easily fall off. Falling off a log is not a behavior, it is the effect of gravity on an unstable object or person. Can a rock walk on a log? No. A person can do it, but not a rock, so walking is a behavior.

When you're looking for a target behavior to increase or decrease, make sure it *is* a behavior. For instance, you might think you want to increase "not talking." But, is "not talking" a behavior? Can a rock engage in "not talking?" Sure, they do it all the time. "Not talking" is not a behavior in and of itself; it is the absence of a behavior. What is it that you want your student to do instead of talking? Perhaps you want to increase "taking notes during lectures," or "being on-task and completing assignments," or "quietly orienting towards the teacher during a lesson," rather than simply "not talking." Think about the positive things you want your students to do, the behaviors you want them to engage in.

On the other hand, you may want to decrease observable behaviors such as "talking out in class without raising a hand." This is an observable behavior, because we can see it and a rock can't do it. To decrease the "talking out" behavior, you would simultaneously want to increase the "raising hand" behavior. We'll be looking at exactly how to do this later on in the book. Right now, let's look at some of the other characteristics of behavior.

Behavior is Measurable

There are various ways of measuring behavior. We can count or quantify observable behaviors using the dimensions of the behavior.

▨ Frequency

One dimension is *frequency*: how often did the behavior occur within a specified time frame? Did your student complete five single-digit addition problems in one hour? Or scream three times in five minutes? Or eat one green bean during the twenty-minute lunch period? All of these behaviors can be counted.

▨ Duration

Another dimension of behavior is *duration*: how long does the behavior last? We measure duration from the *onset* of the behavior (when it starts) to the *offset* (when it stops). If a child screams only once per day, but the duration is forty-five minutes, it is a very different experience from having a student scream six times a day for a duration of less than one second per utterance. Of course, we would be working toward no screaming at all, but on our way to that goal it is important to know not only the frequency of the behavior (how often), but also the duration of the behavior (how long it goes on).

▨ Intensity

Intensity is another dimension of behavior. A child may bite himself on the hand when under stress to the degree that the skin is broken, or deep marks are visible and continue to be visible five minutes after the bite. Another child may press his teeth to his hand softly, leaving no visible marks within two seconds of removing his teeth from his hand. Intensity makes a big difference, and it is important for us to measure it. We need to know if the behavior of concern is getting better in any way, including whether the intensity is decreasing, in addition to looking for a decrease in frequency or duration.

Latency

Finally, we look at the dimension of *latency*. How long is the gap or delay between what *triggered* the behavior and the behavior itself? If there is a five-minute lag between the teacher telling the class to clean up and Sarah beginning to clean up, there is a five-minute latency. She may need a five-minute warning before time to start cleaning up to become acclimated to the idea of transitioning. If Jacob engages in the behavior of ripping up his work paper after a seven-minute latency (seven minutes after being presented with a work paper) then we can plan to insert an intervention as early as possible, well within those crucial first six minutes. This might mean offering help, explanation, or encouragement at the time of giving him the paper, depending on the function of the behavior. (More on that later.)

Behavior Impacts the Environment

What we do every day—our behavior—makes a difference, doesn't it? We may not always be aware of what impact a behavior has, but the impact is real at some level. Whether we berate or praise our students, we affect how they respond to us. If a student throws a chair, or turns in a homework assignment, or crawls under a desk, or raises a hand to answer a question, all these behaviors have an impact on you, on your class as a whole, and on what kind of a day everybody has. Behavior definitely impacts the learning environment.

Behavior is Lawful

We're not talking about legal or illegal behaviors here. Obviously not every behavior complies with the law, but all behavior is *lawful* in that it follows natural laws. Examples of the natural laws of behavior include the functional relationship between cause and effect, or between removing reinforcement and extinguishing behavior. The science of behavior analysis provides a lot of information about this, and we'll get into it more deeply later. For now, just know that we can count on behavior to follow certain natural laws.

Behavior is Seen and Unseen

Some behaviors are readily observable and easy to monitor, describe, and document. Other behaviors are hidden. It takes a behavioral detective to discover what is going on behind the scenes with behaviors which are seen and unseen: *overt* and *covert*.

▇ Overt Behaviors

Behaviors we observe and measure are public or *overt* behaviors; they can be seen. We can all see that Jacob is frowning, or screaming, or throwing pencils. It is overt. Many of the behaviors that cause problems in the classrooms are overt or observable behaviors, and they are usually easy to measure.

▇ Covert Behaviors

Things like thinking and feeling are also considered by many behaviorists to be behaviors, but they are private or *covert* behaviors. Covert behaviors are unseen. We may think we know how Jacob feels based on the frowning, screaming, and pencil-throwing overt behaviors, but we don't, not really. He may be feeling angry because he got an "F" on his spelling test. He may be feeling frustrated because he doesn't know how to do a problem and doesn't know how to ask for help. He may be hungry, or tired, or depressed, or in pain. Any of these covert thoughts or feelings could have triggered the overt behaviors we observed. Since we do not yet have the power to read minds, we can't know for sure what someone else is thinking or feeling. We can ask, and hope that they tell us the truth if they can. We can watch what they do and hope to get clues about what's going on with them, using our keen observational skills. But no matter how much we might like to, we can't really get inside someone else's head.

When we have a nonverbal student, we really need to be behavior detectives in order to figure out what they might be thinking or feeling. It's important that we do this. Every student deserves to be understood, and by seeking to understand their needs, we can help improve their behaviors.

Problematic Behaviors

Behavior is not good or bad in and of itself. Everybody behaves, all the time. What is there about behavior that gets people in trouble? When behaviors become problematic it's either due to *behavioral excesses* or *behavioral deficits*.

Behavioral Excess

Behavioral excesses happen when someone does something too much, so that it gets in the way of their daily life or functioning. For example, walking is just a behavior, but when a person walks out of the classroom in the middle of a lesson, or walks into the street without looking for cars, or repetitively paces back and forth for hours on end, that's excessive.

Talking is just behavior, and of course we want our children to learn how to talk. But when someone talks incessantly on the same subject for hours, or blurts out answers in class without waiting to be called on, or shouts obscenities at a police officer, we're talking about a problem of behavioral excess.

Behavioral Deficit

Behavioral deficits, on the other hand, occur when people are not doing things—usually things that their teachers or society believe they "should" be doing. For instance, if someone doesn't brush their teeth or take a shower with any regularity it may not seem problematic to them, but you can be sure this deficit will be noticed by others.

If someone fails to respond when a parent says, "Stop," or a teacher says, "Sit down," or a police officer says, "Take your hands out of your pockets so I can see them," a behavioral deficit can become a serious problem.

Behavior is Communication

In order to help our students decrease their behavioral excesses and fill in the gaps of their behavioral deficits, there is something else about behavior that will be important to remember: behavior is communication.

Behavior means something. It is a way to communicate when the words are not there. When babies cry, we don't refuse to take care of their needs because they didn't "use their words." Infants don't have words, so we accept crying as their communication. It's up to us to figure out whether they need a bottle, a diaper, or a hug.

Our students don't always have words, either. Of course, we already know our nonverbal students don't talk. We need to provide them with alternative communication systems that work for them.

What we don't always remember is that sometimes our verbal students don't have words, either. When stress increases, it decreases our ASD students' ability to form words and sentences. They may even become completely nonverbal. We don't always know what causes increased stress for them. Maybe someone is bullying them on the bus or playground. Maybe they forgot their homework and don't know how to tell you. Maybe their parents had an argument that morning. Maybe a dog barked and startled them on the way to school, or a bee buzzed past their ear and they froze. We don't know. But we do know that when stress goes up, language skills go down. Yes, even your student who lectured nonstop for an hour yesterday on the respective strengths and weaknesses of one brand of vacuum cleaner over another may be completely nonverbal today.

When verbal communication is unavailable, other behaviors kick in to try to get the message across. Maybe the buzzing of the fluorescent lights plus the sound of the timer ticking away has just become unbearably painful. Screaming can communicate when words fail, and as an added bonus, screams can block out painful auditory stimuli. To the teacher it seems random, but there is communication behind the behavior. It's up to us to figure out what the behavior means, or the function of the behavior. (More about the function of behavior later.)

ACT I, Scene Two Summary

In this scene we learned that behavior is observable (except when it isn't). It is measurable by frequency, duration, intensity, and latency. It is usually overt or public, but many also recognize the impact of covert, or private behaviors such as thoughts or feelings. Behavior becomes problematic when there are behavioral excesses (they're doing something we don't want them to do, or they're doing something too much), or behavioral deficits (they're not doing the things we want them to do). We learned that behavior is communication, and it is our job to try to figure out what our students are trying to tell us with their behaviors.

In Their Own Words

"I was in the third grade when my unique condition of Asperger's started rearing its head (although I wouldn't know what it was until later). I remember I was fairly young, only about eight years old, so it was hard to convey or express my emotions, but I do recall that the teacher's explanations did not interest me at all. So, instead of listening to my third-grade teacher, I would walk around the room. The teacher sent my parents a note about me. Instead of realizing it might be autism, they attributed it to misbehavior and I was punished. I learned in time, however, that my problems were related to Asperger's."

~ Joseph, diagnosed with Asperger's syndrome as an adult

What Can We Learn from Joseph's Story?

Don't assume that a child who behaves differently is purposefully misbehaving. You may have students who have not yet been diagnosed, but who still exhibit signs of autism. Give them the benefit of the doubt.

ACT I, Scene Two Vocabulary

behavior	behavioral deficits	behavioral excesses
covert	duration	frequency
intensity	latency	overt
quantify	rock test	self-injurious behavior (SIB)
special day class (SDC)		specific learning disability (SLD)
trigger	verbal behavior	

 ACT I, Scene Two Discussion Topic

Think about a behavior you have observed which you consider to be a problem behavior. Would you describe it as a behavioral excess or a behavioral deficit? Describe it to your small group, including your estimations of the frequency, duration, latency, and intensity of the behavior.

ACT I, Scene Two Questions

1. Which of these is a behavior?
    A. Running in high heels.
    B. Falling down.
    C. Both A and B.
    D. Neither A nor B.

2. Which of these is not a behavior because it fails the "rock test" (a rock could do it)?
    A. Being quiet.
    B. Staying on task.
    C. Both A and B.
    D. Neither A nor B.

For questions 3–6, use the words *duration, frequency, intensity,* and *latency* to fill in the blanks.

3. Logan continued to swing for approximately five minutes after the bell rang at the end of recess. This describes the _____ of his response following the stimulus of the bell.

4. Olivia hit her leg with her hand fifteen times per minute. This describes the _____ of her behavior.

5. Ian pounded the wall with sufficient force as to be heard clearly from across the room and from the hallway outside, and to dislodge the clock from the wall causing it to fall. This describes the _____ of his behavior.

6. Addison stood at the back of the classroom, spinning around in a tight circle, for seven minutes. This describes the _____ of the behavior.

For questions 7 and 8, use the words *deficit* or *excess*.

7. Rob asked sixty questions during a one-hour speech therapy session. This is an example of a behavioral _____.

8. When his name was called, Rob did not respond verbally, pause his behavior, or turn to look at the speaker. This is an example of a behavioral

_____ .

For questions 9 and 10, use the words *overt* and *covert*.

9. Mallory felt hurt and angry when the other girls wouldn't let her play ball with them at recess, and she decided to take their ball. This is an example of a(n) _____ behavior.

10. Mallory grabbed the ball from her classmates and threw it over the wall. This is an example of a(n) _____ behavior.

Scene Three

Language: Learning the Lines

Every good show starts with a good script, so let's learn our lines, the language of behavior. The field of applied behavior analysis (ABA) is filled with jargon that sounds mysterious and confusing to the uninitiated. We're going to make sense of it, starting with the basic vocabulary. Later we'll look at ways to use what we have learned to set our students' stage for success.

Stimulus Response

Let's start with behavioral terms that you may have heard: *stimulus* and *response*. A stimulus is something that happens, an event, something that can be detected by the senses. A bell ringing, an assignment written on the board, a pat on the back, these are all *stimuli*. When you say, "Take out your spelling books," that is a stimulus. The *response* is the behavior that usually follows the stimulus. You expect that your students' response to the stimulus of your direction will be to take out their spelling books.

People respond to stimuli all day long, without thinking about it. Our phone vibrates (stimulus), so we pick it up (response). The timer buzzes, we turn off the oven. We hear a siren, we pull over. Children hear a bell, and they line up after recess. It's all stimulus and response.

Discriminative Stimulus (S^d)

Now let's talk about the *discriminative stimulus*, or S^d. This is a very particular stimulus, in the presence of which a given response has been reinforced. When a teacher says, "Line up for recess," those students who line up get to go out to recess. They may also receive thanks, a smile, or praise. Their teacher's approval and going outside serve to reinforce lining up behavior. They are more likely to repeat this response the next time she presents the S^d of "line up for recess."

Present the S^d for the Desired Behavior

Presenting the S^d for the behavior we want is like giving our students the cue for their lines or actions. It's another way to set them up for success. Sometimes it's as simple as giving a verbal direction such as "line up for recess." In other situations, where the undesired behavior has been going on for a long time, it may be necessary for the teacher to do some pre-setting of the stage to guide them toward the desired behavior.

For example, let's say that a class of seventh graders had a history of coming in to class and gathering into clusters to talk or horse around. Many minutes were wasted daily while the teacher asked them again and again to be seated. After everyone was finally in their seats, she began her lesson, usually five to ten minutes late, which cut into their instructional minutes. This teacher wanted her students to start working immediately, but she knew she would have to make some changes in order to get the desired results. Here's what she did.

First, before class started, she put a "quick-write" topic on the board, usually a simple writing prompt or unfinished sentence for them to complete.

Then, she placed a half-sheet of lined paper on each desk. Using a half sheet served two purposes: it saved paper, and it let the students know this was a short task and they were not expected to write a lot. She also had a cup of pencils available on her desk, so that everyone could get right to work even if they had lost their own pencil. (After losing all of her attractive pencils the first week, she switched to large, primary pencils used by first graders. Seventh graders would rather not be seen using the "baby" pencils, so only those with a true need borrowed them, and they seldom failed to return them.)

Finally, she stood at the door and greeted each student as they entered, asking them how they were and pointing out the assignment on the board. This forced students to enter one at a time rather than in groups, greatly reducing the carryover of social "break behavior" into the classroom.

This teacher's actions—providing a clear, written assignment, the materials needed to complete the task, and a verbal reminder at the door—were her S^d. These stimuli were designed to evoke, or call forth, the desired response or behavior. She set up her students for success in a way that included a visual component. This was important not only for her ASD students with visual strength, but also for her students with attention deficit-hyperactive disorder (ADHD) and her students with specific learning disabilities (SLD) such as auditory processing disorders. It would have been easier for her not to do any of those things, but she wanted her students to get the most out of the class, and she was tired of wasting time waiting for everyone to finally settle down and be ready to work. She was willing to change her behavior in an effort to change their behaviors, and it worked.

Here's another example: a kindergarten teacher wanted her students to sit on the carpet for story time without crowding, jostling, or infringing on one another's space. As a way of presenting the S^d for the behavior she wanted, she used colored electrician's tape to make different-colored shapes on the carpet. Each shape was large enough for a child to sit cross-legged on, and spaced far enough apart that if each student sat on a shape they could not easily touch each other. When she wanted her students to sit in certain places for story time, she told one student, "Sit on the blue triangle," and another student, "Sit on the green circle," and so on. This was how she set them up for story time success. In the meantime, because she knew that the tape would curl and be pulled up over time, she put in a request to purchase a special story-time carpet with the colored shapes incorporated into the weave of the rug.

Remove the S^d for Undesirable Behaviors

The last thing teachers want to do is to set up our students to fail. But sometimes we are not aware of the many, subtle ways we do just that.

One kindergarten teacher kept a wide range of manipulatives and free-play toys, such as blocks, beads, counting bears, and dollhouse furniture, in bins on a low shelf which bordered her story carpet. She wanted her students to sit on the carpet and listen to a story after lunch, without getting into mischief by touching the learning materials on the shelves. Each day at story time, several students always chose to sit along the edge that was bordered by the manipulatives shelf. At first, they began surreptitiously reaching into the bins to scramble the small toys with their hands. Later, they took larger toys off the shelf and played with them during the story. This teacher had heard that fidgets could be a useful tool to help students focus their attention, so she did not discourage anyone from taking out toys, hoping it would help them be better listeners. The opposite turned out to be true. Usually the students' attention was on the toys, not on the story, and children would chat while playing together. Conflicts arose when more than one student wanted the same toy. It wasn't long before all of her students went directly to the toy shelf when she said it was story time and chose toys to play with on the carpet. Her after-lunch "story time" looked exactly like a free choice activity time, and she had to shout to be heard. When she asked questions about the story, no one responded. It seemed as if they had never even heard the story, which was, in fact, true.

This teacher had presented the S^d for an undesired behavior, playing with toys during story time, without even realizing it. Placing shelves with bins of toys right beside the story carpet was a visual S^d for playing with toys. She had to find a way to remove the S^d.

The first thing she tried was to attach curtains over the open shelves so the toys would not be as visible; however, they were still within arm's reach. The curtains did little to discourage her students from gaining access to the toys behind them, since they were already accustomed to getting out toys for story time.

Then she rearranged her classroom so that the back of the shelves faced the carpet and the open shelves were on the far side. She also needed to make a new rule, no toys during story time, and a *Social Story*® about the rule. Although at first she needed to remind her students about the rule daily, it soon became part of their new routine, effectively removing the S^d for the undesirable behavior. In addition, she put in a request to purchase low shelves which were hinged together and on wheels. When toy time was over and it was story time, she could close the toy shelves like a book and fasten the clasp so that there was no way for her students to access the toys during story time.

Reinforcement

Reinforcement is what happens when the *consequence* of the behavior, or what happens right after, results in the behavior happening more often in the future. When a student hits another child and that child gives them the cookie from their lunch, he is more likely to hit again next time he wants someone's cookie. The behavior of hitting was reinforced by the consequence of gaining a cookie.

Our goal, though, is to increase the positive or desirable behaviors we want to see in our students. When you smile, thank, or praise your students for lining up quietly, and then let them go out to recess right away because you didn't have to wait for everyone to quiet down, they are more likely to line up quietly the next time.

You've heard it said many times, "Catch them being good." This is the first step: you do need to be watchful and notice when they are behaving the way you want them to. The next step is to reinforce the behavior you like. Let them know why you are letting them go to recess a moment early rather than late. If you have young students who will work for stickers, stars, and happy faces, be sure to tell them what they did to earn the sticker if you want to see that behavior increase. Saying it is just for "being good" is too general and doesn't carry over into the future. Tell them they earned the sticker for working hard even on the difficult problems and for finishing the page; that's more specific. Praising hard work increases hard work. However, praising qualities that are not under the child's control, such as "being smart" or "being good at math," is less effective. Either they are or they aren't, and there doesn't seem to be much they can do about it.

Adults expect to be paid for our work, and children are no different. If we want our students to perform in a given way, we need to provide appropriate payment or reinforcement.

Am I talking about bribing children to do what is expected of them? No, that is something quite different. Bribery is persuading someone to do something wrong on your behalf in exchange for money or other valuables. We do not try to persuade children to behave improperly, but when we pay them in advance hoping for good behavior in the future, it is similar to bribery. It is also ineffective. Say a substitute teacher lets the class go out to recess early and tells them, "Now, I'm doing this nice thing for you, and so after recess I want you to be extra quiet during the math test." Once they've already had their extra five minutes of recess, they have no reason to be extra quiet during math, and there is nothing the teacher can do about that. She can't go back in time and take back the extra recess minutes she already gave them.

What we're talking about when we say we are "reinforcing a behavior" is rewarding the child *after* they engage in the desired behavior, not before. For example, when a teacher says, "First, I need you to work quietly on this math test. Then, after the test is over and everyone was quiet, I will give you five minutes of free time before dismissal."

Saying "first/then" is preferable to saying "if/then," because the word "if" implies that maybe it will happen and maybe it won't. Saying "first" lets the students know that this must happen first, and then something they like will happen.

Objects or privileges which are used to reinforce appropriate behaviors are called *reinforcers*. There are two kinds of reinforcers: *primary reinforcers* and *secondary* or *conditioned reinforcers*. Primary reinforcers are themselves reinforcing, such as food or a chance to play a computer game. Secondary or conditioned reinforcers are not reinforcing in themselves, but they may be exchanged for desired objects. We have been conditioned or trained to find them reinforcing. Money is a conditioned reinforcer; we can't eat it, but we can exchange it for food or whatever we choose to purchase. Grades are conditioned reinforcers; they may be "exchanged" for a diploma or college admission. Points tallied on the board, stars collected on a chart, popcorn kernels filling up a jar—if they can be exchanged for something meaningful to the student, they are conditioned or secondary reinforcers.

Finding the right reinforcement for your students is part of knowing them and knowing what they value. Will they work for a gold star? Lunch with the teacher? Five extra minutes of computer time or recess? A letter or phone call home to tell their parents what a good job they are doing? Whatever it is, make sure it is something they want or it will not be effective.

You might offer a reinforcement *choice board*, a menu of possible reinforcements, where students get to select what they will work for. It is not necessary for teachers to go out and buy a treasure box filled with tiny toys like plastic spider rings which will be lost on the way home or stepped on by barefoot parents in the middle of the night. Privileges are often more valuable to students, and are free. They might work for the chance to do a classroom chore, move their seat to a preferred location, or earn a get-out-of-homework-free pass.

Some teachers use a group reinforcement system, whereby all students' good behavior is reinforced in an "one-for-all and all-for-one" manner. Each time the teacher sees a behavior she wants to reinforce, whether it is the behavior of a single student or the entire class, she adds to a tally on the board, or places a small object in a container. The whole class earns the popcorn party when all the kernels of corn are moved from the bag to the jar, or they earn a game of Hot Lava Balloon Toss (see appendix) when all of the cotton balls have been moved from a box to a jar. Even students who struggle with behavior will get to participate in the group reward, which can motivate them to work harder to help the class reach the goal. When students have behavioral challenges and a history of failing to access reinforcement, they may become discouraged and feel hopeless. If they can't win, there's no point in trying. A group reinforcement system lets them taste success. It means that, regardless of their behavior on a given day, they will not be denied reinforcement as a valuable member of the class that earned the reward. Even if they blow it on a bad day, there is hope. There are few things we teachers provide for our students that are more important than hope.

And no, this doesn't mean that you should give up on changing that student's problem behavior. Add an individual behavior plan to work on the behavior, but don't deny him the opportunity to be a part of something bigger than himself: a class that behaves well and earns rewards. He probably wants to be a "good kid" but can't always control his behavior yet. Let him know that you recognize in him the good kid that you know he is. It's a powerful message.

Punishment

In contrast to reinforcement, *punishment* is defined behaviorally as a consequence that follows a behavior and results in a decrease of that behavior in the future. This is a bit different from the way most people think about the word. The only requirement for a consequence to be considered punishment is that the behavior it follows decreases in the future. We won't really know if a consequence is punishment until we find out if it worked. Did it decrease the behavior? If the answer is yes, then the consequence was a punishment.

Usually we think of punishment as something like being forced to sit against a wall during recess for losing homework. We like to think that taking away recess will decrease their "losing homework" behavior in the future, but this is not always the case. If the child sits on the wall during recess day after day and there is no change in the homework problem, then it is not punishment, because the behavior did not decrease. It is also not effective, and you should just stop.

On the other hand, if a student turns in their homework and you give them a gold star, and after that they stop turning in homework, the gold star served as punishment for that student, because the behavior decreased.

Punishment has been found to be far less effective as a motivator than reinforcement. B. F. Skinner, the psychologist and behaviorist who developed the theory of behaviorism, believed that reinforcement was more effective than punishment. Skinner said, "A person who has been punished is not less inclined to behave in a given way; at best, he learns how to avoid punishment" (Skinner, 1971). We will focus predominantly on positive reinforcement rather than punishment.

Motivating Operations

A *motivating operation* (MO) is a condition or state that changes a student's motivation to do something, usually by making the reinforcer more or less valuable or desirable. There are two kinds of MOs: *establishing operations (EO)* and *abolishing operations (AO)*. As you might guess, an EO will encourage, increase, or establish the desired behavior by making the reinforcer more interesting, and an AO will discourage, decrease, or abolish the behavior by making the reinforcer less interesting.

Arranging Establishing Operations (EO) for Desirable Behaviors

Establishing operations (EO) increase the potency of the reinforcer, making your students want it even more. For example, *deprivation* is an EO because it makes the reinforcement more powerful. A teacher who has a popcorn party every Friday afternoon, and then wants to offer a popcorn party as a reward, may find that it is not very effective. Students know they can just wait until Friday for the usual party rather than working hard to get another one. Another teacher has never had a popcorn party in her classroom. When she uses this as a reinforcer, the state of deprivation (no popcorn parties) makes the reinforcer more potent. Everyone wants to work hard because earning points is the only way to earn the party.

A high school teacher allows his students to get a drink of water from the fountain at the back of the room any time they're thirsty, as long as they go one at a time. During the hottest months at the end of the year he keeps a cooler with ice and cups behind his desk. Students who earn enough points can have a cup with ice and take their water back to their desks. The hot weather serves as an EO for cups of ice. This reinforcer is not effective during the winter months when there is no EO (hot weather) to increase the value of the ice.

Presenting Abolishing Operations (AO) for Undesirable Behaviors

An *abolishing operation (AO)* is another kind of MO, but this is the opposite of an EO. The AO makes the reinforcer less powerful or potent, and therefore less effective. For example, satiation is an AO. Imagine a chronically hungry student who steals food from his classmates' lunch boxes every morning. After he is given free breakfast and snacks, the effectiveness of the reinforcer (stolen food) is reduced, because he is satiated: he is no longer hungry. Providing him with what he needs, food, is the AO for stealing food.

As another example of an AO, one child's functional behavior assessment (FBA) showed that the function of his self-injurious behavior (SIB) of biting his forearm was sensory-seeking. He found the feeling of the pressure of his teeth against the skin of his arm to be reinforcing. The recommendation was for him to wear heavy, long-sleeved sweatshirts to decreases the positive sensory feedback he had received from biting his arm. The long sleeves served as an AO for arm biting, because he no longer got the same sensory feeling he was looking for. At the same time, a safe, resilient sensory chew toy or object was provided to meet his sensory need. By the time summer came around when the sweatshirt would no longer be comfortable, he had become accustomed to meeting his need to bite with the chewable toy, which was always close at hand, rather than going back to biting his own arm.

Response Effort

The *response effort* of any behavior is the degree of difficulty. How much effort is required to engage in a desired or undesired behavior? All things being equal, people are generally more likely to do easier things than things that require hard work. We can use this truth to help our students by making it easier to do the right thing and harder to do the wrong thing.

Decreasing the Response Effort for Desirable Behaviors

It only makes sense that we would want to decrease the response effort for the desired behavior. By doing so we are simply making it easier for our students to do the right thing.

The seventh-grade teacher who put half-sheets of lined paper on her students' desks after lunch was decreasing their response effort. It was much easier for them to sit down and start writing when the paper was right in front of them. Eventually, when the after-lunch quick-write had become an ingrained habit, she started keeping a stack of paper right beside the door next to a cup of pencils, and directed her students to pick up their own paper on their way to their desks. At first, though, she wanted to make sure it was very easy for her students to do the right thing, so she greatly decreased the response effort for the task.

Increasing the Response Effort for Undesirable Behaviors

On the other hand, increasing the response effort for undesirable behaviors means making it more difficult for them to do the things we don't want them to do.

The kindergarten teacher who turned her toy shelves around so that they were facing away from the carpet was doing just this. It had been too easy for her students to just reach right into the shelves and take toys when the open shelves faced the carpet. After she made the change, if her students really wanted to access the toys, they had to stand up and walk around the shelves to find them. This gave the teacher time to redirect them back to the carpet before they got all the way to the toys.

ACT I, Scene Three Summary

Although the language used in the science of behavior analysis can seem daunting, we have explored many of the common terms in this scene. We looked at the relationship between a stimulus and a response, the basic foundation of behavior. We learned that a discriminative stimulus (S^d) is a prompt that lets students know that reinforcement is available when they follow the prompt. We also learned how important it is to present an S^d for what we want them to do, and not to accidentally present an S^d for a problem behavior. We compared reinforcement (adding something that increases the likelihood that the behavior will happen again in the future) and punishment (adding something that decreases the likelihood that the behavior will happen again in the future) and learned that punishment is less effective than reinforcement. We discussed motivating operations (MO) that change a student's motivation. One way of making the reinforcement more powerful is to arrange an establishing operation (EO), such as deprivation, to increase desire for the reinforcement. Alternately, we can present an abolishing operation (AO) to make the reinforcement less potent, such as satiation, to decrease interest in a reinforcer. Finally, we learned the value of decreasing the response effort for the desired behavior, making it easier to do the right thing, and increasing the response effort for the undesirable behavior, making it harder to do the wrong thing.

In Scene Four and the following scenes, we will go into the ABCs of behavior to learn more about why our students behave in certain ways, and what we can do to improve their behavior.

In Their Own Words

"Autism is something that is rooted in the very way the brain is structured. This is a big part of why I prefer identity-first language. I am an autistic person, and that informs every part of my experience in life. Neurotypical people who insist upon person-first language (a person with autism) are misguided, in the way that abled people are often misguided when talking to and about disabled people. You may be well-meaning, but you don't need to say 'Dorian is a person with autism' any more than you would say, 'Becky is a person with Jewishness' or 'Billy is a person with gayness' or 'John is a person with blackness.' People who fit into these groups often choose identity-first language in describing our/themselves because these are identities that come with a fundamental way that experiences are shaped and shared. Our identities shape us in ways that the other aspects of our personalities don't."

~ Anne, diagnosed with autism spectrum disorder as an adult

What Can We Learn from Anne's Story?

In school we are taught to use person-first language. We say, "A child with autism," or "a student on the spectrum." We do this so that everyone on this child's team remembers that we are working with a child, not a diagnosis. However, once students are old enough to understand the concept of person-first language and identity-first language, ask them which they prefer, and abide by their preference. The same goes for an adult colleague or parent who has disclosed that they have autism. It would be the height of condescension to "ablesplain" to an adult that they should refer to themselves as "a person with autism" when they've just introduced themselves as an "autistic person."

ACT I, Scene Three Vocabulary

ablesplain

B. F. Skinner

conditioned reinforcer

deprivation

establishing operation (EO)

motivating operation (MO)

punishment

reinforcer

response effort

secondary reinforcer

stimulus/stimuli

abolishing operation (AO)

choice board

consequence

discriminative stimulus (S^d)

evoke

primary reinforcer

reinforcement

response

satiation

Social Story®

 ACT I, Scene Three Discussion Topic

Choose one of the concepts from this scene. Think of an example from your practice or experience, and share your example with your group. Concepts include:

- Presenting the S^d for the desirable behavior.
- Removing the S^d for the undesirable behavior.
- Arranging EO for the desirable behavior.
- Presenting AO for the undesirable behavior.
- Decreasing the response effort for the desirable behavior.
- Increasing the response effort for the undesirable behavior.

 ACT I, Scene Three Questions

1. What does S^d stand for?
   - A. Stimulus discrimination.
   - B. Discriminative stimulus.
   - C. Systemic deterioration.
   - D. Sensory defensiveness.

2. Things we do to make the reinforcer either more or less valuable or potent are called:

   A. RM (reinforcer motivators).

   B. MO (motivation orders).

   C. MO (motivating operations).

   D. MS (motivational scale).

3. When we make a change that makes the reinforcer more valuable, such as deprivation (i.e., food is a more potent reinforcer when the person is hungry), this is called an

   A. EO (establishing order).

   B. EO (establishing operation).

   C. AO (abolishing operation).

   D. AO (alternative operant).

4. When we make a change that makes the reinforcer less valuable, such as satiation (for example, being able to ask for a break any time it is needed makes running away from a task less reinforcing), this is called an

   A. EO (establishing order).

   B. EO (establishing operation).

   C. AO (alternative operant).

   D. AO (abolishing operation).

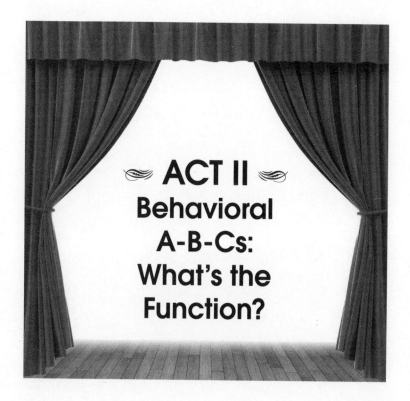

ACT II
Behavioral
A-B-Cs:
What's the
Function?

All behavior has a function.

~ *Jon Bailey and Mary Burch*

I try to write shows where even the bad guy's got his reasons.

~ *Lin-Manuel Miranda*

Scene
Four

Behavior—
Simple as A-B-C

Now we've learned about what behavior is, as well as its characteristics and dimensions. We've looked at how behavioral excesses and deficits can get our students into trouble. We also know that their behaviors are trying to communicate something … but, what? How can we deduce the reason behind their actions, the motivation for the scene, or the *communicative intent*? What's the *function* of the behavior? You may have a lot of experience dealing with behavior problems, but now that you have a student with autism, you suddenly find your tried-and-true strategies may not be as effective. If you want to address these behaviors, you will need to understand the "why" behind the scenes: the function of the behaviors.

If the behaviors are severe, you should call in a professional like a behaviorally trained school psychologist to do a *functional behavioral assessment, (FBA)* or a *Board Certified Behavior Analyst® (BCBA)* to conduct more formal *functional analysis (FA)*. These will help the team come up with a workable hypothesis for the function of the behavior, in order to develop an appropriate *behavior support plan (BSP)*.

Thankfully, most of the behaviors we see in the classroom are not so severe that we need to bring in reinforcements. Teachers can (and do) deal effectively with all kinds of behavioral challenges, managing the behavior before it becomes severe. Knowing the function is key.

Let's look at a couple of examples. Screaming, for instance. Now, there's a behavior that will disrupt a lesson and upset the rest of the class every time. Jacob and Emily both scream. One behavior, one solution, right? Well, not so fast. Let's look at screaming from a couple of different angles to see what we can learn about the possible function of the behavior.

Jacob screamed because he was frustrated by a difficult task and needed help, but he was under so much stress he couldn't ask for it.

Emily, on the other hand, screamed because people were too close to her. She was experiencing sensory overload and wanted everyone to stay away and leave her alone while she tried to self-regulate.

You see the dilemma, don't you? The behaviors looked identical—screaming—but we shouldn't try to respond to both behaviors in the same way. If we rushed over to try to help Jacob, he would be relieved and stop screaming, because he got the help he asked for. If we did the same thing for Emily, on the other hand, she would probably scream all the louder and even take it to the next level by lashing out at the person who invaded her space.

Alternately, if we left both children alone, giving them plenty of space and privacy, Emily would be relieved and stop screaming. Poor Jacob, though, still didn't get the help he needed. His behavior could have escalated into ripping up his paper and throwing his pencil and book.

Clearly, we need to determine the function of the screaming for each child so we can address it appropriately.

Never fear. We have tools to help us solve these mysteries. We'll start at the beginning, with the A-B-Cs of behavior.

Easy as A-B-C

Whenever we talk about behavior, we want to look at the A-B-Cs: *antecedents, behaviors,* and *consequences.* The antecedents might include a *trigger* or a series of unfortunate *setting events* that were in place before the behavior. Setting events are like the off-stage back story that the audience doesn't see. Being hungry, in pain, or afraid of a bully on the bus are all setting events. It's important to get clues about the function of the behavior by keeping track of the antecedents and consequences. This might be very different for two students who exhibit identical behaviors.

A Scream Is a Scream Is a Scream ... Or Is It?

Let's take another look at the cases of Jacob and Emily. Both students screamed in the classroom. The behaviors looked (and sounded) identical, and we might be tempted to treat each behavior in the same way. That would be a big mistake. Let's look at each student's "screaming behavior" with the antecedents to the behavior, and see how they were, in fact, quite different. We'll start with Jacob.

Picture the scene in his special day classroom. It was Tuesday morning, and Jacob was back at school after being absent Monday. The teacher handed out worksheets. The task was not a new one; it was introduced last week and reviewed Friday and Monday, so students were expected to complete this paper independently. Jacob stared at his paper. He looked around the room, then back at his paper. He picked up his pencil, and put it back down again. He scowled. His breathing became ragged and audible, his shoulders rose and fell with each breath, and his face began to turn pink. He glanced toward the classroom aide, who was helping another student. Jacob tapped his pencil on the desk, then rapped it hard like a drumstick. The aide looked up and asked him to stop, then returned to helping the other student. Jacob dropped the pencil, clenched his fists, pounded them on his desk, and began screaming.

You see it, don't you? Jacob's observable behaviors (staring at the paper without working on it, scowling, tapping, pounding the desk) along with the setting event of his absence on Monday, all point toward the conclusion that he had forgotten how to do the problems and he needed help. Because he was usually a verbal student, his teacher and aide assumed that if he needed help he would simply raise his hand and ask for it. However, on this day he seemed to be unable to ask for help. We don't know what covert or private experiences might contribute to his inability to do something he had previously been able to do, namely ask for help. Perhaps he was still feeling weak and sick from his illness over the weekend, and this drained his ability to focus. Perhaps he was not sick at all but there was a family emergency over the weekend and he was still worrying about it. We can't know everything that's going on inside Jacob's head, but we can look at the antecedents and try to prevent the meltdown.

Now, let's look at Emily's screaming behavior.

It was Tuesday morning, and Emily's teacher had just distributed a worksheet. Emily picked up her pencil and began work right away, completing the first two problems in quick succession. The classroom aide walked by, looked over her shoulder, and asked Emily how she was doing. Emily jumped as if startled, shrugged, and leaned forward over her paper. The aide walked away. Emily's neighbor to the left asked her what she got for number one, and Emily swiveled away from her and covered her paper. The boy on her right said, "What are you looking at?" when Emily turned in his direction. Emily faced front again and hunched over her paper, continuing to work. The student on her left peered over her shoulder, and then reached over to pull Emily's paper back into view. Emily clutched her paper to her chest and squeezed her eyes shut, tears leaking out onto her cheeks. The boy on her right pointed at her, laughed, and whispered, "Cry baby!" Now Emily sat silently shaking while more tears came. The girl on her left whispered, "Why won't you help me? You're mean!" and tried again to pull Emily's paper from her tight grasp. The boy on her right whispered, "She's a meanie! Mean little cry baby!" and poked her with his pencil. Emily took a long, shuddering breath and let out a prolonged scream.

Now that we're looking for antecedent behaviors, we can see how Emily signaled that she was in distress and did not know how to handle it. She wanted everyone to leave her alone and let her work in peace, but people kept bothering and interrupting her.

What we can't see are any covert or private behaviors or setting events. Maybe Emily was feeling stressed because she got a problem wrong on yesterday's worksheet and she felt she must get 100 percent. Maybe her "personal space" bubble is large and everyone around her seems excessively close, looming over her. Maybe one or both of the students beside her had been teasing or bullying her on the bus or playground and she was afraid to tell anyone. We don't know, but we do know that Emily needs some privacy and space so she can regroup and try to regulate her emotions without anyone talking to her for a while.

Next time, when her teacher notices these early "Act One" clues (turning away from people, hunching over her paper, shaking, and crying) Emily can be offered a quiet place to work far from other people, before the "Act Three" drama (screaming) can take over.

If we had treated Jacob's screaming and Emily's screaming as if they were identical behaviors, we would still have a lot of screaming. Looking at the antecedents, what happened before, was helpful. We also need to look at what happens after a behavior, the consequence (the "C" in the A-B-Cs), to see if this is holding the behavior in place, or making it more likely to occur again in the future.

In the case of Jacob, if his screaming had immediately resulted in being offered the help he needed, he might be more likely to scream again next time, because it worked. Likewise, if Emily's screaming had caused everyone to leave her alone, she might have used it every time she wanted privacy. In both cases, their teachers needed to make sure the consequences were not reinforcing, so that the same behavior didn't keep happening again and again, by not responding to the screams. At the same time, they needed to provide other ways to communicate their needs instead of screaming.

For Jacob, his teacher began looking for early signs that he didn't understand so she could intervene and offer help before he screamed for it. She also taught him to raise his hand for help, and reinforced that behavior every time he did.

For Emily, her teacher allowed her to choose a different seat away from the two students who were bothering her, and she asked the aide to give Emily space unless she asked for help. She also gave Emily a card that said, "Leave me alone, please," which she could show to request the space she needed instead of screaming.

We need to make sure the intervention fits the behavior and adequately addresses the communicative function of the behavior, or we might as well be blundering around the stage without a script.

ACT II, Scene Four Summary

In this scene, we learned the basic A-B-Cs of behavior: antecedents (what happened before), behavior (what happened), and consequences (what happened after). If we treat every behavior as if it had the same communicative intent or function, we would miss the boat far too often. Rather, we need to use the A-B-Cs to find out what the function of the behavior is—what our students are trying to ask for—so we can help them find a better way to meet that need. In the following scenes we'll go more in depth about the A-B-Cs.

In Their Own Words

"I want to change my anger because that's what gets me in trouble most often. There are many things that make me angry, all of which are out of my control, and then I can't control my anger. Like people telling me to do things when I am in the middle of something else. In school and at home, I am told to do something and then, wham! I'm told to do something else. I can't think of anything except for the list of things I'm supposed to do, and I get overwhelmed. When adults talk condescendingly to me and they don't listen to my side of a story, that also makes me angry. I feel like in school I get singled out a lot and that makes me the angriest. Other kids already think there's something wrong with me, and it only proves them right when a teacher points out something I was doing wrong in front of the whole class. An example of a teacher singling me out was when I was working in class with my laptop open. Many other students had theirs open, too. The teacher came over and shut my laptop. When I asked why, he said, 'You're bothering me.' I was steamed, because I was the only one who got talked to, even though other students were doing the same thing. Overall, I sometimes feel broken, because I don't see things like other people. When my parents or teachers talk to me, they think I don't care, but I do care. I don't want to be in trouble. I like my free time and playing my games, drawing, or playing sports."

~MJS, high-functioning autism behaviors

What Can We Learn from MJS' Story?

It can be very difficult for our students on the spectrum to shift gears and move from one task to another. If they are in the middle of doing one assignment and we interject to remind them of another assignment or ask a question, they may shut down and become unable to do either one, or over-react.

As teachers, we must be vigilant in our efforts to treat all students fairly and with respect, and to refrain from drawing attention to a student's weaknesses in front of peers. When a teacher picks on a student, the rest of the class understands that bullying is acceptable, or at least that it is acceptable to bully that particular student.

Many students on the spectrum already feel broken before they even walk through your door. You have the power to build them up, or to tear them down. Use that power wisely and kindly.

ACT II, Scene Four Vocabulary

antecedent	behavior support plan (BSP)
Board Certified Behavior Analyst® (BCBA)	
communicative intent	function
functional analysis (FA)	functional behavioral assessment (FBA)
setting event	trigger

 ACT II, Scene Four Discussion Topic

Think about a behavior in your own life that you might want to change, such as eating unhealthy snacks. Does something happen before you choose an unhealthy snack that might have prompted or triggered the behavior? Was there a setting event that made you want the snack more? Is there anything that happens after you eat an unhealthy snack that might make it more (or less) likely that you will make unhealthy snack choices again in the future? Is there anything you can do differently that could support the change you want to make? Discuss with your small group.

ACT II, Scene Four Questions

1. What do the letters stand for in A-B-C?
    A. Applied behavioral contingencies.
    B. Analytical behavior consultation.
    C. Antecedent, behavior, consequence.
    D. None of the above.

For questions 2-4 use the words *antecedent*, *behavior*, and *consequence*.

2. After Liam hit his brother, his brother game him the toy he wanted. This describes a(n) _____ that may make this behavior more likely to recur.

3. Liam used a closed fist to strike his brother on the upper arm. This describes Liam's _____ .

4. Liam's brother went into Liam's room and took a toy without permission. This describes the _____ .

5. A setting event takes place after the target behavior. TRUE or FALSE?

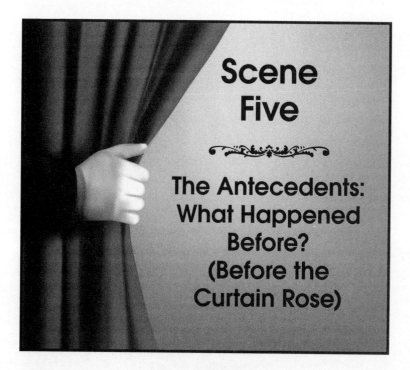

Scene Five

The Antecedents: What Happened Before? (Before the Curtain Rose)

"A" is for Antecedent

When we examine behavior to learn more about how to make meaningful changes, we always start with the antecedents, or what happened before the behavior. Antecedents include *triggering events,* specific events that seem to spark the behavior. They may also include setting events, like being hungry or anxious, or feeling tired or sick. Perhaps something is going on at home, on the bus, or on the playground that we know nothing about, but is affecting behavior.

Setting events can also be sensory experiences like the scent of disinfectant, the sound of a distant lawn mower, or the flickering of an overhead fluorescent light.

Antecedent Examples

Let's look at the antecedents and setting events for the five students we met in Scene Two. We'll start with Anthony, who acts out in class.

Example One: What Happened Before Anthony Acted Out?

Anthony entered the classroom Monday morning, and his teacher could already tell he would have a bad day. How could she tell? She knows her students well, and here are the cues she picked up on.

Anthony is usually cheerful and greets each adult when he arrives at school after a weekend or vacation. He asks repetitive questions about their weekends, and is eager to tell about his own weekend to anyone who will listen. Although he does not make as much eye contact as most typical students his age, Anthony occasionally glances toward the person he is talking to, he keeps his head upright or tilted slightly to one side, and he has a pleasant smile on his face. He immediately notices if there is anything new in the classroom, and shows curiosity by asking many questions.

However, today was one of his "bad days," which occur approximately once a month, usually on a Monday. Today, Anthony entered the room with his head down and a blank expression on his face. He did not make even fleeting eye contact with anyone, and turned away when his teacher tried to meet his eyes. He did not initiate questions or conversation, and when anyone spoke to him he ignored them, shrugged, or mumbled, "I don't know." These were the initial clues his teacher noticed.

When it was time for the first assignment of the day, writing about his weekend, Anthony sat and stared at his desk without getting out his journal or a pencil. When prompted by the aide a second time, he brought out his journal, but not a pencil. His breathing became louder, he puffed out his cheeks and blew air between his lips, and his face turned pink. He started fidgeting with his hands, flicking his fingers, and twisting his wrists in a circular motion. Then his loud breathing and blowing turned to a monotonic hum. He began rocking back and forth as if in a rocking chair, gripping the sides of his desk with both hands. The classroom aide walked over to him and reminded him to have "nice hands, Anthony, quiet mouth, quiet body."

Suddenly, he stood up and began pacing rapidly back and forth at the back of the room, shaking his hands at his sides, and his humming escalated to a prolonged moan with each exhalation. The aide approached him again and put her hand on his arm to lead him back to his desk. Those were the observable antecedent behaviors which led to more serious "acting out."

There were setting events, private or covert experiences going on with Anthony, as well. This was one of the weekends when his father failed to show up for their scheduled custodial visit, without calling to let them know he wouldn't be there. Anthony's mother was angry at her ex-husband all weekend because of this. Anthony picked up on her anger, but not on who she was angry with, and he assumed it must be his fault. We can't always know what's going on in our students' lives, but when we do get a heads up from a parent that the child had a bad weekend or night, we can be ready to cut him some slack. Communication between home and school is key.

Example Two: What Happened Before Destiny was Disruptive?

Whether it's time for a small group lesson at the whiteboard or a full-class activity using the overhead projector, Destiny is always ready. She seems to love being part of discussions and demonstrating her knowledge, as evidenced by the frequency and enthusiasm with which she tries to answer every question. When she is called on, she takes the opportunity to expand her answer into a lecture on the topic, or on a somewhat-related topic of her own preference. When she is not called on, she shows her disapproval by rolling her eyes and sighing audibly. When another student gives an incorrect or incomplete response, in her opinion, she expresses exasperation by stomping a foot or slapping her palms on her lap or desk, or she calls out the correct answer with an expression of disdain.

On this day, after several instances of waving her hand without being acknowledged, Destiny began calling out the answers without raising her hand. When the teacher ignored her and called on another student who gave the wrong answer, Destiny scowled and shouted the correct answer loudly. When the teacher asked her to be quiet, she shouted that the teacher hated her and that the other students were all idiots. Finally, she burst into tears and ran from the room.

Example Three: What Happened Before Daniel was Defiant?

The first observable antecedent for Daniel was being presented with an academic task, a page of mathematical word problems, which he was to complete independently. He looked at the page and sat quietly without picking up his pencil, as if in defiance of his teacher's instruction.

Notice that Daniel's first evidence of defiance—not working—is actually a non-behavior rather than a behavior. It is what he is not doing, rather than what he is doing, that is the problem. This is an example of a behavioral deficit like the ones we talked about in Scene Two.

When pressed to complete the work, Daniel made negative statements such as, "No," "I can't," and "I don't want to." When told that he would lose his recess if he did not complete the task, his behavior escalated. He talked back, argued, and shouted, "You can't make me!" and "Yes, I will, too, go to recess!"

Example Four: What Happened Before Sophia's Self-Injurious Behavior?

Sophia is in a small group of three students all morning. The groups rotate together from station to station, and students work with the teacher at one table, with one of the classroom aides at another table, and finally at an independent work station. When Sophia is given a task in the small group with an adult, she finishes it quickly. The other two students in her group have significant behavioral concerns and one in particular regularly screams or hits the aide between tasks or when unable to complete a task independently. Because of their needs, and Sophia's quiet compliancy, the majority of the adult's attention is directed toward the others in the group and Sophia is left to do her work on her own. She typically sits in her seat without moving or vocalizing after her task is finished. There are books to read and paper and crayons available in a plastic bin for students to use when they finish their work before it's time to move to the next station. Sophia has never requested these materials.

During the station rotation period, Sophia often exhibits three different types of self-injurious behavior (SIB): hand-biting, face-slapping, and head-banging. We'll examine the antecedents for each of them separately.

Sophia sat quietly after completing her work, touching her hand to her mouth with the side of the hand between the thumb and wrist in direct contact to her lips. After approximately two minutes of pressing her hand to her mouth, she pressed her teeth to her hand with greater and greater pressure, until eventually she was biting her hand quite hard.

On another occasion, immediately after another student had slapped the classroom aide, Sophia slapped her own face.

When another student screamed loudly and unexpectedly, Sophia struck her own forehead down upon the table with a loud smack.

Example Five: What Happened Before Aiden's Aggressive Behavior?

Aiden's teacher says that he often comes in after the lunch recess with a "chip on his shoulder." What does she mean by a "chip on his shoulder?" What she observes is that when he is in line waiting to come into the room, he complains frequently about being bumped or pushed by others. On this day, she also observed that he had pushed the students standing directly in front of and behind him, while shouting at them to stop pushing him. His facial expression looked angry: he had a deep frown, his eyebrows were lowered, and his eyes were narrowed as he glanced quickly back and forth between the two students closest to him in line.

As soon as he walked into the classroom he began making negative comments: the room was too hot, the pictures on the bulletin board were "stupid," the book the teacher was about to read to them was "boring." Although he settled down briefly when the teacher began to read the next chapter in their book, he soon began making rude mouth noises, muttering under his breath, and then calling out negative comments, until his teacher gave him a verbal reprimand. At this, Aiden yelled, swore, and got up and stomped back and forth at the back of the classroom. The classroom aide touched his arm in an attempt to lead him back to his seat, and he lashed out with his fists and dropped to the floor, flailing his legs and indiscriminately kicking people and furniture close to him.

Those are Aiden's observable antecedent behaviors. But what about before he lined up? Did something happen? In order to gather more data to better address the problem, we need to observe what happens during the unstructured period after lunch (or have a team member observe for us). This should occur daily for at least a week to note any patterns of behavior, because the very presence of a new adult in the area taking notes is unusual and may result in changes in behavior. Keep on observing each day until the observer is no longer of interest and everyone is acting as they usually do. In this way we can find out what went on before the behavior.

In Aiden's case, after multiple observations, it was noted that he spends the majority of his time after lunch walking around the perimeter of the quad with no apparent purpose. One day (which corresponded to an outburst after lunch), a group of boys was observed to follow him around the perimeter for a time, and then to overtake him and stand directly in his path, keeping him from completing his self-determined circuit. Although the observer could not hear what was said by the boys, this had the appearance of a bullying attempt and was reported to the vice principal. School and district bullying response protocol was subsequently followed.

ACT II, Scene Five Summary

In this scene, we have looked at the "A" in the A-B-Cs of behavior, antecedents, and the many ways in which events that happened beforehand can affect our students' behavior. We learned that unseen or covert setting events, such as feeling hungry, tired, sick, anxious, or afraid, can set our students up to fail. Finally, understanding these antecedent events is the key to turning the tables and setting the stage for success. In later scenes, we will take a closer look at how we can manipulate antecedent events to set our students up for success, but first we'll learn more about understanding and clearly defining problem behaviors.

In Their Own Words

"One year in elementary school, we had a project to construct a model of a mission building. (This was before we knew I had autism.) Our teacher told us not to make them too big because there wouldn't be room for all of them if they were huge. She said, 'Think small.' Since I had a skill with sculpting small objects with modeling clay, I made a very small mission, no bigger than two or three inches. I wanted it to be perfect, so I kept smashing it down and doing it over again, for hours and hours. When I brought it to school my teacher took one look at it and said, 'Well, you obviously didn't spend any time on that.' Not true. She gave me a 'D' while the missions which were desk-sized and larger all received passing grades, even though those kids ignored her instruction to 'think small.' I thought I had worked hard and done exactly what she asked, and she thought I had a bad attitude and poor work habits."

DW, 26, diagnosed with autism spectrum disorder as a teenager

What Can We Learn from DW's Story?

Our students on the spectrum are very literal, so be sure that your instructions reflect what you actually expect from your students. Also, don't make assumptions about a student's effort based solely on the finished product. And certainly, don't make disparaging remarks in front of the student and peers.

 ACT II, Scene Five Vocabulary

triggering event

 ACT II, Scene Five Discussion Topic

Think about a student you have observed who exhibited a behavior that seemed baffling or inexplicable at the time. Now think about an antecedent, setting event, or triggering event that may have preceded the behavior and affected it. Share your insights with your small group.

ACT II, Scene Five Questions

1. What does the "A" stand for in A-B-C?
   A. Applied.
   B. Analyst.
   C. Academic.
   D. Antecedent.

2. After Diego did his homework, his mother gave him a cookie. Was getting a cookie an antecedent? YES or NO?

3. Antecedents occur before the problem behavior. TRUE or FALSE?

For questions 4–7 use the words *antecedent* or *setting event*.

4. Noah was hungry after school when his mother took him on a few errands. After the second errand, when she told him they still had to go to the bank, Noah began to scream. Noah's hunger was a(n) _____ .

5. Being told they had to go to the bank was a(n) _____ .

6. After going to the bank, Noah's mother bought him an ice cream cone. He accidentally dropped it on the ground and then he kicked his mother. Dropping the ice cream was the _____ to kicking.

7. Noah was tired and hungry when he dropped his ice cream. These were the _____ (s).

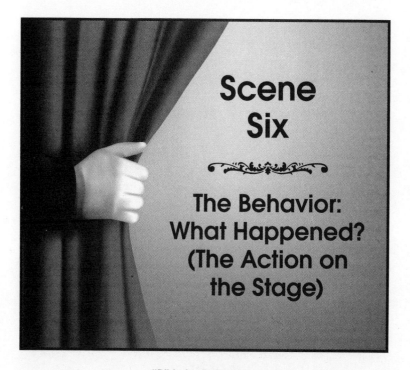

Scene Six

The Behavior: What Happened? (The Action on the Stage)

"B" is for Behavior

We may think we already know what the behavior is, but let's look at how we describe problematic behaviors. When we gather data about how often the behavior occurs, it helps if everyone on the team is counting the same behavior. If we try to count a problem behavior we call "having a bad attitude," we won't know what to count. It is too vague. Most of us assume we know it when we see it, but "bad attitude" doesn't really describe any particular behavior. It means different things to different people. We need to be specific rather than general, defining what the target behavior *is*, as well as what it is *not*, and describe it clearly enough that everyone on the team (classroom aides, support staff, student teachers, interns) knows what we're looking for. We also need to be able to explain to the student what it is they are doing that we don't like if we want them to change their behavior.

For example, instead of saying, "Mia has a bad attitude towards school work," we might write, "When given an academic task, Mia (1) rolls her eyes,

(2) sighs audibly so that her breathing may be heard by people across the room, (3) leans back in her chair or turns away from her desk, and (4) mutters quietly under her breath." To be clear, we might add, "Behaviors not incompatible with working, such as (1) looking around the room briefly, (2) quiet breathing which is not audible to someone across the room, (3) a posture which is relaxed but does not interfere with working on the task, and (4) asking questions related to the task or making comments appropriate to the situation, are not included in this behavior." Now Mia knows what people mean when they say, "Fix your attitude!" A note: under (4) we added "making comments appropriate to the situation" as not being included as an instance of "bad attitude." If Mia whispers to her friend, "Did he ask you to the prom?" it is not related to the assignment, and it is not appropriate during class time, but in it is not an indication of "bad attitude." To many teen-aged girls, whispering about boys is appropriate to the situation (being in class together) and, while it is an unwanted behavior, it does not fall under the description of "bad attitude."

Examples of Behavioral Definitions

We need to choose one behavior to address when there are multiple behaviors. Once we find the one we want to target, we need to define it clearly. Let's look at our five students again and develop clear, behavioral definitions for each problem behavior.

Example One: Defining Anthony's Acting Out Behavior

"Acting out" is another nebulous term, meaning different things to different people. What, precisely, did Anthony do that we consider "acting out?"

After the loud breathing, puffing out his cheeks and blowing, then rocking back and forth in his chair, then standing up and pacing around the room, his behavior *escalated*: it increased or became worse. When the aide placed her hand on Anthony's back and tried to guide him towards his desk, Anthony broke away. He ripped up the papers on his desk, threw his chair down, and ran to the back of the room. He stood with his face to a corner, pressing his forehead to the wall while emitting a prolonged, high-pitched wail.

We've observed a number of behaviors here. Which one should we target to describe for a behavior change plan? Obviously, throwing his chair is an extremely problematic behavior that we do not want to see repeated. Conversely, loud breathing is a minor behavior that is probably barely even on your radar. When we choose a behavior for change, we need to focus on the behavior that will make the biggest impact. Because he threw the chair down towards the floor, did not direct it toward any person, and this was the first time he has done anything like this, it may be a single occurrence that won't happen again. If we decide to document only "chair-throwing" behavior, and Anthony never throws a chair again, it will look like there's no problem. Month after month, our data shows zero occurrences of the problem behavior. Success!

Meanwhile, back in the classroom, Anthony may be pacing, yelling, and ripping paper daily without escalating all the way to the chair-throwing stage. The classroom continues to be disrupted, even though the data shows success.

Instead of focusing on the most severe—but least frequent—behavior, let's look at the precursor behaviors (remember the "A": antecedents). This way we may be able to stop the behavior before we see flying furniture.

The loud breathing is the first antecedent behavior we observe. You might want to describe and take data on that behavior, or you might want to just be aware of it and use it as an early warning sign that you can address before it escalates.

Rocking back and forth is a mannerism that often signals something is wrong. If you try to eliminate the behavior, though, you may find that a new, and more problematic, behavior will emerge. Don't try to enforce sitting still when you have a student who rocks to self-regulate, like Anthony, but do recognize it as another early warning sign.

If you are unable to fix the problem by discovering and eliminating sources of stress when you see these two antecedents, loud breathing and rocking, then the next behavior may occur. In Anthony's case, this is pacing around the room. We know that whatever is wrong is really bothering him now, so this is a good behavior to count and monitor, to prevent the subsequent behaviors of tearing up papers, screaming, and throwing his chair.

Describe this behavior clearly. For example, "Anthony stands up and walks back and forth in the classroom for more than five seconds, with no apparent purpose." (We say, no "apparent" purpose because we assume that pacing serves a purpose for Anthony, even though that purpose is not apparent to the observer.) We also need to describe what does *not* constitute the behavior: "Rising briefly and returning to his seat within five seconds, or walking for a specific purpose (such as going to sharpen a pencil) and then returning to his seat, are not included."

Now we have an easily understood definition of the target behavior (the behavior we want to change). With this description we can go on to measure and work on reducing Anthony's pacing behavior for the purpose of preventing future instances of yelling, paper-ripping, and chair-throwing. But that's another scene.

Example Two: Defining Destiny's Disruptive Behavior

What, exactly, does Destiny do that disrupts the lesson? The series of behaviors starts with excessively raising her hand to answer every question, then escalates to calling out answers without being called on, correcting her classmates' answers, and challenging and arguing with the teacher. Ultimately Destiny calls the teacher names, shouts that the teacher "hates her" and "never calls on her," cries, and leaves the classroom without permission.

Which of these behaviors warrant defining so we can keep data on it? Frequently raising her hand is a behavioral excess; there is nothing wrong with this particular behavior, the problem is how often she engages in it. We may not consider this to be very disruptive, depending on how vigorously this is done, and we do not want to discourage hand-raising behavior in general.

The ultimate behavior of leaving the classroom without permission is potentially quite dangerous, as it could result in running into the parking lot or street or becoming lost. If this occurs, it will be important to prioritize this behavior because of the risk involved. The behavior could be defined as, "Destiny leaves the classroom without permission." Simple. You might add, "Leaving the room with the entire class as for recess, with a small group to the library or other destination as directed, or to the restroom or office with permission, are not included."

If Destiny only ran out of the room once, you might not consider her to be at significant risk for elopement. (*Elopement* is the behavioral term for running away or leaving without permission.) If it is rare, and the campus is well-fenced to prevent access to the street, you may want to target one of her other behaviors to focus on.

Calling out answers without waiting to be called on may seem like a rather mild behavior in the grander scheme of things, but any teacher who has a Destiny would disagree. Teachers are aware of how much time this behavior can siphon away from other students, not to mention how it disrupts the flow of the lesson. Also, if unchecked it can escalate into more disruptive behaviors or even potentially dangerous elopement. So let's focus on this behavior, which might be described as, "Verbally responding to questions or vocally commenting without being called on by the teacher. Not included are joining in choral responses when the teacher has indicated that a choral response is desired, responding after the teacher has acknowledged her, and comments or conversations outside the group lesson or direct instruction setting." This clear definition will help us address and reduce or eliminate the problem behavior.

Example Three: Defining Daniel's Defiant Behavior

Let's take a look at Daniel's defiance. How will we describe it so everyone on the team can recognize the behavior we're focusing on? First he did not begin work when given a worksheet (behavioral deficit) and he mumbled, then shouted negative statements. When pressed to complete the work, Daniel ripped up the paper, swore at the adult and shouted statements such as, "You can't make me!" and "Yes, I am going to recess!" Finally, he ran to the office on his own without being sent, and paced or sat in the outer office until an administrator or staff member talked to him and eventually sent him back to class.

The ultimate behavior, running to the office, is not seen as dangerous because he has never attempted to leave the campus or go anywhere other than directly to the office, presumably in a preemptive strike before the teacher could send him there.

Let's focus on what happened before that stage, notably the negative comments which escalated from mumbling to shouting. We might start with the negative mumbling and describe his behavior this way: "When given an academic task, rather than beginning work on the task, Daniel makes negative comments such as, 'No,' or 'This is too hard,' or 'I won't.' Not included are requests for help or clarification, or neutral comments or questions about the paper or other topics." Now we know which verbal behaviors to document and count, and which ones are not problematic enough to focus on at this time. Addressing the difficulty early may keep it from becoming over-dramatized later on.

▨ Example Four: Defining Sophia's Self-Injurious Behavior

Naturally, we are concerned about Sophia's self-injurious behavior (SIB). We must never ignore any self-harm by assuming "that's just what some people with autism do." Her SIB may be a strong attempt to communicate that something is wrong, or that something is missing, or that she is in pain. How do we describe it so everyone recognizes it? Here are behavioral definitions of three kinds of self-injury Sophia engages in at different times:

(1) "Sophia bites her hand with enough force to leave a mark which is still visible more than ten seconds after removing her hand from her mouth, and which may or may not break the skin. Not included are light touches of the teeth to the hand which do not break the skin, and which do not leave visible marks lasting more than ten seconds."

(2) "Sophia hits her own face with her palm with sufficient force that the sound of the slap may be heard across the classroom and the skin is visibly pink following the slap. Not included are touching her face with her hand or fingers gently enough so that the contact is not audible by a person within one foot of her, leaving no visible marks or discoloration."

(3) "Sophia strikes her head against a firm surface such as a table, wall, door, or another person, with sufficient force that the sound may be heard across the room, or that it causes pain to the person she strikes. This does not include gently tapping or leaning her head against surfaces or objects with no audible force or which can only be faintly heard by a person who is in close proximity."

Notice that we have addressed intensity in each description. This helps clarify which behaviors are considered self-injurious and which are not.

Example Five: Defining Aiden's Aggressive Behavior

Aiden's aggression is definitely problematic. It not only disrupts the classroom learning environment, but it puts his classmates (and staff) at risk of being hurt. The target behavior might be described in detail like this: "Aiden engages in verbal outbursts including negative comments and name-calling. When touched by another person, such as an adult attempting to physically guide him back to his seat, he falls to the floor, hits out with his fists, and kicks out with his legs, indiscriminately striking nearby persons and objects. The target behavior is striking other people with his fists and/or feet. The intensity is medium to high, based on proximity to his fists and feet, i.e., closer objects or people are struck with greater force and those who are farther from him are grazed with little force. Accidental contact while moving normally through the room or area, such as brushing against or tripping over another person in passing, is not included."

ACT II, Scene Six Summary

In the previous scene we looked at antecedents to behavior (what happened before), and now we've described behaviors clearly enough that everyone on our team knows exactly what the behavior is, as well as what it is not. In Scene Seven we'll move on to the "C" in the A-B-Cs of behavior: consequences.

In Their Own Words

"When I was in elementary school I had a teacher that I thought did not like me. I didn't know why, because I liked her. I started studying how friends behave so I could do something friendly that would make her like me better. Friends call each other by their first names, rather than the formal 'Mrs.' I noticed her full name written on an envelope on her desk, so I called her by her first name as a gesture of friendliness. As you might imagine, this did not go over well at all. My attempt to be friendly was seen as disrespectful and a behavior problem."

~DW, diagnosed with autism spectrum disorder in middle school

What Can We Learn from DW's Story?

Don't assume the worst. If you have students with autism who do not understand the unwritten rules of social conduct, their awkward blunders may be innocent and without malicious intent. Try explicitly teaching the social rules that their typical peers already know, so they can avoid making the same mistake again.

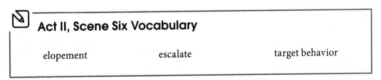

Act II, Scene Six Vocabulary

elopement	escalate	target behavior

ACT II, Scene Six Discussion Topic

Think about a problem behavior you have observed. Describe it clearly in behavioral terms, including what the behavior is as well as what does not constitute the behavior. Share with your small group.

ACT II, Scene Six Questions

1. What does the letter "B" stand for in A-B-C?
   A. Behavioral.
   B. Behavior.
   C. Board Certified.
   D. None of the others.

For items 2–4, is this a clear behavioral description? YES or NO

2. Charlotte is rude to classmates, siblings, and adults—both at home and at school—90 percent of the time when someone talks to her.

3. Liam uses a closed fist to strike his brother with sufficient force as to cause pain and/or bruising. Gentle pats, taps, and "fist bumps" which do not cause pain or bruising are not included.

4. Abigail harms herself or others when she is under stress.

5. TRUE or FALSE? *Elopement* is not considered an appropriate target for behavior change unless the students are in high school and/or are old enough to get married without parental consent in their state of residence.

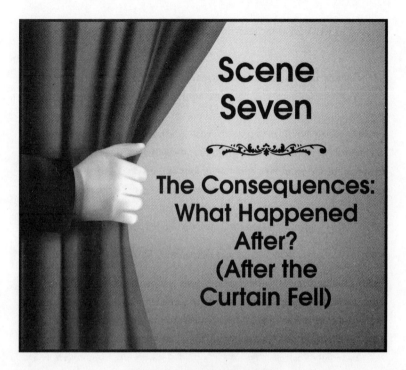

Scene Seven

The Consequences: What Happened After? (After the Curtain Fell)

"C" is for Consequences

What happened after the behavior? When the scene is over and the curtain drops, it's not over yet. The consequences are important, even though they can't change the behavior that just happened (unless you have a time machine). However, consequences can affect the likelihood that the same behavior may occur again in the future. If we don't want to keep seeing the same behavior we need to make some changes, including changing the consequences (or what happened after the behavior).

If a student does something that results in a *reinforcing* or pleasant (desired) consequence, such as praise, a gold star, or a positive phone call home, she is more likely to do the same thing in the future in hopes of gaining the same reward.

If she does something that results in an *aversive* or unpleasant (undesired) result, such as being yelled at, or put in time out, or sent to the office, then if she wants to avoid those consequences, she may choose not to do those things in the future.

One size does not fit all, though. We may think that one thing will be reinforcing and another thing will be aversive, but that doesn't mean our student feels the same way. One girl's gold star is another girl's garbage.

If your student is acting out in an attempt to escape or avoid a non-preferred task, and you send her to the office, she may view that as a reward. Next time she wants to get out of an assignment she's likely to engage in the same behavior that got her sent to the office last time, because it worked.

Another student may hate the unstructured, physically challenging, and highly social atmosphere of the playground. If you tell him that he will miss recess if he does not turn in his homework, you may never see another homework assignment again. My advice is to never take away recess as a consequence. The students who hate being outside will find it reinforcing, and the ones who need active movement the most will have a hard time coping through the afternoon without recess. For adults, the law provides that employees must be allowed regular breaks during their work day. Our boss can't take away our break just because he's mad at us. By the same token, recess should be every child's right, and not a privilege to be earned.

Remember, consequences include everything that happened right after the behavior, not just the things we plan. For instance, let's suppose that one day little Ava was washing her hands at the classroom sink before lunch, when a fire alarm went off as she turned on the tap. The sound was painful to her super-sensitive ears. Now, she refuses to touch the cold water tap on that sink. She has no problem turning on the water at other sinks, and she willingly washes her hands at that sink if someone else turns it on for her, but she will not touch that tap. The unexpected and unplanned consequence the last time she turned on the tap—the loud alarm—affected her behavior in the future.

Any of our students' most baffling behaviors, which make no sense to us, may have been associated with consequential occurrences the child remembers, but we do not. In cases such as Ava's, it could take some serious detective work to try to figure out what happened. Sometimes we will never know.

Fortunately, knowledge of the past, while enlightening, is not necessary in order to move forward and address behavioral excesses and deficits. There is much to be learned by documenting observable consequences, and usually our detective work pays off.

Examples of Consequences

Let's look at the consequences that followed each of our five students' problem behaviors and see how they may have kept the behaviors in place. In future scenes, we'll talk about interventions, but for now, we're simply observing the consequences; what happened after the behavior happened?

Example One: What Happened After Anthony Acted Out?

Immediately after Anthony ripped his paper and threw his chair down, he ran to the back of the room and placed himself in the corner, pressing his head against the wall and moaning. This was another part of his behavior chain, and not a consequence, since he did it himself. The teacher and aide quickly determined that no other students had been hit or hurt by the chair. By a predetermined action plan, the aide and Anthony's classmates evacuated the room and went to the library to continue their work. The teacher gave Anthony a few minutes to calm down on his own. When he was able to hear her, she reminded him of the rules he had broken ("Work quietly" and "Be safe") and she filled out a referral slip and escorted him to the office. He sat calmly in the office for fifteen minutes until the vice principal could meet with him. Anthony nodded in the affirmative when asked if he had, indeed, thrown the chair, but offered no explanation. When asked, "Why?" he shook his head, shrugged, and looked down without speaking. Eventually, he was sent back to his classroom as he appeared to be docile and not dangerous to himself or others. By this time, journal writing was over and he joined his reading group in progress, with no further behavior problems.

Do you see the major problem with this scenario? That's right, he escaped the journal writing activity. If his goal was to get out of writing about his weekend, then his behavior was successful for him. It worked. Although we can't be sure this was the function of his behavior without conducting a functional behavior assessment, it's a pretty good hypothesis to start with.

Example Two: What Happened After Destiny was Disruptive?

The initial consequence of Destiny's behavior of raising her hand for every question was that she was called on more frequently than her classmates, at least until it became excessive. Maybe this was because Destiny seemed so eager to respond, and also because the teacher knew she could count on Destiny to have the correct answer. Later, the teacher called on her less frequently in order to give others a chance, and Destiny began calling out the answers and correcting her classmates more often and loudly.

The consequences followed a sequence: the first few times, her teacher accepted and acknowledged that her answer was correct without mentioning the fact that Destiny had failed to raise her hand. The next several times it happened, her teacher acknowledged that she was correct, but also stated that Destiny should have raised her hand. By now Destiny may have assumed that she held an unspoken position as co-teacher or leading expert in the field, for whom the hand-raising rules do not apply. Later, when the behavior continued, her teacher told Destiny that she simply must not call out answers without waiting to be called on, pointing out that other students should also have a chance to respond. When Destiny argued that she knew the answers and the others didn't, her teacher engaged in a back-and-forth argument, during which Destiny's voice became progressively louder, higher, and more strident. Destiny stomped her foot, called the teacher a "tyrant," and yelled, "You hate me!" and "It's not fair!" The teacher reprimanded Destiny, and directed her to move to the back of the class and be quiet. Destiny burst into tears and ran out of the classroom. When Destiny was found crying in the girls' restroom, she was sent to the office where she told her side of the story to the vice principal at great length. After forty-five minutes, she was sent back to class. A note was written to her parents detailing the incident, and Destiny repeated her story to the home audience. If she had been seeking drama or attention, she got what she was looking for.

Example Three: What Happened After Daniel was Defiant?

After Daniel mumbled, shouted, paced, and finally ran to the office, he waited there until an administrator was able to see him. When asked why he was in the office, he said he didn't know. When asked if he was in trouble with his teacher, he said maybe. He did not elaborate, and the administrator called the teacher. She recommended that Daniel should spend his recess time doing the paper he had refused to do in class.

During recess, Daniel sat against the wall with his paper and pencil and watched the other boys play a game of soccer. When his teacher saw that he had not done the paper she told him to take it home for extra homework. For several days the paper rode back and forth in his backpack, accompanied by other papers he had not completed in class, until his teacher called his mother. The next day the papers were returned, in an adult's handwriting. When asked who did the work, Daniel shrugged. The ultimate consequence of his behavior was that he successfully avoided the task.

Example Four: What Happened After Sophia's SIB?

Because Sophia's self-injurious behaviors have occurred frequently over time rather than being a single incident, each is described as the behavior typically manifests.

Usually, when Sophia bites her hand, the adult closest to her removes her hand from her mouth, tells her not to bite herself, and gives her a book or paper and crayons to distract her. Sophia accepts the materials offered, and she looks at the page numbers in the book or writes strings of numbers with the crayons until it is time to switch to the next center. The consequence of biting her hand was receiving objects of interest to her.

When Sophia slaps her face (following a classmate slapping an adult nearby), an adult holds her hands down and says, "Nice hands," or "No hitting." Meanwhile, the student who slapped the adult has been removed from the group and his behavior is dealt with by the teacher in another part of the classroom. Sophia returns to her task. From Sophia's point of view, the consequence of slapping her face was the removal of the peer who slapped.

After Sophia strikes her head against the table (following a classmate screaming nearby), an adult intervenes and gently holds her so that she is unable to continue to hit her head on the table, using the safe technique staff have been trained in. At the same time, another adult responds to the student who screamed. If his screaming continues, he is removed from the classroom. Once the sound has stopped, Sophia returns to her task. The consequence of hitting her head on the table was the removal of the painful sound, her classmate's scream.

Example Five: What Happened After Aiden's Aggressive Behavior?

After Aiden fell to the floor and hit and kicked the aide, the classroom was evacuated and students and aide went to the library.

When he was alone with the teacher, Aiden lay quietly on the floor in the fetal position. His teacher asked him to get up, and he showed no response or awareness. She took his arm to try to help him stand and return to his chair, and he lashed out with fists and feet, undirected, and then curled up more tightly. She paused, tried talking to him again with no response, and touched his arm gently to get his attention. This resulted in Aiden lashing out again. She left him alone and worked at her desk nearby, allowing him to recover and self-regulate in his own way.

Eventually, Aiden stood up and sat in a chair without assistance. When asked why he hit or kicked, he looked at the floor and shook his head without speaking. When the teacher continued to ask him questions about his feelings or behavior, he put his head down on his desk and cried quietly.

Because of his school's policy regarding aggressive behavior, Aiden was sent home for the remainder of the day, and an independent education program (IEP) meeting was scheduled to discuss whether his behavior adversely affected his own or others' education. The immediate consequence of his aggression was the removal of other students, the aide, and academic demands.

What's the Function?

How can we learn more about which consequences might be reinforcing, and which might be punishing? We need a working hypothesis about the function of the behavior. What is the communicative intent? It must be providing some benefit for them, or they wouldn't do it. Maybe it's helping them escape from something aversive or painful. Maybe it's helping them get something they want or need. Maybe it's giving them some kind of sensory stimulation which is pleasing to them but could be inexplicable to us. We can't know just by looking at the behavior. A functional behavior assessment (FBA) with your school psychologist or a functional analysis (FA) with a Board Certified Behavior Analyst® (BCBA) can help determine what function the behavior serves for the student. Based on hypotheses generated by the behavior assessment team, you can start putting in place procedures that will help increase positive (desired) behaviors and decrease negative (undesired) behaviors. Fortunately, many classroom behaviors are not severe enough to require the behavior team, and may be managed successfully by the teacher.

ACT II, Scene Seven Summary

We know the A-B-Cs of behavior are just the preliminary building blocks, or the "prequel" to effectively dealing with behavior. In Scene Seven we looked more closely at the "C" in the A-B-Cs, consequences. We saw how intended and unintended consequences may affect future behavior, and how planned consequences must be individualized; one size does not fit all. Usually teachers can make needed changes in their own classrooms to improve student behavior. In the case of severe behaviors, it is recommended to call in the school psychologist or BCBA to help determine the function of the behavior and make a behavior plan with appropriate interventions. In Scene Eight we'll look at immediate interventions teachers can put in place when the behavior recurs before the behavior plan has been fully implemented.

In Their Own Words

"In high school, I kept my pencil moving on the paper at all times, even when we were not meant to be taking notes. I did this to re-channel my nervous energy. I had an algebra teacher who interpreted my behavior as a sign of inattention. I was repeatedly ordered to stop doodling. As a result, I was completely unable to focus in class. There was a buildup of nervous energy that would have been worked out via the non-distracting stim of doodling. The 'unwanted behavior' of doodling decreased, but the following semester I was in the remedial math class because I had been set back so far. The ultimate consequence to me as a student was that I was not able to learn at my natural pace and in my own way, and a subject that I previously had mild struggles with became one that I felt I could never catch up in or get a handle on."

~Cat, diagnosed with autism spectrum disorder as a college student

What Can We Learn from Cat's Story?

Don't assume that students who doodle or fidget are not listening to you. If they can demonstrate that they are learning the information, then be lenient about allowing non-distracting movement or doodling during lectures.

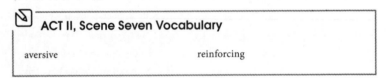

ACT II, Scene Seven Vocabulary

aversive   reinforcing

Act II, Scene Seven Discussion Topic

Think about a behavior that you have observed in a classroom or other setting. What happened right after the behavior? Do you think that consequence would *increase* or *decrease* the likelihood that the child will repeat the same behavior in the future? Share with your small group.

✉ Act II, Scene Seven Questions

1. What does the "C" stand for in the A-B-Cs of behavior?
   A. Continuous.
   B. Contract.
   C. Contingency.
   D. Consequence.

For questions 2–4, use the words *increased* or *decreased*.

2. William hates going outside to recess. His teacher tells him if he does not finish his math paper he must stay inside during recess. Now his math paper completion rate has dramatically _____ .

3. Emily loves to read but has a poor history of turning in required book reports. She often talks about wanting her father to be proud of her, and seems to crave positive attention from him. Her teacher promised to send a good note to her father whenever she completes and turns in three book reports. Now Emily's book report completion has significantly _____ .

4. Liam always wants to be first in line. He often pushes other students in line when he is not first. His teacher says that he cannot always be first because their class has a system where everyone gets a turn. However, she tells him that after one week of no pushing in line she will give him a three-second head start to recess on his next turn of being first. Now Liam's pushing behavior has greatly _____ .

5. Making recess contingent on good behavior is a good idea; taking away recess should always be the first consequence that a teacher tries with every student. TRUE or FALSE?

Scene Eight

The Interventions: What Do We Do When It Happens?

t happens. A student engages in a behavior that disrupts class or interferes with learning, and we need to do something; it's up to us to *intervene*. To intervene has been defined as "to come between, to hinder or modify, or to change an outcome to improve functioning." An *intervention* is systematically applied in behavior analysis in an effort to improve socially significant behaviors to a meaningful degree (Baer, Wolf, and Risley 1968).

Long-term interventions which are part of our behavior plans may include such things as antecedent manipulations (setting the stage, preparing for success) and specific strategies to put into play (token economy, behavioral contract, self-management techniques) which we will explore further in later scenes. Right now, let's talk about immediate interventions. What do we do, right there on the spot, when the behavior occurs again before we've had a chance to put our plans into action?

As teachers, we are daily called upon to intervene, to make a change that makes a difference, so our students can keep learning and growing. It may be as subtle as giving our students "the look" when they are starting to step out of line, or as serious as sending students to the office or detention, or even referring them for suspension or expulsion. The better able our students are to respond to subtle interventions, the less likely they are to be subjected to the more serious ones.

Unfortunately, our students on the autism spectrum are often unaware of, or misinterpret, facial expressions or tone. When a teacher gives "the look," most of the class snaps into line, quickly putting away the rulers they had been sword-fighting with, folding their hands, and assuming an angelic expression. Our ASD students are the lone stragglers who continue to laugh and brandish their rulers. They may complain that they are always the ones in trouble when "everyone else was doing it, too," but the fact remains that they got caught while their neurotypical classmates knew when to stop.

So we can expect that, along the path to learning better behaviors, there will be times when our students with autism get caught in the act of doing the wrong thing. How do we respond when this happens? Our response can go a long way toward assuring that the same thing doesn't keep happening again and again.

The first thing to remember is a cliché: "Keep calm and carry on." One reason a saying becomes a cliché is because of the truth in it. When the teacher remains calm, the student who is misbehaving, and the rest of the class, all find it easier to stay calm themselves.

The next thing is to become a behavior detective. Can you see a trigger or setting event which may have caused the behavior, and if so, can you remove the trigger or intervene to lessen its effect? One special education teacher noticed that her student, Emily, screamed several times a day. By observing and taking notes, she realized that Emily's screaming happened right after the school bells rang and when someone used the electric pencil sharpener which was right behind her desk. She also screamed on rainy days when the class had indoor recess and they were being particularly noisy in the confined space of the classroom. Emily did not scream during quiet times, her teacher noticed. She decided to change two things: first, she moved the electric pencil sharpener across the room so that it was not near

Emily's desk. Second, her teacher created a quiet place for Emily to retreat to by placing a beanbag, pillows, books, and headphones under a table. Two minutes before a bell was scheduled to ring, Emily's teacher invited her to go to the quiet place. Emily's teacher also found Emily a Social Story* (Gray 2015). The story helped Emily understand the reason for school bells, such as fire alarms, and that she would be safe. Emily's teacher also taught her that when she hears a loud noise that hurts her ears, she can cover her ears and say, "That's too loud," instead of screaming.

Finally, we must fit the intervention to the behavior. You don't want to send your student to the office every time a behavior occurs while you are in the process of making changes to improve the behavior. Change doesn't happen overnight, and there will be instances of the undesired behavior along the way. If you know it's going to happen again during the process of working to improve it, you can have a plan to respond appropriately rather than reacting impulsively. You don't want to ignore or under-respond to behaviors which may be dangerous to the student or others, though. Teachers have a responsibility to keep our students safe, and to maintain an environment where everyone can learn.

Extinction—Don't Try This at Home

That is, don't try *extinction* in your classroom, unless you are working with a behavior specialist or behavior analyst who is trained in this principle of applied behavior analysis.

You may have heard that you should *ignore* bad behavior and then it will magically go away. Although this misconception is based on a scientific principle, extinction, the process is far more complex. According to Miltenberger, "Extinction occurs when a behavior that has been previously reinforced no longer results in the reinforcing consequences and therefore, the behavior stops occurring in the future" (Miltenberger 2012).

An example of extinction is seen when a man goes to visit his friend, rings the doorbell, and there is no response. He knows his friend is at home and expecting him, so he rings the doorbell again, and a third or fourth time. Finally, he knocks and his friend immediately answers the door. The next time he visits he rings the bell once before knocking, and after that he never rings the doorbell again. Doorbell ringing behavior has been *extinguished*, because it was not reinforced by his friend answering the door. This is fairly simple and straightforward. However, in the classroom extinction is not so simple, nor is it automatically successful.

Imagine William, a student who yells, "Teacher!" whenever he needs help. At first, his teacher came over to help him when he shouted. Later, she responded by reminding him to raise his hand while walking over to help him. Every time he yelled, "Teacher!" she helped him; the words she said on her way, the verbal reminders to raise his hand, were meaningless. It was all part of his routine for getting help: (1) I yell "Teacher!" (2) She says something about raising my hand, and (3) she helps me. The important connection William made was that (1) leads to (3). The teacher's reminder (2) was immaterial to the link between yelling and receiving help, so he continued to yell. Yelling was reinforced; it worked for him.

Eventually the teacher realized that all of her reminders had not changed William's behavior at all. He still yelled, "Teacher!" every time he needed help, only now she was tired of it. She had heard of extinction, and decided to ignore him whenever he yelled at her. She believed that he was yelling for attention, and that if she stopped giving him attention, he would stop yelling. It seemed pretty straightforward to her, so she put her plan in place.

The next day, when William got stuck on a math problem, he yelled, "Teacher!" as usual, but this time she ignored him. He tried yelling louder, and with greater frequency: "TEACHER-TEACHER-TEACHER-TEACHER!" She walked away and continued to ignore him. Now his behavior escalated, and he slammed his math book against his desk. She pretended that he didn't exist, although his classmates were now having trouble concentrating. He threw the book on the floor and stood on top of his desk, screaming "TEACHER! HELP ME!" at the top of his lungs. She wondered if she was perhaps not ignoring him effectively enough, and tried even harder to refrain from reacting to his behavior. William's next step was to tip over his desk and the desks of the two students beside him. Now she couldn't possibly ignore him, as the safety of her other students was at stake. She finally acknowledged him and sent him to the office.

Do you see the problem with off-handedly trying to use ignoring to put behaviors on extinction in the classroom? When students inappropriately seek attention, it's usually because they need attention. William did not know how to do his math problem. Do you know what else he did not know how to do? He did not know how to appropriately ask for help. All the times he had shouted, "Teacher," and she had helped him, her actions spoke much louder than her words. She may have been saying, "Raise your hand," and "Don't shout at me," but what she did was to give him what he needed. Since she never specifically taught him to appropriately request help, he kept doing what worked for him. Then, when she suddenly withdrew all attention from him and completely ignored the request that she used to respond to, William didn't know what to do. His behavior escalated as he became more and more confused, hurt, and angry by her inexplicable behavior. Eventually, when she couldn't possibly ignore him anymore, he got two things: first, he was removed from the classroom to the office (which removed the math problem as well); and second, he was removed from the Twilight Zone of being invisible to his teacher. Imagine how it must feel to have someone act as if you are not there, no matter what you do or say. What William learned from this was that yelling, "Teacher!" was no longer effective in getting his teacher's attention, but that tipping over desks was effective. The danger is that next time he needs help, he might skip the yelling and go straight to the behavior that worked.

Now we know we shouldn't simply ignore bad behavior (unless it is part of a behavior extinction plan supervised by a school psychologist, behavior specialist, or Board Certified Behavior Analyst®). So, what should we do when our ASD student engages in the undesired behavior we are trying to reduce or eliminate? If we don't have a response plan already in mind, we are apt to react on the spur of the moment, and our actions could make the behavior worse instead of better.

So, what should we do?

Teach the Skills They Need to Succeed

Usually, students do the wrong thing for one of two reasons: they don't know how to do the right thing, or the wrong thing has been working for them. In William's case, the wrong thing (yelling "Teacher!") was the only way he had ever asked for help in the past, so he didn't know another way. Also, it had always been effective, so he had no reason to change.

William's teacher needed to teach him how to raise his hand to request help, not just remind him. Like many students on the spectrum, he did not benefit from *incidental learning*, observing what other students do in a similar situation and imitating them. She decided that, even though everyone else already knew how to raise their hand to ask for help, William needed direct instruction in this skill. She started by posting classroom rules, including "Raise your hand," and having a discussion about what each rule meant. She had several people model raising a hand and waiting to be called on before asking for help. Later, if William called out, "Teacher!" from across the room, she immediately turned and gave him attention, but she didn't help him yet. She reminded him of the rule about raising hands and waited expectantly. As soon as his hand went into the air, she came to him and gave him the help he needed. Eventually she reduced giving him attention for calling out by simply raising her hand and pointing to the rule, not looking at him until after he had raised his hand.

Examples of Interventions

Let's look at some immediate interventions for our five example students, starting with Anthony.

Example One: What Do We Do When Anthony Acts Out?

The plan for Anthony is to help him self-regulate when he is under stress so that he can control his own behavior. Allowing him to rock in his seat, which does not interfere with the classroom or with learning, is one way to let him calm himself down. However, if the stressor remains, his ability to self-regulate by rocking alone may diminish. If he gets up and starts to pace, it may be time to intervene. It is important that all staff members are instructed not to touch Anthony when he is upset; touching him at this point has resulted in escalation of undesired behaviors such as ripping papers and tipping his desk over. Rather than touching him, an adult may offer Anthony a break, which is what his behavior is telling them he needs. He also needs an acceptable way to ask for a break. An aide may offer him a card that says, "I need a break," which he can use as a temporary escape from the assignment. This does not mean that he never has to do the journal writing, just that it will be postponed until he feels calmer. Do not make him do the work during recess, however. He needs this break from the classroom more than ever. Later, the journal writing can be substituted for a learning center activity or done at another appropriate time. If it is likely that the subject of the writing assignment was responsible (at least in part) for the behavior, the teacher may wish to change the topic. If Anthony's mother called the teacher to say that he had a rough weekend, then "How I Spent My Weekend" will not be a good idea. Try something related to his interests, such writing about "Dinosaur's Favorite Weekend."

If the behavior escalates too quickly or if the teacher did not have advance warning that he had a difficult weekend, the teacher will find herself in the position of responding to the behavior rather than preventing the behavior. Having a pre-established evacuation plan in place is something many special education teachers have in case a student has an unexpected outburst or tantrum that affects the entire classroom or might endanger classmates. An aide quietly and calmly leads the rest of the class to a predetermined place, either the playground or the library or other location. They should have a planned course of action, such as listening to the aide read a story aloud, or practicing hopping on one foot and then the other while counting by twos, fives, or tens. This should not be an extra free recess, but should in some way provide a learning or enriching experience in an alternate setting. Some teachers even have a bag near the door with books and other materials to take with them so that learning continues while they are out of the classroom. Some periodically stage surprise trips out of the classroom when there is no behavioral outburst, just to get students used to the idea at a non-stressful time.

The teacher remains with Anthony to ensure his safety. At first, she keeps her distance and sees that once the room is empty he becomes calmer and his breathing starts to return to normal. She does not rush to communicate with him yet, because she knows he will continue to feel the after-effects of the adrenaline rush he experienced during his outburst. She does other work while waiting for him to calm down, and takes her cue from him and his body language. Has his breathing returned to normal? Have excess body movements quieted down? After a time, when he seems ready to hear her, she suggests he sit in the quiet place under the library table and listen to music. Once he is settled and calm, she signals the aide to bring the rest of the class back inside.

It is tempting to want to push a student with autism to talk about their feelings, or to ask them why they acted that way, or what they could do differently next time. Anthony's teacher understands she must not do this. Right after an outburst, she lets Anthony rest without pushing him to talk about it. Communication is difficult for him even in the best of times, and may be impossible when he is under stress.

Because she has been paying attention to his behavior, Anthony's teacher is likely to recognize the precursors of his outburst in advance next time. Even before the pacing starts she can remind him that he can use his "break" card if he needs it (she will have taught him what it means and how to use it during a non-stressful time). Importantly, she is always sure to honor the card when he plays it. She knows better than to try to push Anthony to do more work before taking a break when he plays the break card ("Just do five more problems and then you can take your break"). This could be harmful to his faith in her and in the power of the break card. Once she has taught him that this is a self-regulation tool he can use to avoid a full meltdown, she needs to let him take a break when he asks for one. If she worries that he will never work again if he can play a break card any time he wants to, she reminds herself that this is a short-term, emergency plan and will not be needed forever. Many students would rather stay with their classmates when they can do the work, and only play the break card when something in the environment is too much for them. If Anthony plays the card often, his teacher will be looking closely at what was going on right before he played the card, looking for patterns and clues. If she can fix the reasons he needs the card, he won't need to play it.

Example Two: What Do We Do When Destiny Disrupts?

We saw that reminding Destiny to raise her hand and give the other students a chance to answer was not effective. She argued when confronted and escalated when ignored. A long-term solution involving antecedent control procedures and various strategies would ultimately be implemented. In the meantime, how should her teacher begin to respond when Destiny continues to disrupt the class?

Having rules posted in the classroom is an important part of setting the stage for success. For Destiny, this is vital. Her teacher prepared a special lesson about rules and pointed out the rule to "raise your hand," which was rule number four on their classroom list posted on the wall. She ensured that all the students, including Destiny, understood the rule, and that the rule applied to everyone. Then her teacher told the class that she was going to change her own behavior about that rule. From now on, when any student failed to raise their hand before talking out or answering a question, the teacher would not talk to the student. Instead, she would silently point to the rule on the wall, and then call on someone who had raised their hand (but not the person who had called out, even if they raised their hand while calling out or immediately afterward). If there was a second outburst from the same student, the teacher would point to the rule, then put her finger on her lips and with the other hand hold up four fingers to indicate that the rule that was being broken was rule number four, "Raise your hand." Again, she would call on someone who had raised their hand without breaking the rule. If there was a third outburst, the teacher would place a pre-arranged sticky note on the student's desk with a drawing of a hand and the number four as a visual reminder. Continuing to ignore the rule after several gestural and visual prompts would be seen as being disrespectful of the teacher and classmates, and "Be respectful" was another of their classroom rules.

Destiny's teacher decided that if Destiny raised her hand without calling out, she would call on her every single time on the first day or two. She wanted to reinforce Destiny's quiet hand-raising behavior as often as it occurred initially. Later, she would gradually reduce the number of times she called on Destiny until the frequency was comparable to that of her classmates.

Destiny's teacher also discussed rule number one in their classroom, which was "Be respectful." She told the class that if someone chose to be disrespectful (such as name calling, interrupting, arguing, or repeatedly shouting out answers after reminders), then that student would be removed from the group temporarily to a seat at the back of the room, so that they could still hear the discussion but would not be a part of the group. After a brief time away from the group, the student could return when they were ready to be respectful. When this rule was invoked, the teacher would point to the rule on the wall and hold up one finger to indicate that rule number one, "Be respectful," was being broken, and point to the chair at the back where the student should sit. After approximately five minutes of respectful listening, the teacher would invite the student to return and be included in the discussion again.

The most difficult part for Destiny's teacher was learning not to argue with Destiny. As a teacher she was used to having the last word in any discussion, and Destiny was determined that she, herself, would have the last word. It took some self-control for the teacher to ignore Destiny's attempts to engage her in lengthy discussions rather than letting herself be drawn into an argument, but she succeeded and Destiny learned that trying to argue no longer worked.

Posting rules, reminding everyone about them, having a clear understanding of the consequences of breaking the rules, and consistency in follow-through are all important interventions. We will discuss other antecedent manipulations to set the stage for success in advance, as well as specific evidence-based strategies to support appropriate behavior in a later scene.

▪ *Example Three: What Do We Do When Daniel is Defiant?*

When Daniel first begins to exhibit defiance, e.g., when he is given an assignment and does not work on it, it is important to determine whether he truly understands what he is expected to do. Some students have gaps in their academic abilities, so that even if they are able to do some higher-level tasks, they may be unable to do other tasks which seem to be easier and so are assumed to be mastered. Others have memory problems, and may have forgotten how to get started on tasks that they were able to complete successfully the day before. They may be embarrassed to ask for help and would rather be seen as the "bad kid" who gets in trouble than to be seen as the "dumb kid" who doesn't know how to do the work. Many students with autism, even verbal students like Daniel, find themselves unable to formulate questions or to ask for help when needed. Staring at a paper without working is the only sign that Daniel does not know what to do.

Rather than prompting him to get to work, work faster, or "think harder," his teacher decided to review the work he was being asked to do and make sure that these were problems he had done independently and correctly in the past. As needed, she modified his work to ensure that there was nothing new or too difficult for him, given his past performance. She also decided to offer help immediately at the first sign of "defiance" or not getting to work quickly on his own. She sat down beside him and talked him through the first problem step by step, praising him for the parts he was able to do himself. Then she had him do the next one while she was still next to him, so she could easily help him again if needed. Finally, she told him that she would be circulating around the room and would check back in with him to see how he was coming. She drew a star by each of the correct problems they had done together, and then asked him how many he thought he could do by himself before she got back to him. Daniel said two, so she made a small dot after the second problem down on the page. When she had made her rounds of checking on the other students and got back to his desk, she praised him for the work he had done, drew a star by each correct problem, helped him make corrections as needed, and set a new goal for how much he might do before she returned again.

Daniel seemed more confident and produced more work, and his teacher realized that his difficulty was probably related to his inability to ask for help rather than actual defiance of authority.

Example Four: What Do We Do When Sophia Engages in SIB?

When any student engages in self-injurious behaviors (SIB) the most import-ant thing is to keep the student safe, and bring in the behavior analyst, school psychologist, or behavior specialist to conduct an assessment of the function of the behavior. While waiting for the results, the teacher acts to keep the child safe and to prevent the behavior whenever possible. Sophia's teacher looks at each of the three types of SIB that Sophia engages in as separate behaviors with unique characteristics.

Hand biting appears to happen during times when Sophia has completed her work and remains at the station while her teammates continue to work on their tasks. She may be bored, but lacks the skills to ask for something to do or to find an activity on her own. Sophia does not attempt to access the mate-rials provided for students who finish early, but after she bites her hand and is given an activity, she engages in the activity without further SIB. Her teacher instructs the aides to keep an eye on her, and as soon as she finishes her task, immediately present her with one of the activities (book or drawing materi-als). Eventually, she wants to teach Sophia to request one of the activities by using a picture icon card; however, her immediate goal is to keep Sophia safe. Presenting her with materials to keep her occupied decreases hand biting in the short term.

Face slapping tends to occur after a classmate has slapped an aide. It is important to address the other student's behavior with a separate functional assessment, as this is a serious behavior that should not be allowed to continue. (When in doubt about the seriousness of a behavior, imagine the child doing the same thing as an adult. Would it be dangerous, or grounds for legal action or incarceration? If so, then address it now, while the child is young.)

In the meantime, as a stop-gap measure, the teacher changes groups so that the student with a history of slapping the aide is not in Sophia's group. This appears to reduce her stress level and her face-slapping behavior.

Head banging has occurred in response to a loud noise near her. This is often another child screaming near her, but it has also occurred when the bell rings while she is seated directly under it. Because the child who screamed most often was also the child who frequently slapped the aide, this child has been removed from Sophia's group, so that any screaming he engages in is not right next to Sophia. Also, they have arranged the classroom environment so that there is no chair or work station placed directly below the bell that rings for lunch, recess, and fire drills. Because there are several aides in this classroom, Sophia's teacher has assigned an aide to be near enough to Sophia so as to be able to intervene and stop her from hitting her head in the event of an unexpected loud noise. Classroom staff have been trained by the county office of education in safe ways to hold her and keep her safe when she tries to bang her head against surfaces, and to keep themselves safe if she attempts to bang her head against their head or face. Because such an aide assignment can be stressful, Sophia's teacher makes sure all of her aides have been trained, and she rotates aide assignments so that different staff members are assigned to work with Sophia at different times throughout the day. Staff rotation also helps prevent a student from becoming overly attached to only one aide and refusing to work with other aides.

Reducing unexpected noises and the aide rotation was somewhat successful in the short term. In the long term, following the recommendations of the functional behavior assessment and behavior plan will be important for Sophia's continuing safety.

Example Five: What Do We Do When Aiden is Aggressive?

When behavior escalates to the point of physical aggression, it is important to act quickly and calmly to keep everyone safe. When Aiden's teacher evacuated the classroom, using the pre-determined plan, she was acting to keep her students and staff safe. The next time, however, she wants to intervene before the aggression if possible. She instructed her aides that they should not touch Aiden, even if kindly meant or in a supportive way, as this tends to trigger an increase in physical aggression. This was especially true when he was already upset.

Aiden's teacher recognized that a negative attitude (i.e., scowling, making negative comments, overreacting to normal jostling by peers) usually preceded aggression. She decided that as soon as he came into the classroom with this attitude, she would offer him an alternate activity instead of sitting with his classmates and listening to the book after lunch. He could go to the library corner or quiet place and put on headphones to listen to music or just block out noise. Being alone gave him time to recover from whatever had happened on the playground.

At the same time, his teacher followed up with the principal to ensure that bullying was being addressed schoolwide, as well as regarding this particular incident. Aiden had access to a counselor trained in working with students who have been targeted for bullying attempts, and district bullying protocol was followed. On the occasions that he talked to his teacher or the counselor about bullying on the playground, they listened and believed him. They did not try to minimize his feelings with platitudes such as "Boys will be boys," or "Don't react and they'll get bored and quit bothering you," or "You just need to grow a thicker skin." Statements such as these can be damaging, and send a message we don't want to send.

When we say "boys will be boys," we are saying that boys can get away with teasing, bullying, or hurting others because of their gender.

When we say "don't react and they'll get bored and quit bothering you," we are saying that whether or not the bullying continues is up to the bullies; they will only stop if they get bored, and he can't count on anyone else to protect him. We are also suggesting it is Aiden's fault because of his reaction, which is probably outside of his control.

When we say "you just need to grow a thicker skin," we are blaming the victim for not being strong enough to withstand repeated bullying. Children do not need to grow a thicker skin in order to feel safe at school. Adults need to protect them.

This is the message that Aiden's teacher wants to give him: that he will be believed and protected, that the bullying is not his fault, and that it will not be tolerated.

Long-term interventions and strategies will be put into place, but in the short term, allowing Aiden respite and understanding when he shows that he is upset will go a long way in preventing escalation and aggression.

ACT II, Scene Eight Summary

In Scene Eight we discussed immediate interventions, or what teachers can do when problem behaviors occur in the classroom. These are not long-term solutions to prevent the behaviors, but they can help everyone to be safe in the interim, including the student who is misbehaving. Now that we've looked at short-term interventions, it's time to make some long-range plans to change the behavior. We know that a stop-gap "bandage" approach will not be sufficient for significant problem behaviors. In ACT III, we will be looking into antecedent control procedures: changes we can make in the classroom environment so that the undesired behavior is unnecessary or unlikely to recur.

In Their Own Words

"During recess I would not play with other children, but instead would walk around the perimeters of the playground. It wasn't that I didn't like other children, but what they did didn't interest me because I found it basic and cliché. I've never had any interest in things that the general crowds liked. My parents could tell you that I had an unusually intense interest in super heroes, motion pictures, and martial arts, which are still my primary interests in life."

~ Joseph, diagnosed with Asperger's syndrome as an adult

What Can We Learn from Joseph's Story?

If someone has an intense interest, they may not connect with their classmates. Try to find someone else with the same interest, so they will have something to connect about. Some schools have clubs that meet weekly after lunch, such as a chess club, anime club, comic book club, astronomy club, and so on. If you start a club about your student's interest, others who share the same interest may join. It could be the start of a beautiful friendship.

ACT II, Scene Eight Vocabulary

extinguish	extinction	ignore
incidental learning	intervention	

ACT II, Scene Eight Discussion Topic

Think about a time when you observed a behavior in class that you didn't know how to handle. How did you intervene? If you were not the teacher, how did the teacher intervene? Would you have handled it differently based on what you are learning now? Share your insights with your small group.

ACT II, Scene Eight Questions

For each question, choose GOOD IDEA or BAD IDEA.

1. A child complains of being bullied on the playground. Her teacher tells her to toughen up and learn to laugh it off or ignore it rather than letting it bother her. GOOD IDEA or BAD IDEA?

2. A child bites his arm whenever he is left alone with no work to do. His teacher decides to put the behavior on extinction by ignoring him every time he bites his arm. GOOD IDEA or BAD IDEA?

3. A student hits her head against sharp corners of doors, desks, and filing cabinets, and her teacher doesn't know why. The teacher puts cushioned bumper guards on all sharp edges and corners and increases supervision with close adult proximity during passing periods when the student must walk through areas with unprotected sharp corners. She also immediately schedules an individualized education program (IEP) meeting to discuss the self-injurious behaviors (SIB). She refers the student to the school psychologist, behavior specialist, or Board Certified Behavior Analyst® (BCBA) at her school and requests a functional behavior assessment (FBA) to help form a hypothesis about the reason for the SIB. GOOD IDEA or BAD IDEA?

4. A student who sometimes wanders around the classroom instead of working becomes aggressive every time an aide puts a hand on his shoulder, arm, or back to try to make him sit back down. The teacher assigns a bigger, stronger male aide to shadow him and to physically guide him to his seat whenever he tries to get up during work periods. GOOD IDEA or BAD IDEA?

5. A teacher notices that she is raising her voice with her class more often than she likes. She is concerned that her students don't remember the rules of the classroom that they talked about on the first day of school. She makes sure that the rules are posted on the wall, and she holds a class discussion to remind everyone of the rules. She asks students to talk about what the rules mean and why they have them, in their own words. She also promises them that in the future she will try to remember to point to the rule that is being broken silently, without yelling at them. She also promises not to call out the name of the student who is breaking the rule, because she doesn't want to embarrass them. She also asks the class to help remind her by silently pointing to the rule, and holding up fingers to show which rule is being broken, any time she forgets and yells instead of pointing to the rule. They agree. GOOD IDEA or BAD IDEA?

ACT III
Antecedent Control Procedures:
Setting the Stage

Progress is impossible without change, and those who cannot change their minds cannot change anything.

~ George Bernard Shaw

You have within you the strength, the patience, and the passion ... to change the world.

~ Harriet Tubman

Scene Nine

Ecological Assessment: The Sets and Props

n ACT III we'll be talking about *antecedent control procedures*, or manipulating antecedents to influence the target behavior. In other words, we're doing something before the misbehavior happens, with the hope that the changes we make will change the outcome. This is how we set the stage for success, and set our students up to choose a better behavior to get their needs met.

In Scene Nine we'll focus on the main stage on which our students perform, the learning *environment* or *ecology*, which is the classroom. Your room is the set on which they play, and your learning materials are the props they use. Because our students on the autism spectrum often have difficulty with change and may perform differently in different arenas, we want to do our best to set up the stage and props in a way that makes it easy for them to shine. If needed, a school psychologist, behavior specialist, or Board Certified Behavior Analyst® (BCBA) may come in to conduct a formal *ecological assessment* to determine how a student functions in different environments, but you don't need to wait for that. You can informally evaluate your own classroom to find things you can change that might make it easier for your students to succeed. What works? What doesn't work? When evaluating the environment, we should consider the interaction between all relevant factors, which include the classroom (the set for your production) and the learning materials (the props your students will use in their performance). The people are also an important part of the learning environment, but we'll talk more about that in Scene Ten. First, let's look at the set.

The Set

Look around your classroom. Consider how the chairs and desks are arranged. Where is your ASD student placed within the room? Many teachers seat their special needs student front and center, as close to the teacher as possible. For some, this is ideal, especially if you have a student who has trouble seeing the board or hearing. However, if you have an ASD student with heightened peripheral awareness, as many have reported, this could be the worst possible placement. For these students, the presence of anyone behind them may be distressing, and can trigger a *fight, flight,* or *freeze* response. These students usually learn better when they are seated either at the back of the room or on one side, where they may subtly turn their back towards the wall while still able to see the teacher and the rest of the class.

Next, think about traffic flow. How will your ASD child get from the door to their desk? Try to minimize the need to weave through a maze of other students' desks along the way. Also, avoid placing this student in an area that gets a lot of traffic, such as right by the pencil sharpener, waste basket, or other frequently-visited areas.

Your classroom may be divided into different areas with different purposes. Think about how you can make the purpose clear to your students, with no ambiguity. Label these areas, such as an art area, science lab, book nook, quiet zone, and so on. Some primary teachers change the purpose of a table by changing the color of plastic table cloths. For example, a green table covering means it's the snack table, the white one means it's the art table, and no table covering means it's the math table.

Even in a classroom for older students with very little extra space for learning centers, it is possible to set up mini-centers with activities for students to choose when they finish their assignment. These may be placed around the perimeter of the room on top of bookshelves or short filing cabinets, or even on windowsills. If you have room for a standing dowel topped by an upside-down clothespin to hold a small sign next to a file folder, you have room for a center. Many teachers use colorful folders and laminate them after writing the activity instructions on the front. Inside the folder is the paper they will need, or a worksheet with instructions. After reading the directions on the folder, students take a paper and return to their own desks to do the activity.

One example is an art center. The sign on the dowel (or on the outside of the folder) identifies it as the art center and states that it may be used when students finish their work. You might have a wipe-off board on which you post a different drawing prompt every day, such as, "Draw your favorite animal," or "Draw what you see when you look out this window," or "Draw a picture of an imaginary creature." You could tie this center to your academic subjects, such as, "Draw a picture of a character from the book you are reading," or "Draw a picture illustrating the water cycle," or "Draw a picture of one of the founding fathers signing the Declaration of Independence." After students read the drawing prompt, they take a blank sheet of paper from the folder and return to their seats to complete the task. Very little room is needed since they don't actually work at the center, and you may set up several similar stations along one counter or windowsill.

Another center could be a library center, where students may choose a book to read at their desks. This requires more space, but most teachers already have a shelf dedicated to books students may read. If you have enough room, you could create a library corner with a beanbag chair or large pillows where students can relax while they read. If not, they may take a book back to their desk.

A quiet zone could be set up underneath a table at the side or back of the room, with pillows and headphones to block noise. This is an ideal place for a student to calm down when upset. If you can identify the precursors to a meltdown and send your student here first, you might be able to prevent it.

A sensory center includes a variety of materials that provide sensory stimulation activities which students with autism may find calming. Many students have sensory integration challenges; their systems either over-react or under-react to typical sensory experiences. In the classroom it may appear that they are seeking or avoiding certain places, things, or activities that include a strong sensory component, such as a listening center. Does your student crank the volume all the way up, or turn it down to a whisper? Do they reject wearing the headphones because they are say they are too tight, or too heavy?

Many students have problems with visual sensory input. Imagine that you are entering your classroom for the first time, from this student's point of view. Visually, is the space distracting? Are there bright colors and patterns on every wall? Of course, you don't want your classroom to look like a barren, empty box, but you can look for ways to simplify while you beautify your room. Try to avoid multiple busy patterns, such as plaids and stripes, and a bombardment of many different, bright colors everywhere. Many children with autism see colors differently than their neurotypical peers, and for some the color red can vibrate with special intensity. Muted colors have been described as having a more calming effect.

If your classroom has horizontal venetian blinds, these may be distracting for a couple of reasons. Some students find the stark contrast of the parallel lines painful to the eye, especially on a bright, sunny day. Other students have a strong fascination with the order of parallel lines, and may stare at them instead of doing their work. Still others will be intent on figuring out how they work—what happens if I pull this string? Or pull these strings together? Or flip each of the slats in opposite directions? You may find them out of their seats fiddling with the blinds on a daily basis. You may not have the option of removing the blinds, but if your student is overly focused on them, you can keep them pulled to the top if possible.

It seems every open house or parent night has one thing in common: mobiles hanging from the ceiling or tied to the light fixtures. It makes a strong visual impact, and parents enjoy seeing their child's artwork hanging in the room. If this kind of display is part of the culture of your school's open house routine, you don't want your students' parents thinking your classroom is boring or that you just don't try as hard to make it fun. If you feel you must suspend objects from the ceiling for the occasion, by all means, do so. But please don't leave the mobiles up for very long after the event. These things can be highly distracting, especially when a breeze makes them move. They may even trigger anxiety when your ASD student is startled by unexpected movement in the periphery of their field of vision.

Some positive, helpful visuals in the classroom include labeling classroom materials, objects, and the shelves or cupboards where they belong. A place for everything and everything in its place can be comforting to a child with autism.

Posting classroom rules is also important; everyone needs to know what is expected. Display them prominently and review them frequently, even daily if needed. It's easy to point to the rule list and hold up the number of fingers to show which rule they should remember and follow.

A list of things students may do when they finish their assignments should also be posted. Many behavior problems crop up when students don't know what to do. Often, students with autism have academic strengths which surpass their social and problem-solving abilities; they finish their classwork quickly, but can't figure out what to do next. This can be a behavior problem just waiting to happen. Head it off by making sure everyone knows what to do when they finish their work.

Specific rules for various classroom areas should also be posted. What is the rule for the pencil sharpener? Perhaps it is turning the handle ten times, or holding the pencil in the electric sharpener for a count of five. Many students respond surprisingly well to a simple "STOP" sign placed on cupboards, doors, or areas that are for teachers only.

Think about *auditory* stimulation as well as visual stimulation. What does your classroom sound like? You may be accustomed to the hum of the fluorescent lights, the scratch of pencils on paper, the squeak of markers on the board, the shuffling of feet, and the murmuring of voices that are present even during relatively quiet work times, but these things will be magnified to your student with auditory sensitivity.

During unstructured times there are often competing sounds such as music playing, someone reading aloud, small groups with multiple voices talking at the same time, even the distant sound of a leaf blower or siren. All of this can be extremely difficult for auditory-avoiding students with autism.

Many teachers create a visual system to control classroom noise levels. One such idea is to make a stop light which the teacher can change to show a red light, yellow light, or green light. When the red light is showing, there should be no talking at all, such as during a test or when the teacher is giving directions or reading aloud. When the yellow light is showing, student talking is acceptable, but they should raise their hands and take turns. When the green light is on, such as during rainy day recess, free choice time, or while getting ready to go home at the end of the day, students may converse freely with one another. During this time, you may allow a student who is bothered by noise to put on ear buds or headphones to block out part of the noise. It is up to the teacher to use the lights consistently, so that everyone knows what they mean and that they are still in force. One mistake teachers make is to set it to red and just leave it there, hoping that this will mean they will have a quiet classroom for the rest of the year. This does not work. If you forget to change it for several days, it will lose its power to quiet down the class. When you have taught it, practiced it, and use it every day, their behavior falls under the control of the stoplight.

Any time you have a student covering their ears or shouting that it's too noisy or too loud, it's time to re-evaluate the noise levels in your room and do something about it.

What about *olfactory* sensitivity? Many students on the spectrum are put off by normal smells and odors. Even your best, most expensive perfume or cologne applied minimally may be objectionable to your student who is overly sensitive to smells. Did you pop popcorn in your classroom? Your student may still smell it days later, along with your half-finished cup of coffee, the disinfectant that was used to mop the floors last night, and whatever you had for lunch. Unfortunately, we can't create a totally scent-free environment, but at least we can be thoughtful about what we bring into the room, such as avoiding artificial, chemical air freshener sprays.

The Props

In a play, the props (or properties) are the things the actors use onstage, beyond mere decoration. We are not talking about the paintings on the wall or the books on the bookshelves, those are just set dressing. Props are actually used by the actors, and they make a difference in the plot. A prop may be the bell the master rings to summon his butler, or the tray the butler carries in with the morning mail, or the musket hanging over the mantelpiece which will be used in ACT III to subdue the villain.

In your classroom, your props are the learning materials your students use, from pencils and paper to globes, overhead projectors, television sets, boards and markers, and even the classroom pet or plant.

Because many ASD students are strong visual learners, providing a wide range of visual aids and hands-on manipulatives is always a good idea. The idea of a *fidget basket* is gaining popularity in many schools. This is a container filled with small objects your students may hold and manipulate with their hands to help them to focus. Not only your students with autism, but also students with attention deficit-hyperactivity disorder (ADHD) and specific learning disabilities (SLD) often benefit from having a fidget to hold. However, you can't expect that students automatically know how what a fidget is and how to use it properly. A fidget is not a toy, and should never be used as such. If you have toys in your classroom, make sure they are in a separate area and are not mixed in with the fidgets. Post rules and share a Social Story© about fidgets. Here is an example of a Social Story®:

A fidget is something small that keeps my hands busy so I can listen and learn. Holding or touching a fidget helps me pay attention better. A fidget is not a toy. Toys can distract me from learning, and fidgets help me listen and learn. How can I tell if something is a fidget or a toy? If I look at it, or use it in a way that makes my friends look at it, it's a toy. If it gets dropped, bounced, rolled, or tossed, it's a toy. If I hold and move it quietly in my hands, if it helps me focus, and if it keeps my hands out of trouble, it's a fidget. Fidgets are useful tools to have in the classroom.

Providing a box or basket of fidgets students may use to help them focus can be a good idea, as long as everyone knows the rules, and the difference between a fidget and a toy. Don't just put a bunch of small toys in your fidget box, or things that can be tempting to bounce or examine. This is the one thing in your classroom that you want to be boring. Any small object, such as a block, a beanbag, a paper clip, a small bit of smooth plastic, or a sturdy balloon filled with sand may be a fidget. Training your students how and when to use fidgets is an important step toward success.

A *sensory box* is another useful prop. Unlike fidgets, which should only appeal to the tactile sense to avoid becoming a distraction, sensory box objects should appeal to all of the senses. The sensory box is not used during a lesson, as a fidget is, but may be kept in the quiet zone for students to use to self-regulate or to avoid (or recover from) a meltdown. Include visually stimulating objects such as a kaleidoscope, or a snow-globe or lava-lamp type of bottle with slow-falling beads, glitter, or liquids (make sure the bottle is unbreakable cannot be opened). Auditory-stimulating objects might include a rain stick or headphones to listen to music. *Tactile* objects might be soft and furry, or lumpy and bumpy, or squishy and squeezable. Students who seek *proprioceptive* (deep muscle and joint) input may want to snuggle under a heavy quilt. For *olfactory* (odor) sensory-seekers, consider small plastic bottles, each containing a cotton ball which has been soaked in vanilla, rose oil, or other pleasant scents.

Classroom Ecology Examples

Let's look at each of our five students and see how their teachers changed the classroom environment or ecology (the set and props) to set them up for success.

Example One: What Changes Can We Make so Anthony Doesn't Act Out?

Changing the Set:

Sometimes Anthony needs a break, a special place to get away from it all so he can calm down—especially after an upsetting weekend. While he's trying to adjust to being back in school, his mind is still on the weekend. He can't seem to get much work done, and at times this has escalated into acting out behaviors. His teacher creates a "quiet zone" in a corner of the room with a bean-bag chair, sensory basket, stuffed animals, and small weighted quilt.

Anthony is given a "break" card on his desk on Monday morning and told that if he needs it, he can play the card and go to the "quiet zone" for a few minutes. There is a timer in the zone, and he is invited to choose how many minutes he needs, between one and seven. He usually chooses seven, which is also his age, and sets the timer himself. When the time is up, he returns to his desk and is better able to focus on his work.

At first his teacher worried that he would lose out on instructional time if she let him use break cards. She soon saw, though, that he was more productive after a break than he had been when required to stay at his desk for the entire period. She saw the benefit of giving him a break.

Changing the Props:

As well as making the classroom change by adding a "quiet zone," Anthony's teacher also looked to see what changes she could make in her teaching materials that might help Anthony. She had a regular pattern for journal writing prompts every morning, and the Monday prompt was always, "What did you do over the weekend?" Anthony had a history of difficult weekends, either because of the changes to his routine when he stayed with his father, or the disappointment when his father did not pick him up. Because of this, his teacher started offering options for Anthony's writing prompts, and she wrote them on cards. She let him choose whether to write about his own weekend, or to write about Dinosaur's weekend, or several other options. Having this choice seemed to relieve some of the stress Anthony had been exhibiting related to the weekend writing prompt. He was more engaged in the writing process when she put a dinosaur stamp on his paper or allowed him to have a small toy dinosaur on his desk (as long as he didn't play with it).

Example Two: What Change Can We Make so Destiny Doesn't Disrupt?

Changing the Set:

Destiny's classroom had originally been set up in rows, and Destiny had been seated in the front row, center seat, with the rest of the class behind her. Her teacher wondered if this proximity to the teacher and the board might have reinforced Destiny's apparent feeling that she was a co-teacher. Her teacher rearranged the desks as an experiment, with desks facing one another in a circle. Destiny was placed in a position approximately forty-five degrees to one side of the teacher, neither directly beside her nor directly across from her. From this position Destiny could easily see her teacher as well as all of her classmates, but it seemed to reduce her attempts to take over the lesson somewhat.

Changing the Props:

Destiny's teacher also tried a new way of deciding who should answer questions during discussions. She brought in a cup and a small box. The cup was filled with wood craft sticks (Popsicle sticks). Each stick had the name of a student written on it, one stick per student. When she had a question for the class, the teacher drew one stick from the cup, and that person was selected to answer the question. Then that stick was placed in the box. When all of the sticks had been drawn and moved to the box, she knew that every student had been given one chance to answer a question. Then she put them all back in the cup and everyone got a second turn to answer a question. If a student whose stick was drawn was unable to answer a question, or had an idea they were unsure of, they had two options: they could poll the class and ask by a show of hands how many agreed with the answer they thought might be correct, or they could ask a friend, calling on someone they thought might know the right answer. In this case, the students who know the answer must raise their hands quietly to be called on by the student whose stick was pulled. This provided Destiny with practice in quiet hand-raising.

If she still had trouble raising her hand instead of calling out answers, Destiny's teacher provided her with a sticky note posted on her desk as a reminder. She also allowed Destiny to hold a small, plastic figure of a hand as a physical reminder to raise her hand. Finally, Destiny was given a 3" x 5" card and asked to make a star on the card every time she raised her hand without calling out. At the end of the day her teacher made a note of how many stars she had that day, wrote an encouraging note on the back, and let her take the card home. This seemed to help Destiny focus on remembering to raise her hand quietly without blurting out answers.

Example Three: What Can We Change so Daniel Won't be Defiant?

Changing the Set:

Daniel's teacher asked him where in the classroom he thought would be best for him to learn, and he said he'd like to sit at the back, not too close to any other students. This surprised her because she assumed he would want to be near the front, but she respected his preference. She told him she would let him try sitting in the back, and if she saw that he seemed to work well there, that would be his new place permanently. Although she had been concerned that he would not pay attention in the back row, she found that he seemed to be more focused on classroom discussions instead of turning around to tell students behind him to stop bothering him.

Changing the Props:

The next thing Daniel's teacher did was to take a good, hard look at the work she had been assigning Daniel. She believed it was right on the mark as far as his ability level, but he kept saying he couldn't do it. Was it really too hard for him? Was he missing key skills that he needed to master before moving forward?

She was tempted to discount this idea, because she already used an approved assessment to determine academic placement, and it had been appropriate for her other students.

But Daniel was not the same kind of learner that her other students were. Sometimes he was able to do a problem when it was presented in a certain way or on a particular kind of work sheet, but other times he seemed genuinely confused. When the same kind of problem was presented differently, such as in a word problem, horizontally rather than vertically, or copied from a book rather than on a worksheet, he seemed perplexed. He was not a flexible learner, and he couldn't carry over what he had learned in one format to another way of expressing his knowledge.

His teacher decided to plan specific lessons to demonstrate that problems presented in different ways could still be solved using the skills he already has. She reviewed again the clues to look for in word problems. These reviews were useful to her whole class, but were especially needed by Daniel. She also created work sheets for him that alternated the same problem presented in different ways, always with the same answer, to help him stretch his flexibility without extra stress.

In addition, Daniel's teacher created a *choice board* of phrases he could use to communicate when he needed help or what kind of help he needed. This put communication in his hands at a time when stress made communication difficult if not impossible for him. The choice board was in the form of a file folder, with phrases written inside such as, "This one is too hard," "I forgot how to do this one," "I need a break, please," or simply, "Help, please." Daniel could raise his hand or hold up the folder, and the teacher or an aide would come to him. He needed only to open the folder and point to the phrase that communicated his need, and they responded accordingly.

Later, after he had some practice asking for help using the file folder, his teacher decided that it didn't need to be so complicated for Daniel. She simplified it so that he raised his hand for any kind of help, and he raised his "break" card if he needed to go to the quiet zone.

Example Four: What Can We Change so Sophia Doesn't Self-Injure?

Changing the Set:

Changing the small groups was an important step in making the environment safer for Sophia. When she is not near a student who screams and slaps, she engages in SIB less frequently. Sophia's teacher asked her principal if the school bell on the wall could be removed or muted somehow to reduce Sophia's extreme startle response of striking her head against the table when it rang near her. Unfortunately, state regulations required the bell in the room to be at a set volume. Instead, Sophia's teacher rearranged the classroom so that no work centers were placed under the bell, putting her own desk and file cabinets in that part of the room. This reduced the effect somewhat.

Changing the Props:

Because Sophia had not yet demonstrated an ability to request, staff were instructed to be aware of when she finished her task at a work station and immediately offer the free-choice materials of books or paper and crayons. This eliminated the hand biting that she had engaged in when she had finished her work and had nothing to do.

The next step was to teach her to request the items herself, which is an important move toward autonomy and independence. For the initial stage, the staff members had only one item at each center, either books or paper and crayons. A picture icon of that item was also on the table next to Sophia. As soon as Sophia had finished her work, the staff member placed the icon in her hand, and then held out her own hand to accept the icon. If necessary, Sophia was gently physically guided to put the icon into the adult's hand. Within one-half second of the icon being placed in the adult's hand, the free choice activity associated with the icon was immediately given to Sophia. Over time, less guidance was required, and eventually Sophia would hand the icon to the staff member as soon as she had finished the task.

Example Five: What Can We Change so Aiden is Not Aggressive?

Changing the Set:

In Aiden's case, the set, or learning environment, included the school yard as well as the classroom. His teacher wanted to put a change in place that would help him feel safer outside. The first step was enlisting administrative support in recognizing and effectively dealing with bullying schoolwide. Part of that plan included ensuring that there were constructive, engaging activities for all students to participate in during the long break after lunch. They set up stations with activities such as shooting baskets and running relays and obstacle courses, as well as tables for checkers, chess, and "cup stacking" activities. A music area was also provided where students could listen or dance. Each of these areas had the rules of the area posted and were monitored by staff and volunteers. Students were encouraged to choose one of the many options.

For Aiden, they created an option of walking the perimeter of the school yard, with a rule that walkers could not be stopped or obstructed. This allowed Aiden a familiar routine with support staff monitoring that no one interfered with walkers on the path. All students were encouraged to try new activities and eventually Aiden tried some of the other choices, even though walking was his preferred option.

The area where students line up outside before entering the classroom is also included in his learning environment, and so rules were created to indicate how far students were to stand from one another to avoid crowding. Aiden was particularly sensitive to other people in his space, and he interpreted normal jostling as hostile pushing. A row of circles was painted in the area where his class lined up, with ample room between them, and the rule was one student per circle. This helped him feel safer in line, and further reduced his aggressive outbursts.

In the classroom, Aiden's teacher created a "safety zone," which was a desk facing the corner on the far side of the room. Because the changes being made in the school yard would take many months to be completed, during the interim his teacher allowed him to spend time in the safety zone during after-lunch recess if he felt unsafe or stressed. He often went there immediately after lunch, and listened to the chapter being read aloud to the class from this distance. When the story was interesting to him, he joined his classmates rather than listening from afar. Over time, he used the zone less frequently, and his aggression decreased significantly.

Changing the Props:

The school provided playground activity materials and posted signs with rules for the activities as part of their schoolwide anti-bullying campaign. They had analyzed the discipline referral data and saw that most fights and bullying attempts occurred during recesses, especially the longer, unstructured time after lunch. Armed with this knowledge, they were willing and ready to purchase materials that would provide fun, structured activities appealing to different interests and abilities. They also devoted sufficient staff resources and recruited and trained parent volunteers to monitor the yard during these times. These materials (or props) went a long way toward reducing the kinds of problems that frequently occur when students have too much unstructured time to fill.

In the classroom safety zone, Aiden's teacher wanted to avoid the appearance of it being considered a "time out" area where students went when they were in trouble. She made it attractive by placing a padded "teacher chair" in that area, and by putting photographic posters of tranquil island beaches and ocean waves on the walls. There were headphones attached to a CD player with classical music such as Mozart, as well as calming sounds of nature to choose from. There was also an hour glass similar to a lava lamp full of colorful falling liquid, which could be turned over to watch the colors moving. On the wall above the safety zone was a visual timer. Any student could sign up to request a break in the safety zone when needed; however, the teacher had the authority to override if she determined that another's need for the zone was greater. If she bumped someone from the zone for a needier student, the student who was bumped got a pass to be first in line for the next turn in the zone. She had reserved the after-lunch time slot every day for Aiden, since that was the time when he had been most likely to act out aggressively. This option after lunch, combined with the structured activities outside, served to reduce his aggressive outbursts significantly.

ACT III, Scene Nine Summary

By making changes to our classrooms and our learning materials—the set and props of our students' show—we can make a big difference in their performance. Antecedent control procedures like these make it possible to prevent many problems before they happen.

Now that you've conducted your own informal ecological assessment by looking at your classroom environment and materials to prevent problems, the next step is to manage your cast and crew. Staff training means getting everyone on board to help you set the stage for success.

In Their Own Words

"In one class in high school I was moved to sit front-and-center in the classroom. I was unable to focus in class because I was continuously trying and failing to block out all the students behind me. I constantly felt nervous and on edge because there was so much movement behind me and to either side."

~CD, diagnosed with autism spectrum disorder as an adult

What Can We Learn from CD's Story?

Ask your students with autism where they feel most comfortable sitting. Don't make them sit at the front of the room if they're not at ease there; their enhanced peripheral awareness could put them on hyper-alert. Allow them to sit at the back or along one side of the room if they prefer, where they can turn their back toward a wall to feel more protected.

ACT III, Scene Nine Vocabulary

antecedent control procedures	ecological assessment
ecology	environment
fidget basket	fight, flight or freeze
quiet zone	sensory center

Act III, Scene Nine Discussion Topic

Within your small group, choose one person to describe a student they are working with who has behavioral challenges. As a group, brainstorm possible changes to the environment or materials that might be helpful.

Act III, Scene Nine Questions

1. Antecedent control procedures are interventions put in place every time the behavior happens, immediately after the behavior. TRUE or FALSE?

2. Antecedent control procedures include changes we make in an effort to prevent problem behaviors; these changes may include environmental changes in the classroom and the learning materials. TRUE or FALSE?

3. Sensory integration challenges, such as sensory-seeking and sensory-avoiding, may increase the likelihood of some unwanted behaviors and should be considered when making changes in the environment. TRUE or FALSE?

4. All ecological assessments must address alternative energy sources such as solar and wind. TRUE or FALSE?

5. An ecological assessment looks at the environment and materials which are part of the learning ecology. TRUE or FALSE?

6. To help prevent meltdowns for a student who exhibits sensory integration challenges, consider:

   A. Creating a "safe zone" or "quiet zone" in the classroom.

   B. Providing access to a "sensory box."

   C. Seating the student in the part of the classroom where they feel safest.

   D. Any or all of the above.

Scene
Ten

Staff Training:
The Cast and Crew

Training your "cast" (your students) and your "crew" (aides, support staff, and volunteers) is vital to the success of any behavior plan. Everyone in the room must be on the same page, and respond to inappropriate behaviors in the same way, to avoid confusion. Once students realize that their undesired behaviors will always be followed by the same consequences, the groundwork is laid for behavior change.

The Cast

When you have a student who frequently has behavioral outbursts or meltdowns, the other students in the room need to know how to respond and what to expect. They need to know that the adults in the room know what to do and will keep everyone safe. This is why you need a *Plan B* already prepared.

Be careful how you present this, because you do not want to imply that only one student has behavior problems. Never target an individual student by name, such as saying, "When Aiden has a temper tantrum, here is what everyone else will do …" This is a violation of his privacy and confidentiality. It sets him up for social conflicts with his peers, and it is deeply disrespectful. Always maintain confidentiality.

Depending on the age of your students, you might want to write a Social Story™ or social article about various emergency procedures. If you use the guidelines provided by Carol Gray, creator of the Social Story™, your story is more likely to be effective. Here is an example of a Plan B Social Story™ for younger students:

PLAN B = SURPRISE!

In Room Five, we have a plan for what we will do each day. We can look at our schedule and see what will happen next. This is our Plan A.

Sometimes there is a surprise. The schedule changes, and we have Plan B. It's different, and that's okay. When it is time for Plan B, we try to listen to our teachers. They know what to do.

Maybe we will go to the library. Maybe we will have a surprise popcorn party. Maybe we will go outside for a fire drill.

We don't know what the surprise will be, but our teacher knows. We try to listen and follow directions. Later, we will go back to our schedule. Our teacher is happy when we listen and follow directions for Plan B.

Here is an example of a Plan B social article for older students. It can be modified to fit the reading comprehension and interest level of students from upper elementary to high school.

OUR PLAN B

In our classroom, we have a plan for every day. Our schedule is on the wall so we can see what will happen next. It is Plan A, what we expect to happen today.

Sometimes something unexpected happens, and we need to change the plan. That's when we go to Plan B. Maybe there is a fire drill, and we have to stop reading and go outside. Going outside is our Plan B for the fire drill.

Maybe there is an assembly during math time. When that happens, we go to the auditorium instead of math. That is our Plan B for assemblies.

What if someone gets sick and throws up in the classroom? Do we have a Plan B for throwing up? Yes. First, we should try to look away, keep working, and pretend that it is not happening. This is kind and respectful. Someone who is throwing up can't help it, and we don't want to make them feel worse by staring or talking about it. Our teacher or another adult will help our sick friend, and everyone else can keep working. If our teacher says, "This is too much throwing up, we need to go to Plan B," we will go with another adult, our Plan B manager, to a different place in the school. Then our sick friend can have privacy, and our teacher can help. We try to line up quietly and follow our Plan B manager. Maybe they will take us to the library, or to another place in our school. Our Plan B manager will tell us what to do when we get there. When it is time to go back to class, they will take us back.

Sometimes a student gets very upset about something. When that happens, it is important not to stare or talk about it. We give our friend privacy, just like we would if they were throwing up. Being very upset can be a private thing, and our friend might need some time alone with the teacher to calm down. Our teacher might say, "Time for Plan B," and we go with our Plan B manager. This gives our upset friend time to calm down, with our teacher there to help. It is kind and respectful to leave quietly, without saying or doing things that might make our upset friend feel worse.

Sometimes the change is a surprise reward. Maybe our teacher will say, "Everyone worked hard all week. Our Friday afternoon Plan B is a popcorn party!" Maybe our teacher will say, "Thank you for being kind and respectful. Today's Plan B is going to recess five minutes early." We never know what Plan B will be, and that's okay.

Even though we have a schedule and a Plan A at school, sometimes things change. It is okay if something different or unexpected happens, because we have a Plan B. There is always an adult who knows the plan and who is there to help.

Of course, you will need to modify any story to fit your classroom and to suit your students' needs, but the important thing is to make Plan B a part of your classroom vocabulary. Label your daily schedule Plan A, read it every morning, and refer to it throughout the day. Calling it Plan A reinforces the idea that sometimes change happens. Starting on the first day of school, consider reading the Plan B story regularly, and use the vocabulary with your students each time you stray from the expected schedule. You want your students to know that Plan B is not chaos; it is managed change. It can even mean a fun surprise, such as a game of Hot Lava Balloon Toss (see appendix) for the last few minutes of the school day. If you do not have a classroom aide, be sure to talk to your administrator and arrange in advance who would help you evacuate your classroom if needed.

Planning ahead with your class will make things go more smoothly in case you do need to evacuate the class because of a severe behavioral outburst. You should try to have several pleasant Plan B experiences under their belts beforehand, including evacuating the whole class to go with an aide for a walk around the school yard for some purpose. Perhaps you want them to keep their eyes open for birds they can learn about on the internet back in class, or wildflowers that they can draw. Maybe you want them to count how many pieces of litter are on the ground as baseline data before a program to try to keep the playground clean and litter-free. Whatever the reason, give your students multiple opportunities to go to Plan B in advance of any emergency situation.

In the midst of an emergency situation where one student is out of control and having a meltdown, praise students who are going on with their work, and let them know that you see how respectful they are being.

Modeling and reinforcing how to respond calmly when a student is having a meltdown is a vital part of maintaining a classroom that stays in control no matter what. Show your cast how you expect them to perform, and they will rise to the occasion.

The Crew

Your crew includes your classroom aides and support staff, classroom volunteers, administrators, and other resources and specialists such as the *speech-language pathologist (SLP)*, *occupational therapist (OT)*, school psychologist, behavior specialist or Board Certified Behavior Analyst® (BCBA), and any other school personnel who work with your students.

Everyone in your crew needs to know how to respond consistently to problem behaviors. At the same time, confidentiality must be maintained.

Those who are on the student's individualized education program (IEP) team, such as other teachers the student goes to, SLP, OT, school psychologist, and behavior specialist or BCBA, already have access to confidential information. If the student has a behavior support plan (BSP) in place, each IEP team member should already have a copy. If a BCBA is on the case, be sure to follow their recommendations.

Classroom aides will become privy to confidential information about students' behaviors just by being in the room every day. They see who acts out and who is disruptive, defiant, or aggressive. Even though confidentiality will have been covered during their initial training when they were hired, you will need to remind them regularly that what they see and hear in the classroom is confidential. They are not to talk about any student's behavior in the staff lounge, or with other aides or staff members, or with any parents, ever—including the child's own parent or relative. If anyone asks your aide about any child's behavior or any other information about a child, your aide must refer them to you. As the teacher, you are the communication point and you are responsible for disseminating information.

Plan regular staff training sessions with your aide or aides. This may not be easy because of schedules, but some creative planning will help you find the time. You must not ask them to come in early or stay after their work day or hold a meeting during their legally required breaks. They are paid by the hour, and teachers do not hold the purse strings to approve overtime pay for your staff. If you're not sure how many breaks they must have and how long the breaks must be, check your district's classified staff union agreement. If they are mandated to have a ten-minute break during their work day, and they take their break during a twenty-minute lunch period, that doesn't mean they get a twenty-minute break. You may hold a staff meeting during ten minutes of the lunch period.

During your staff meetings, let them know what behaviors are being targeted for change, and how you want them to respond if the behaviors occur. Remind them about confidentiality and provide them with a written agenda of the meeting to serve as a reminder of what was discussed with a summary of how to respond to behaviors that they can refer back to. Of course, do not include any student's name on the agenda. At the beginning of the meeting, praise your staff for specific things you have seen them doing well. If necessary, remind them of things that they may not be doing at the level expected in a way that no one feels singled out or embarrassed. Then, after going through the agenda, end the meeting with praise and gratitude for the job they are doing, and remind them of how much their work benefits the students.

Cast and Crew Training Examples

Let's look at each of our five students and how their classmates and staff should be trained to respond to their problem behaviors.

Example One: How Should Others Respond when Anthony Acts Out?

When Anthony rocks in his seat or paces back and forth, his teacher quietly praises other students who continue to work without reacting to Anthony's behavior. She never draws attention to Anthony with these comments; for example, she would never say, "I like how you're not staring at Anthony," or "I like how you're working in spite of all the distractions." This unnecessarily draws attention to Anthony during a time that he is trying his best to self-regulate, and it would only make matters worse. Instead, his teacher very quietly comments on positive work habits of students who are ignoring Anthony, such as, "Thank you for working quietly," or "I can see that you're really focused on your work." She models calm ignoring of the behavior. If one student is overly distracted and turning around to stare at Anthony, the teacher may position herself between Anthony and the "gawker" to interrupt the line of sight, while nonverbally redirecting that student to task by pointing to their worksheet.

Meanwhile, classroom aides give Anthony space, as they discussed in their staff meeting. They know not to touch or talk to Anthony when he seems upset. Touching him usually escalates the behavior. If they all continue working calmly, he is often able to self-regulate by rocking or pacing at the back of the room, and then return to his task. If this is not the case and his behavior continues to escalate, the teacher will call for Plan B, and the aides will escort the students to the library. On the way out, an aide picks up the Plan B bag with a read-aloud book that supports their social studies curriculum and paper and pencils to draw their response to the book after hearing it. When Anthony's teacher calls the library to tell them Plan B is over, the aides bring the class back to the room, and everyone goes back to Plan A.

Example Two: How Should Staff Respond when Destiny Disrupts?

We have learned that Destiny has a history of arguing when the teacher tells her to raise her hand, and her behavior escalates when she is ignored. Her teacher had to remind herself not to argue or get drawn into debates. Destiny's classmates were praised and reinforced for raising their hands, without referencing Destiny's behavior. Although there are no aides assigned to this class, the teacher lets parent volunteers know that they are not to engage with any student if they try to initiate an argument about the rules or the lesson.

Sometimes, during the behavior change process, behaviors may escalate as the student tries harder and harder to control the situation. This is called an *extinction burst*, when behavior gets worse before it gets better. If

Destiny's behavior escalates to the point where it is necessary for her to be sent to the office, it is important for the office staff to know how to respond. After discussing it with her school administrator, Destiny's teacher provided a file folder for the office to keep on hand in this case. On the front of the file folder it said, "This work is to be done quietly in the office. Do not talk to the office staff; they have work to do and are not available for conversation." Inside the file folder on the left side her teacher had written these prompts:

1. Write your name, today's date, and the time at the top of your paper.
2. Write one to five sentences describing how you feel right now.
3. Write one to five sentences telling what happened just before you were sent to the office.
4. Write one to five sentences with an idea of what you might do differently next time.
5. After you finish, write what time it is at the bottom of the paper.
6. Give the folder with this paper to the secretary.
7. Go back to class. Your paper will be reviewed later by an administrator and/or teacher.

Destiny's teacher laminated the file folder, put several blank sheets of paper inside, and gave the folder and several pencils to the school secretary. Any time Destiny came to the office, office staff were instructed to hand her the folder and a pencil, and leave her alone to complete the task. If Destiny tried to tell someone her story, they were instructed to say, "No talking," and point to her work folder without interacting with her. The first few times, Destiny tried hard to get an adult to pay attention to her so she could tell them her side of the story verbally, but each time she was redirected to her folder and reminded that the staff had work to do. At a time chosen by her teacher, she and Destiny would review the paper, the teacher would acknowledge Destiny's feelings, remind her of the rule she had broken, and briefly discuss what could have been done differently to have a different outcome.

It is important to note that Destiny's teacher knew that writing was one of Destiny's strengths, and that she often wrote stories during her free time. She would not have used the same plan for a child who struggled with handwriting or written expression. An opportunity to draw a picture of what happened would be more appropriate for someone who likes drawing but not writing.

Example Three: How Should Staff Respond to Daniel to Avoid Defiance?

Daniel's teacher told her aides that taking away Daniel's recess was not an option; he would not be required to stay in or to finish classwork outside on the wall, but would be permitted to play regardless of his classwork completion. He really needed this time to move and be free from academic tasks. She also asked her staff to stop using phrases such as, "You can do it, try harder." If he showed that he needed help by raising his hand or indicating a request for help in his communication folder, they were to immediately provide him with help, and then gradually fade out the support as he gained confidence in his ability to do it on his own. If he played the "break" card, staff were instructed not to try to get him to do more work before allowing him a break, but immediately let him go and set the timer in the quiet zone for the length of break time indicated by the behavior plan. His teacher assured her staff that the support and breaks were only going to go on as long as he needed them. Eventually they would be phased out when he was able to be successful and comfortable without them. In the meantime, staff were instructed not to override or modify the plan, because the plan was designed to make it unnecessary for Daniel to act defiantly. When his needs were met without defiance, he would be able to learn at his own pace and in his own way.

Because his classmates noticed that Daniel got to go to the quiet zone and it looked appealing, they also wanted to go there. Their teacher opened up the zone for other students to use when they had finished their work using a sign-up sheet.

Example Four: How do we Train Staff to Respond to Sophia's SIB?

In cases where there is risk of significant harm to the child if the behavior continues, such as Sophia's self-injurious behavior (SIB), it is important to follow the advice of the behavioral professionals assigned to the case. In Sophia's case, the school district's board-certified behavior analyst (BCBA) trained the teacher and staff in how to respond appropriately to keep Sophia safe and to prevent injury to herself or others. Because Sophia did not have a functional communication system, this was the first thing that was addressed, using the *picture exchange communication system (PECS)*. All staff members attended PECS trainings, and later in their staff meetings they discussed and practiced what they had learned. Sophia responded well and quickly mastered phase one, learning to communicate by looking at, picking up, and handing a picture icon to a communicative partner in exchange for the desired item pictured on the card. This effectively eliminated hand biting at school, except in the rare instances when she had no activity or task to do and there was no PECS icon within easy reach, and/or no adult nearby to hand the icon to. Eventually she would be taught to seek out the icon for what she wanted even if her PECS binder was in a different place, and to find an adult to give the icon to. Until she mastered this, classroom staff remained nearby and ensured that a PECS icon was available when she had finished her task.

Regarding both the face slapping in response to the sound of a classmate slapping an aide and the head banging in response to loud noises, staff were instructed to try to prevent injury by interrupting the behavior; for example, placing their hand or arm between Sophia's hand and her face as soon as a classmate slapped an aide, and blocking her from striking her head against the table when a loud noise occurred (using the approved techniques they had been trained to use safely). In order to reduce the need for these behaviors, the classmate who engaged in slapping and screaming was seated as far as possible across the room from Sophia to reduce the effect of their behavior, while the school psychologist conducted a functional behavioral assessment (FBA) in partnership with the BCBA to significantly reduce or eliminate slapping and screaming behaviors. In addition, staff were asked to pay attention to where Sophia was working in relation to the alarm bell before each recess or lunch break signaled by the bell. They planned to have her assigned to the station furthest from the bell at those times of day to reduce the effect of the loud noise. She was also offered noise-blocking headphones, which she sometimes tolerated and sometimes refused.

In Sophia's case, there was no need to train her classmates in how to respond to her behaviors, as they appeared to be unaware.

Example Five: How should Staff Respond when Aiden is Aggressive?

The most important thing Aiden's teacher wanted her staff to know was that they should never touch or lay hands on Aiden, especially when he was upset. He was highly sensitive to touch and experienced tactile defensiveness, so that what seemed like a gentle pat on the back or hand on the shoulder felt to him like an attack. This defensiveness, coupled with heightened peripheral awareness, is why he so often complained of being shoved or pushed in line; normal jostling and proximity of peers was interpreted as hostile. Staff were made aware of the fact that he prefers to be last in line with a lot of space between the next student and himself. If he fell slightly behind when walking in line, they allowed it rather than urging him to hurry and take up the slack. As long as he was moving in the same direction without stopping, was within sight, and was not late to class, letting him lag a bit behind was preferable to increasing his agitation by being forced to walk too close to his classmates.

Regarding the new playground procedures, school staff members received training on the various activities and the rules for each. This training included all teachers, aides, and volunteers who monitored break time, recess, lunch, and before/after school. Administration monitored discipline referrals to determine whether implementing these playground activities resulted in fewer fights and other behavior problems during these previously unstructured times.

ACT III, Scene Ten Summary

In Scene Ten, we talked about how and why to train our classroom aides and students to respond to problem behaviors in ways that will help, rather than reacting in ways that could make the behavior worse. Next, we'll learn how to be the prompter, providing cues for the behavior we want to see.

In Their Own Words

"When I was seventeen, back in high school, there was a day when an announcement came over the speakers to leave the classroom immediately and go with our class to the main field. So I did. They didn't say to bring our backpacks, so I left mine in the classroom. Instead of telling us to go back to class, after a while they told us we needed to leave campus and to wait for the busses or call our parents. I didn't ride a bus and my phone was in my backpack in the locked classroom, so I couldn't call home. It was noisy, chaotic, and disorganized. So I found two of my teachers who are really nice and I just stayed with them. Since my mom didn't know to come pick me up, they drove me home. I was never scared. I just found someone I could trust and stayed with them."

~Sean, 20, diagnosed on the spectrum as a preschooler

What can we Learn from Sean's Story?

When there is an emergency situation at school, all staff need to be especially mindful of our students on the spectrum, and make sure they know what to do and where to go. When a student knows they can trust a certain staff member, they might seek them out when they need help. You could be one of those teachers that students trust and turn to in need.

ACT III, Scene Ten Vocabulary

extinction burst

occupational therapist (OT)

Plan B

icon

picture exchange communication system (PECS)

speech-language pathologist (SLP)

ACT III, Scene Ten Discussion Topic

Brainstorm with your small group various ways to fit staff training into an already-full school day. Should you even try? Why or why not? Discuss.

ACT III, Scene Ten Questions

For each question below, choose GOOD IDEA or BAD IDEA.

1. Your classroom aide read somewhere that children with autism like to be squeezed, and she saw on television that Temple Grandin created her own squeezing machine. Now every time one of the students seems agitated or stressed out, she wraps her arms around them in a tight squeeze and just holds on tight, no matter how much they protest. GOOD IDEA or BAD IDEA?

2. Your BCBA® told you to let one of your students lag back at the end of the line and come straggling in several feet behind his classmates, because she says he is bothered by being too close to other people and she thinks it will reduce incidents of him hitting his peers. This does not fit with your teaching style; you feel it is important for him to learn to stand and walk in line with everyone else. In addition, you know that your fellow teachers can be highly critical in the staff lounge, and you don't want his next year's teacher to complain that you didn't teach your class how to walk in line. Because you have far more teaching experience than the BCBA®, you decide to disregard her recommendation and make him walk in line like every other boy his age. If he hits someone again, you will send him to the office like always. You do not inform the BCBA® that you have decided to

ignore that part of the behavior plan, because you assume you will never see the BCBA again. In any case, it is her job is to change the student's behavior, not to tell you how to do your job. GOOD IDEA or BAD IDEA?

3. You know you should train your staff, but you have two part-time aides rather than one full-time aide, and they come in at different times. It works best for you to hold the training after the students leave for the day, so you tell the morning aide you would appreciate it if she could come back for the training. You tell her it is not required, but that it is very, very important and you hope she will decide to come in on her own time. GOOD IDEA or BAD IDEA?

4. Your student tells you that most of the other girls in class have been bullying her. You have never seen this happen, and the other girls are good students and don't seem like the "bully type." You ask the other girls what has been going on and they say that the girl is bothering them, but they are not bothering her. You tell your student that because there are no witnesses, and the other girls deny it, there is nothing you can do. You tell her to avoid them or to ignore them if they bother her again. If they do not get a response from her, they will probably stop bothering her. GOOD IDEA or BAD IDEA?

5. Your BCBA has presented a BSP that your aides don't understand and don't want to implement. You're not sure you understand it well enough to explain it in a way that will get them on board. You ask the BCBA to schedule a training for you and your aides at a time when your students can go watch a film about their history lesson with another class. Your administrator approves and volunteers to drop by the other classroom to ensure there is sufficient staff to handle both groups of students. GOOD IDEA or BAD IDEA?

6. A boy in your class tells you someone is bullying him, but he doesn't know the other boy's name or class. No one has observed this and there are no witnesses. You assure your student that you believe him, and that you will

take action to keep him safe. Then you consult with your administrator to begin following the district-wide bullying protocol, increase observation during unstructured time, and implement a bully-proof social skills unit with your class. GOOD IDEA or BAD IDEA?

Scene Eleven

Providing Cues: The Prompter

Every production needs a prompter: someone to provide a cue when the actors forget their lines. You will be the prompter for your students, available to offer support when needed, but hoping the prompts won't be necessary for long.

In Scene Three we learned the language of stimulus and response. We learned that the discriminative stimulus (S^d) is a cue to let students know that a particular behavior may been reinforced, because it has been reinforced in the past. Your students know that every time you pick up a kernel of unpopped popcorn and approach the popcorn jar, you are more likely to reinforce their on-task behavior by putting the kernel into the jar. They immediately get to work, hoping to fill the jar and earn their popcorn party. Picking up the popcorn is the S^d for being on task. If you want to bring forth certain behaviors, you need to present the S^d for the desired behavior.

Presenting the S^d for the Desired Behavior

Let's see how our five students' teachers prompted or cued them to do the right thing by presenting the S^d for the behaviors they wanted to see.

Example One: How to Prompt Anthony to Do the Right Thing?

Do this:

Presenting the S^d for Anthony to engage in the desired behavior included a verbal instruction such as, "Time to do your dinosaur sentence-writing," as well as presenting the physical paper with the dinosaur stamp on it. His teacher also offered a choice, "Do you want to do the writing idea on the board, or your dinosaur sentence paper?" This put a certain amount of power in Anthony's hands without giving him blanket permission to choose whatever he wants to do.

Example Two: How to Prompt Destiny to Do the Right Thing?

Do this:

Destiny's teacher learned that a nonverbal prompt was preferable to a verbal prompt because Destiny argued when given an opening statement. To avoid a debate, her teacher used nonverbal prompts, such as raising her own hand, pointing to the posted rules, and holding up the number of fingers to correspond with the rule that Destiny was breaking. This presented an S^d for following the "raise your hand" rule.

Example Three: How to Prompt Daniel to Do the Right Thing?

Do this:

Daniel's teacher said, "Get out your folder," as the S^d for Daniel to use his communication choice folder. It was simple and direct, and the first step in the behavior chain that included opening the folder and pointing to the statement for what he wanted to say. By keeping it short and simple, and by taking the steps one S^d at a time, Daniel's teacher helped Daniel do the right thing. Later, when she wanted him to raise his hand to ask for help without using the choice folder, she used a nonverbal prompt by raising her own hand as a cue for him to raise his hand.

Example Four: How to Prompt Sophia to Do the Right Thing?

Do this:
Sophia's teacher wanted her to communicate that she has finished her work and needed the free-time materials rather than biting her hand when she finished her work. Placing the picture icon of the free-time materials into her hand and then guiding her to give it to the adult working with her was the first S^d presented to evoke the desirable behavior. Later, the icon was placed on the table and the aide slid it closer to Sophia's hand as a prompt to pick it up.

Example Five: How to Prompt Aiden to Do the Right Thing?

Do this:
When Aiden appeared to be upset, rather than waiting until his behavior escalated, his teacher said, "It looks like you may be having a rough day. Feel free to take a break in the safety zone." Later she simply pointed to the break card on the corner of his desk as a prompt to use it.

Examples of Removing the S^d for the Undesirable Behavior

We talked about what to do: present the S^d for the desirable behavior. But sometimes that's not enough. We need to make sure we are not accidentally setting them up to do the very thing we don't want them to do. We need to avoid or remove any S^d for behaviors we don't want to see. Here are some examples of what not to do with our five students.

Example One: What to Avoid to Help Anthony Do the Right Thing

Don't do this:
Don't talk too much. When he was under stress, Anthony lost the ability to process language. He also takes things literally. His teacher removed an S^d

for acting out by refraining from making comments that included a negative prediction, such as, "Calm down or you're going to get out of control." Since he can't process a lengthy sentence when he's under stress, all he hears is "... out of control." His subsequent behavior demonstrated the fulfillment of the prophecy. His teacher needs to avoid talking too much, using long sentences, and especially using negative language when Anthony is already upset.

Example Two: What to Avoid to Help Destiny Do the Right Thing

Don't do this:

Don't argue. Destiny loves to engage in back-and-forth discussions, debates, or arguments with her teacher, and she is very good at it. Her teacher learned to avoid presenting the S^d for arguing by refraining from responding verbally to Destiny when she called out answers without raising her hand. Her teacher stopped the arguments by removing herself as a participant; you can't argue with thin air.

Example Three: What to Avoid to Help Daniel Do the Right Thing

Don't do this:

Don't ask rhetorical questions. Daniel's teacher has learned not to offer him a choice that she doesn't want him to take. She used to say things like, "You are really asking for it now, mister! Do you want to go to the principal's office?" Many students with autism are very literal, concrete thinkers, and Daniel is no exception. To him, this was a clear invitation to go to the principal's office. Since he wanted to escape the task anyway, he was happy to accept her offer. As he ran off to the office, his teacher—not realizing that he was simply responding to her unintended S^d—believed that he had run away without permission. Now that she has learned not to present an S^d for an undesirable behavior by asking him if he wants to go to the office, scenes like this are no longer played out in her classroom.

▦ Example Four: What to Avoid to Help Sophia Refrain from SIB

Don't do this:

Don't seat a student who screams and slaps near Sophia. Observation had revealed that the S^d for slapping her own face was another child slapping the aide, and the S^d for striking her head against the table was the onset of any sudden, loud noise near her—such as a child screaming. Her teacher removed the S^d by moving the child who slapped the aide and screamed to a different rotation group, so that Sophia was not near the student.

▦ Example Five: What to Avoid to Help Aiden Do the Right Thing

Don't do this:

Don't touch Aiden, and don't ask questions. When he comes in with a "chip on his shoulder," Aiden's teacher and aides know now that they shouldn't try to touch him, ask him questions, or press him to talk about what may have happened or how he is feeling. Questions increase his stress, and touching him leads to behavior escalation. Removing these stimuli help prevent a potential outburst.

Using Motivating Operations to Prompt Desired Behaviors

In Scene Three we learned about motivating operations (MO), which can serve to make reinforcers more (or less) valuable. Establishing operations (EO) increase the desirability of the reinforcer, such as deprivation: hunger makes a snack more reinforcing and lack of a computer at home makes access to the computer at school more reinforcing. Abolishing operations (AO) make certain reinforcers less potent. An example is satiation: a student who just had lunch is less likely to work for a box of raisins as a reward, and one who just got back from the computer lab and has computer access at home is less likely to work for an extra five minutes on the classroom computer.

Let's look at how two of our example students' teachers used motivating operations to prevent undesired behaviors. An EO was arranged for Anthony and an AO was presented for Sophia.

Example: How Can an EO Prevent Anthony from Acting Out?

Anthony's teacher wanted him to write sentences every day as part of the writing standards for his grade level. The writing prompts that motivated his classmates to write on Monday mornings, the opportunity to tell about their weekends, was more stressful than motivating for Anthony. How could she increase his motivation to do the task? In other words, what establishing operation (EO) can she put into place to increase the power of the reinforcer? Anthony's teacher knew how much he loved dinosaurs. For him, having a dinosaur stamp on the top of the paper and being allowed to write about Dinosaur's weekend instead of his own motivated him to complete the task. Dinosaurs were his EO.

Example: How Can an AO Reduce Sophia's Hand Biting?

We observed that Sophia bit her hand when she had finished her work and wanted the free-time materials (book or crayons and paper) because she did not yet have the skill to request what she wanted using verbal language or picture icons. While she was being taught functional communication skills, her teacher needed to make some changes to ensure Sophia's safety until she was able to ask for what she wanted without biting her hand.

One thing her teacher wanted to do was to present an AO, or an abolishing operation, to make hand biting less reinforcing for Sophia. The immediate plan was to provide satiation of the requested item, the free-time materials, so that there would be no need to bite her hand while waiting for someone to notice she had nothing to do. The adults kept the free-time basket right beside Sophia and the moment she finished her work it was immediately offered to her. Because her desire for something to do was satiated, hand biting to request the items was abolished. She had no need to bite her hand, because the materials were always available. This also reduced the effort required to gain access to the materials.

Using Response Effort to Prompt Behavior Change

In Scene Three, we learned that response effort describes the level of difficulty of any task. We saw how we can support behavior change by decreasing response effort for the desired behavior (making it easier to do the right thing) and increasing the response effort for the undesired behavior (making it harder to do the wrong thing). This is an important part of setting our students up for success. Let's look at how the teachers of three of our example students used this to their advantage with Daniel, Destiny, and Aiden.

Example: How Can Decreasing the Response Effort Increase Daniel's Desired Behavior?

The function of Daniel's defiance appeared to be to escape a difficult task, especially one that was above his ability level or that he had forgotten how to do. Acting defiantly by yelling, swearing, and tearing up papers had been effective in removing him from the classroom and from the task. His removal from the task was the reinforcer, but Daniel's teacher wanted him to use another, more desirable behavior to meet the same need. She realized that the important thing was to give him a way to get his needs met more appropriately, which meant giving him a break. Right now it is not about getting the teacher's needs met by making him stay on task. We already know that leads to outbursts. So, what could Daniel's teacher do to make it easier for him to escape a task that he was frustrated with? Providing him with a "break" card made it easy for Daniel to communicate his need to temporarily escape, even when his stress level made speech difficult for him. Because his teacher and staff were trained to respond immediately by letting him go to the quiet zone as soon as he played the card, he learned that the break card worked. This was a powerful lesson for Daniel. It was much easier for him to use the card than to stomp his feet, yell, swear, and carry on when he was upset. Before long he was using the card every time he became too stressed to use his words, and the outbursts were greatly reduced. Later, his teacher was able to gradually increase his time on task and decrease his time in the quiet zone.

Example: How Can Increasing the Response Effort Decrease Destiny's Undesired Behavior?

Sometimes, after Destiny tried and failed to engage her teacher in a debate, she cried and ran to the office. She had a history of spending more than thirty minutes talking to the principal, vice principal, or school secretary, telling them all about what happened and how she felt about it. This had become problematic, as the office staff and administrators were busy. They were also frustrated because her repeated, lengthy visits did not appear to change her classroom behavior. It had been very easy for Destiny to run from the room and go to the office, or to escalate her classroom behavior until she was sent to the office so that her teacher could teach the other students. Now her teacher wanted to increase the response effort required for her to tell her story to someone in the office. The file folder with instructions on how to tell her story in writing, instead of sitting and talking to an adult, did just that. Destiny's teacher knew that writing was a strength of Destiny's and that she enjoyed it, so the writing aspect of the task was not aversive. However, it was still more effortful than simply talking, so substituting the written report for verbal reporting increased the response effort for the behavior.

Example: How Can Decreasing the Response Effort for Reporting Bullying Help Prevent Aiden's Aggression?

The functional behavior assessment (FBA) revealed that Aiden's after-lunch aggression usually followed incidents of bullying attempts on the playground. Aiden had not reported any of the bullying attempts, and they were only brought to light after observations. Now yard-duty staff have been trained to pay close attention to situations and areas of the playground where bullying has occurred as part of the schoolwide bullying prevention program. Because the school instituted a highly structured activity plan for the after-lunch break, discipline problems overall have decreased significantly; however, Aiden continued to be targeted for bullying attempts and he did not report them due to his difficulty expressing what happened when under stress. Because the bullying attempts were often subtle and may not be observable to staff from across the yard, it was important for Aiden to learn to report such incidents.

His teacher wanted to reduce the effort required to report bullying. She created a daily half-page worksheet titled, "How are you doing?" above a scale from one ("Terrible!") to five ("Awesome!"). As each student walked in after lunch, she handed them the page to do before class started. Their only task was to write their initials above the number that showed how they were doing. If they wanted to, they could write or draw anything else to elaborate on their response, but this was optional. At the bottom of the page there was a box to check if they needed to report a bullying incident, either as a witness or as the one who was targeted. When Aiden, or any student, reported feeling terrible, she cut them some slack in the afternoon. If anyone had checked the box about reporting a bullying incident, she made time the same day to talk privately about it and help the student complete the school's bullying reporting form. She always let her students know that it was safe to report bullying to her and that she would believe them and maintain confidentiality. She also made sure that district protocol related to bullying reporting was followed. All Aiden had to do was to write his initials and check one box in order to start the bullying reporting process. Because of this, and because his teacher promised to help him with the paperwork and interacting with the administrator, it was easy for Aiden to report any bullying attempts before his stress elevated and his aggressive reactions escalated.

ACT III, Scene Eleven Summary

In Scene Eleven, we saw how the concepts and terms we learned in Scene Three may be put into practice to prompt our students to do the right thing (and not to do the things we wish they wouldn't). These included presenting a discriminative stimulus (S^d) for desired behaviors and removing the S^d for undesirable behaviors. We learned how motivating operations (MO) can affect the potency of a reinforcer, such as arranging an establishing operation (EO) to make a reinforcer more potent, or presenting an abolishing operation (AO) to make a reinforcer less potent. We also learned about increasing or decreasing response effort to make it easier for our students to make good choices and harder to make poor choices. All of these are ways teachers can prompt the behaviors you want to see in your classrooms. In ACT IV, we'll learn about three evidence-based strategies that work.

In Their Own Words

"In high school, I didn't make eye contact because I was trying to take in the information and to block other distractions. Also, eye contact was distressing to me. I had a teacher who insisted that I make eye contact. So, instead of paying attention to the material, I was focused on trying to make eye contact whenever the teacher turned my way, even though I couldn't hear what he was saying when I was looking at his eyes."

~Cat, diagnosed with autism spectrum disorder as a college student

What Can We Learn from Cat's Story?

Don't insist on eye contact. Instead of saying, "Look at me," try saying, "Listen to me." Your students with autism may be better able to listen if they are not looking at you.

 ## ACT III, Scene Eleven Discussion Topic

With a partner, discuss the pros and cons of using a "break" card for a student who misbehaves to escape a task. How would you defend the use of such a card to a teacher who fears her student will never do any assignment ever again if given the option of requesting a break?

ACT III, Scene Eleven Questions

1. A teacher has a student who pokes his eyes when he is frustrated and over-whelmed with his seat work. She decides to have him present a "break" card to request a break when he gets stressed out, rather than poking his eyes. The "break" card is one of twenty-five picture icon cards, which are placed randomly in a five-page communication binder on a shelf at the back of the classroom. The student is told that when he needs a break he should go to the back of the room, get out the binder, find the page with the "break" card on it, and present the card to an adult. GOOD IDEA or BAD IDEA?

2. Students in Mr. Taylor's class are allowed to eat in class during the last half hour of the school day, so they bring candy, cookies, and chips. He notices that the noise level during this time has become increasingly loud, and he has to shout to be heard. He has read that positive reinforcement, offering something of value as a reward for appropriate behavior, can be a useful tool. He decides to offer his students a small box of raisins as a reward for studying quietly during the last half-hour of the day. GOOD IDEA or BAD IDEA?

3. A motivating operation (MO) can be either an establishing operation (EO) or an abolishing operation (AO). TRUE or FALSE?

4. Decreasing the response effort for doing the right thing decreases the likelihood that your student will do the right thing. TRUE or FALSE?

5. Increasing the response effort for doing the wrong thing decreases the likelihood that your student will do the wrong thing. TRUE or FALSE?

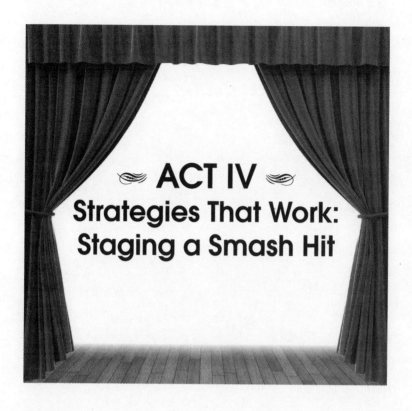

ACT IV
Strategies That Work:
Staging a Smash Hit

The way to get started is to quit talking and begin doing.

~ *Walt Disney*

And will you succeed? Yes you will indeed! (98 and ¾ percent guaranteed.)

~ *Dr. Seuss*

Scene Twelve

The Token Economy: Paying the Players

If we want to stage a smash hit, we need to do what works. That means using *evidence-based practices (EBP)*. When a practice or technique has been studied and shown to be effective with many students, we can feel confident using it in our classroom.

One of these evidence-based practices or strategies is the token economy. A token economy is one kind of reinforcement delivery system, or a way to give your students what they want in exchange for the behaviors you want. Remember, this is not bribery, it's positive reinforcement— your students are getting paid for their efforts. In a token economy we use conditioned reinforcers, or *tokens*, which will be exchanged for *backup reinforcers*, the objects or privileges that students may purchase with their tokens.

Five Steps for a Successful Token Economy

There are five essential components of a successful token economy, according to Miltenberger (2012). If you want a successful token economy, you need to include all five.

▨ Step One: Which?

We need to determine which desirable behaviors will be targeted to be increased. Choose a behavior that is *socially significant*. This is one that will benefit the students themselves, not only the adults in their lives. It should allow the student greater access to reinforcement. For example, learning to raise one's hand is a socially significant behavior. While it is beneficial to the teacher, acquiring this skill also benefits the student. Students who know how to do this can gain attention, approval, and reinforcement from their teachers in appropriate ways. This skill may also help the student access less-restrictive educational environments, such as a general education classroom as opposed to a special education classroom.

On the other hand, let's look at a goal of learning how to sit at a desk without shuffling feet, moving hands, or fiddling fingers. This may benefit a teacher who wants a very quiet and controlled classroom, but it may not be beneficial for the student who needs physical movement in order to pay attention. This would not be a socially significant goal, nor would it be an appropriate one. If moving feet and waving arms is so extreme as to create a risk of harm (such as accidentally bumping, kicking, or hitting others who are nearby), or if it is intrusive enough to be significantly distracting to classmates, that's different. It may be appropriate to create a goal which replaces the large movements with a *functionally equivalent replacement behavior (FERB)*. A FERB is a different behavior which serves the same function, or meets the same need, as the undesirable behavior. It might include providing the child with an elastic band around the legs of their chair, so they can bounce their feet on the band without making noise on the floor. It might mean providing small, quiet, and non-distracting fidgets that the student may fiddle with. The goal is to find a replacement behavior that serves the same need—one that is functionally equivalent. Remember, we are talking about meeting the child's need, not the teacher's need.

Choose behaviors to reinforce that are tailor-made to each child's needs. Even if you are doing a whole-class token economy, you will still need to individualize what each student is working for. If you pay everyone for academic achievement or for generally good behavior, then your students who are already good at academics or naturally quiet and attentive will become rich easily. Meanwhile, the students who may be most in need of motivation will continue to feel like they just can't win. This may also create resentment among classmates. A student who is an excellent reader but who struggles with physical education might earn tokens for persistently trying every PE activity. If you have a natural athlete who does great in PE but is a poor reader, give tokens for how many pages they read. Students who are very quiet may earn tokens for participating in discussions, while more vocal students earn tokens for attentively listening to their classmates' ideas rather than dominating the discussion. Stay attuned to your individual students' strengths and needs and reinforce accordingly.

Step Two: What?

Next, we decide what tokens your students will earn for engaging in the target behavior. Tokens should be something the teacher can deliver as soon as the student engages in the behavior to be reinforced. The adult must have control of the tokens to avoid *"bootleg reinforcement,"* or sneaking tokens they haven't earned. This undermines your economy. Think about how your choice of tokens will play out in the classroom before you decide. For example, if you have students who take things that don't belong to them, you don't want to fuel their temptation by having stacks of accumulated chips on students' desks within easy reach. Some teachers keep a tally of points at the top corner of their white board under each student's initials. This does not lend itself to a token economy where the student needs an actual, physical token to exchange. More importantly, having points recorded on the board lacks confidentiality. If one student tends to earn fewer tokens than the rest, it can be embarrassing or demoralizing for that child. Points tallied on the board are best used for group goals rather than individual goals.

Some teachers use stickers, stamps, holes punched on a card, raffle-type tickets, or classroom "dollars" copied onto paper. The student's name or initials may be written on the paper, card, or ticket to avoid theft.

Young children with autism often respond well to a token board. This is usually a piece of tagboard which may be individualized for each student. It might be the child's favorite color, or have a picture of their hobby or their favorite character from television. There is also a grid of squares printed on the board, with the number of squares corresponding to the number of tasks they must complete before they can turn in their completed token board for the reinforcer (such as a small snack or access to a preferred toy). Alternately, instead of a grid of squares, there might be a curving path of squares similar to a game board. The card is laminated and hook-and-loop fastener stickers are placed in each square, hook side out. Attach the softer, loop side of the fastener stickers to poker chips, laminated construction paper squares, or small pictures of the favorite character. When the child engages in the target behavior, such as completing a specified number of problems or working for a set amount of time without engaging in the undesired behavior, a token (the chip or small picture) is given to the child to place on a square. Once they have filled every block, they have earned the specified reinforcer.

Step Three: Why?

Why are they collecting all those tokens? What's in it for them? It's all about "pay day"—exchanging tokens for something they want. It's important to carefully choose the backup reinforcers that your students will earn in exchange for their conditioned reinforcers (tokens). Always provide a range of choices and make most of the privileges rather than toys. If you really want to spend your money on toys, spend wisely. Rather than buying dozens of small, plastic toys which will soon be lost or broken, purchase one larger, more expensive toy or appropriate video game that most of your students would enjoy. Keep it in your classroom, and let them earn time to play with it. Other privileges might include running an errand to the office, being first in line, extra time on the computer, use of art materials, time in the classroom library, or having lunch with the teacher. Older students might work for the privilege of eating snacks in class, sitting on their desk or on the floor rather than in their chair, moving their desk to a preferred location, having a day with no homework, or going to another class to read a book to a younger student. Think about what your students like to do. Do you always get raised hands when it is time to choose a game to play on a rainy day or free period? Someone can earn the right to choose the next game. Do they often ask to call their parents to check in? Let them buy a free phone call home, with parent permission. Do they want to help you decorate your bulletin boards, or to have a random dance party at the end of the day? Anything that appeals to your students may be offered as backup reinforcers they may earn.

Step Four: How Much?

Set your token *exchange rate*. How many tokens are needed to purchase each item? Useful items such as pencils or erasers, and simple privileges that don't take too much class time (such as being first to line up, choosing a game, or running an errand) could require fewer tokens. Time-consuming, expensive, and popular items, such as moving their desk, lunch with teacher, reading to a kindergartener, or using the video game or toy you purchased for the class, would require more tokens. Students should have to work longer and engage in the desired target behavior more often before they can earn these big-ticket items.

Think about how many tokens a student might be expected to earn in a typical day, and how many days you want them to work for the most popular items. If you find that you have misjudged, you can always modify the exchange rate from week to week, just the way prices rise and fall in real life.

Step Five: Where and When?

This is their pay day. It's important to schedule a time and place for exchanging tokens, put it on the calendar, and stick to it. Consistency is important here. We wouldn't be happy if our employers were vague about what day we would get our paycheck, or if they forgot to pay us because they had a busy month. We need consistency with our paychecks, and our students need consistency, too. If you have said that they can exchange their tokens on Friday, but you have not scheduled a specific time for it, it is far too easy to find that the dismissal bell has rung and you didn't get around to it. If they can't count on being able to exchange the tokens they worked so hard for, they will be less inclined to try to earn more tokens.

Younger students will need to exchange their tokens more frequently, even daily at first, but weekly may be often enough for your older students.

Getting Started

When you begin a token economy, you need to make sure that your students understand the concept and see the value in it. First, give everyone a free token. Show them the choice board (or whatever you are using to display items they can buy) with a range of one-ticket items, such as pencils, erasers, or a "first in line" ticket. Have each student exchange the token you just gave them for one of the choices. They need to experience the power of the token right off the bat. Then let them know what they need to do to earn more tokens, and that there will be other items that cost more than one token. Ask them for their input about what they would like to buy, and if possible, include their recommendations next time. If they ask for something that is possible but that would be difficult or time consuming, consider including it, but at a very high cost. This shows them that 1) you are listening to them and putting their ideas into play, and 2) if they want the good stuff, they have to work harder to earn it.

Response Cost

Response cost simply means losing tokens for engaging in undesired behaviors. It is the cost of making the wrong response in any given situation. This is not usually recommended, because it is important for students to know that when they have earned a token for good behavior, it is theirs. They can't lose it. It is evidence that they did the right thing that time, even if they did the wrong thing later. What they did to earn the token should not be wiped out. If they engage in inappropriate behavior later, they may lose the opportunity to earn more tokens for a while. Similar to a time-out, this is a "time away" from reinforcement. In addition, depending on the behavior, there may be other consequences. But taking away the tokens they already earned is like saying, "I no longer value the good that you have done in the past." Not only that, but if their behavior escalates after you take away one token (and it very well might), you run the risk of taking away all of their tokens, or even putting them in debt. This is demoralizing and will shut down the good behaviors that earned the tokens in the first place.

An exception to this would be when a teacher is running an economic community in her classroom where students receive "pay checks" for their attendance and productivity, and they "pay" rent for their desks, utilities, and to purchase goods and services. In this kind of a token economy, it may be appropriate to levy "fines" for breaking the community rules. It's like getting a ticket and having to pay a fine in the real world. Just be cautioned to make the fines reasonable and small, and don't pile multiple fines on for a behavior chain or one lengthy outburst. You don't want your students to go bankrupt just because they had a bad day.

Staff Training

Make sure your classroom staff are all up to speed on the token economy system. They need to know when they are responsible for giving tokens, what behaviors earn tokens for each student, and how often to give them. If you have decided not to use response cost in your classroom, make sure your aides know this and that they don't use threats of taking away tokens to try to bring students' behaviors in line. Also, make sure you have a substitute teacher file that explains the system so it can keep functioning even if you are not there.

Token Economy Examples

Here are some examples of different token economy systems and how they worked for our five students.

Example One: Can a Token Economy Keep Anthony from Acting Out?

Anthony's teacher wanted to increase the behavior of requesting a break when needed as a way of decreasing his acting-out behaviors. She gave Anthony a coloring book picture of a stegosaurus named Steggo Star-Us. When she noticed him beginning to show signs of stress, such as fidgeting and rocking, she placed a break card on his desk. Each time he used his break card to ask for a break (instead of pacing, tearing his work paper, throwing materials or otherwise "acting out" when he needed a break), she stamped a star on one of the armored plates on Steggo's back. When all the plates had stars, Anthony earned the chance to wash all of the classroom's plastic dinosaurs. Since he loves both water play and dinosaurs, and because he likes to help, this job was highly motivating for him. When he earned his stars, she posted the completed picture by the sink at the back of the room and moved the box of plastic dinosaurs to the sink area. If there was enough time, she set a timer for ten minutes and he washed the dinosaurs immediately. If there was not ten minutes available at that time, she told him when he would get to do the job and wrote it on a sticky-note to put on the dinosaur chart, saying "after lunch," "after recess," or "tomorrow morning." After he finished washing the dinosaurs, she wrote a positive note on the chart and he took it home.

Here are the steps Anthony's teacher used to develop her token economy:

Step One: Which desirable behavior does Anthony's teacher want to increase?

- Using his break card or his words to request a break during a work period.

Step Two: What tokens will Anthony earn?

- One star on one of Steggo Star-Us' back plates.

Step Three: Why is he collecting tokens? What is the backup reinforcer?

- Washing the classroom toy dinosaurs in the sink for ten minutes.

Step Four: How Much? What is the token exchange rate?

- Ten plates are on the stegosaurus drawing, and he must fill all ten to wash the dinosaurs for ten minutes.

Step Five: Where and When will Anthony's tokens be exchanged for the backup reinforcers?

- At the sink in the back of the classroom, immediately when earned if enough time, or scheduled within one day if there is not enough time.

Using this system consistently, Anthony's teacher found that his outbursts significantly decreased. At first, she watched for early signs of stress before making the break card available to him, because she worried that he would play the card repeatedly when he didn't really need it just to fill up his Steggo Star-Us chart. Later, she switched to reinforcing time on task and work completed, and she made the break card and an "I need help" card always available to him. That way he could be in control of requesting a break whenever he needed it, but he would need to complete academic tasks to earn stars. This was highly effective for him.

Example Two: Can a Token Economy Prevent Destiny's Disruptions?

Destiny's teacher had been frustrated by frequent interruptions when she was trying to deliver a group lesson. When Destiny called out answers and then argued or talked back, it ate up instructional minutes. In addition, while she was arguing with Destiny the other students got into sidebar conversations with each other, whispering and passing notes. The group lessons that the teacher had planned went by the wayside and the entire classroom seemed to be lost.

Destiny's teacher's goal was to complete a group lesson without interruptions or disruptions. She thought about offering Destiny a reward each time Destiny allowed the teacher to complete a lesson without argument, but that idea did not feel right to her. She did not want to put the power of whether or not a teacher is able to teach into a child's hands, and that's what that idea felt like. She also did not want the rest of the class to feel resentful of Destiny. Because Destiny seems to love attention but has the ability to stretch any verbal interaction into a time-eating debate, her teacher wanted to find a way to give her attention without sacrificing instructional minutes. She decided to put a group token economy in place, so that the entire class would be rewarded together.

At the beginning of a group lesson, she told the class that she predicted that they could get through the lesson in thirty minutes. If the lesson went longer than thirty minutes, no one wins; however, if she got through all of her points in less than thirty minutes, the class would get to bank the saved minutes. She dedicated a top corner of the white board to this "minute bank." When the class earns thirty minutes of banked time, they may play one of their classroom games for thirty minutes after lunch on Friday. The teacher considered employing a response cost of taking away a minute from the bank each time the lesson lasts longer than thirty minutes, but decided against it. She realized it would take the class some time to get used to the new plan, and she did not want them getting discouraged at the outset. The first time she put this into practice, she deliberately planned a short lesson so they could be successful.

Before every group lesson, she reminded them of the plan to earn minutes to be spent on a game. Then she wrote on the board the parts of the lesson that must be completed within thirty minutes, so they knew what to expect. For example, for a group math lesson she wrote:

1. Teacher explains new math concept and does three examples on the board.
2. Three student volunteers complete a similar problem on the board.
3. The class determines if it the answers are right, and corrects any errors as a group.

For a literature lesson, the parts of the lesson were as follows:

1. Teacher reads a passage from the class literature book.
2. Teacher asks three questions about the passage and draws sticks to see who answers.

3. Volunteer student reads the next paragraph aloud.
4. Three students ask a question about the paragraph and draw a stick to see who will answer.

After putting the agenda on the board, the teacher wrote down the time that she started the lesson. Throughout the lesson, she used the "draw a stick" technique to see who would answer questions. When a volunteer was needed to read aloud, however, she had students raise their hands if they wanted to read, as she did not want to pressure or embarrass students who struggle with oral reading. If a student's stick was drawn and they didn't know the answer to the question, they could call on a friend or poll the class; however, if they seemed to be taking too long to decide who to ask, the teacher reminded them of the plan to finish the lesson in less than thirty minutes.

When the last item on the agenda was completed, the teacher wrote down the finish time on the board below the start time. The class did the math to determine how many minutes were saved, and she added them to the running tally in the minute bank.

Friday after lunch the class counted the tally for the week. The teacher has several PowerPoint and board games which support the academic standards her students are working on, such as playing Hangman using spelling words. She has made sticks for each of the available games and draws one to see which game they have earned. She has also included one or two non-academic games, such as Lava Balloon Toss, to make it more interesting for the students. After she draws the stick to choose the game and everyone is ready to play, she sets a timer for the number of minutes they earned. When the timer goes off, the game is over, even if they are in the middle of a round.

The teacher found this to be very successful during group lessons. If Destiny interrupted to argue a point, the teacher quietly pointed to the rule and waited for her to stop talking. If other students started talking and laughing amongst themselves, the teacher put a finger over her mouth and looked at them silently, waiting. Everyone realized that they were losing minutes because of these interruptions, and they urged each other to be quiet and let the teacher finish the lesson.

Here are Destiny's teacher's group token economy steps:

Step One: Which undesirable behaviors were targeted to be decreased?

- Time-wasting behaviors such as arguing, interrupting, or chatting with peers during group lessons.

Step Two: What tokens will the group earn?

- Points tallied on the board in a "minute bank."

Step Three: Why are they collecting tokens? What is the backup reinforcer?

- Time to spend playing a game on Friday afternoon.

Step Four: How Much? What is the token exchange rate?

- One-to-one. One minute banked equals one minute to play the game.

Step Five: Where and When will the tokens be exchanged for the backup reinforcers?

- Friday after lunch in the classroom.

This group token economy system was so successful that the teacher started using the minute bank idea at other times of day. If it was time to line up for lunch, she might say, "I think it will take you four minutes to get ready and into a quiet line for lunch. Maybe you will prove me wrong." She then started a stopwatch and waited while the class scrambled to line up. As soon as they were quietly in line, she stopped the stopwatch. If it took less than four minutes, the minutes saved were added to the minute bank. She always estimated a minute more than she thought it would take, so that the class could feel successful. Using this strategy, she never again found herself standing at the front of the line shouting at her class to hurry up and get in line while they moved slowly or horsed around on their way to line up.

Example Three: Can a Token Economy Help Prevent Daniel's Defiance?

Daniel's teacher wanted him to request help when he needs it, rather than saying "I won't!" or other forms of defiance. Because he is verbal, she would like him to simply raise his hand and say that he needs help; however, she realized that when he is under stress he sometimes loses the ability to speak. This is why she wanted to reinforce using a "help" card when he needs help and can't ask with words. To increase using the card or verbally asking for help instead of refusing to work, she created an individual token economy system for him.

Each time Daniel made an appropriate request for help either by asking verbally (if able), or by raising his "help" card, his teacher put a colored paper clip on the edge of the card. She collected paper clips in many colors and kept clips of a different color in her pocket every day to discourage bootleg reinforcement by bringing paper clips from home or saving one from the day before. When he had five colored clips on his card she exchanged them for one larger clip. When he had three large clips, he earned a homework "Trade One/ Toss One" privilege (see appendix).

Here are the five steps in Daniel's token economy:

Step One: Which desirable behavior was targeted to be increased?

- Asking for help using a "help" card or verbally requesting help.

Step Two: What tokens did Daniel earn?

- Paper clips attached to his "help" card.

Step Three: Why is Daniel collecting tokens? What is the backup reinforcer?

- "Trade One/Toss One" homework privileges.

Step Four: How Much? What is the token exchange rate?

- Five small paper clips are traded for one large paper clip, and three large clips earn the privilege.

Step Five: Where and when will the tokens be exchanged for the backup reinforcers?

- As soon as the three large clips are acquired, Daniel may look into his weekly homework packet and choose the two pages he wants to trade or toss.

Daniel's teacher was concerned at first that he might abuse the token economy by repeatedly asking for help when he didn't need it just to get more paper clips. She was ready with an alternate plan if this had happened, in which he would earn paper clips for work completed rather than for requesting help. He could ask for help as often as he liked, but would not earn paper clips unless he demonstrated productivity. As it turned out, Daniel did not ask for help excessively. Eventually, she might still decide to switch to the alternative plan if it seemed that Daniel did not need to be reinforced for asking for help, or she might decide to simply phase out the token economy altogether if it was no longer needed.

Strategies Example Four: Can a Token Economy Prevent Sophia's SIB?

Sophia's face-slapping and head-banging self-injurious behaviors (SIB) had already significantly decreased as a result of removing the triggers by moving a classmate who slapped and screamed to a different group and reducing loud noises in the environment. However, she continued to bite her hand when she did not have something else to do. Her teacher was teaching her to request materials using the picture exchange communication system (PECS) when she had finished her work. She directed staff members to be watchful of any time Sophia had finished her task so they could prompt her to make the request. However, there would always be times in her life when she had to wait for something, and she needed to learn different behaviors to engage in while waiting other than biting her hand. Sophia's teacher implemented a program of *differential reinforcement of other behaviors (DRO)*, which is a way of reinforcing the absence of a behavior such as SIB. In DRO, reinforcement is provided differentially based on whether or not the student engaged in the problem behavior during a moment or period of time. For Sophia, they started with immediate reinforcement rather than a token economy, but later determined that she was able to participate in a simple version of the token economy, or a token board.

Sophia's teacher printed a large 3x3 grid on an 8.5"x11" piece of tagboard. After laminating the card, she placed a hook-side sticker of hook-and-loop fasteners on each of the nine squares in the grid. She also printed up number cards with the numerals one through nine sized to fit in the squares, laminated them, and attached the loop-side of the fastener to the back of each card. Periodically, when Sophia was working or when she was between tasks and did not bite her hand, she was given a numeral token to place on the board. If she bit her hand, the board was removed from her work area for a minute while staff responded to the SIB and prompted communication with the PECS icon. The removal of the board signaled that reinforcement was not available during that minute following her SIB. After approximately one minute, when she was not engaging in SIB, the token board was returned to her area and she regained the opportunity to earn reinforcement for other behaviors (any behavior that is not self-injurious).

When she had placed all nine number cards on her token board, she was given the board to remove the tokens and examine them briefly while she put them back in their envelope. This task was in itself reinforcing for Sophia. She was then offered a favorite number puzzle to complete, after which the token board was put back up and she was given the next work center task.

Later Sophia's teacher expanded the amount of time Sophia needed to be free from SIB in order to earn tokens in two ways. First, after one week, she instructed her staff to provide the tokens after increasingly longer intervals of no SIB. After three weeks, she switched to token boards with sixteen and then twenty-five blocks rather than nine. Sophia readily accepted these new token boards because they represented more numbers, which she loved.

Here are the steps Sophia's teacher used:

Step One: Which undesirable behavior was targeted to be decreased?

- SIB, specifically biting her hand.

Step Two: What tokens would Sophia earn?

- Number cards to be placed on a token board.

Step Three: Why was she collecting tokens? What is the backup reinforcer?

- Time spent manipulating the number cards and putting together a number puzzle.

Step Four: How Much? What is the token exchange rate?

- Placing all tokens on the board equals five minutes to interact with number cards and puzzle.

Step Five: Where and When will the tokens be exchanged for the backup reinforcers?

- Immediately after the last token is earned.

Sophia's teacher found that this was highly effective in decreasing her SIB. Later she began using the token board to reinforce Sophia's use of her functional communication system, for following verbal directions, and for increased engagement with non-preferred activities such as alphabet and pre-reading and writing tasks.

Example Five: Can a Token Economy Help Prevent Aiden's Aggression?

Aiden's teacher wanted to incorporate math, economics, and life skills goals into a class-wide token economy system. In this system, her students earned paychecks for school attendance (showing up to work), and completing assignments (work productivity). In addition, they could earn bonuses for going above and beyond expectations. On the day that she explained the system to the class, she started them off by issuing checkbooks and check registers to each student, and writing them each a paycheck to start on. On Friday, she paid them what they had earned through attendance, productivity, and any bonuses, which they added to their check registers. Then she had them "pay bills," including rent for their desk and their share of utility bills. They wrote checks to pay these bills and learned to do the subtraction required to balance their checkbooks. They could spend whatever money they had left at the store, where they could write checks to purchase goods and services or privileges. These included things that were reasonably priced, such as pencils, erasers, or a "get out of homework free" card. The options ranged all the way up to higher-priced items such as a ticket to a monthly lunch-and-a-movie party in the classroom, or the right to move their desk to a more prestigious location by the window for the week.

When students demonstrated their ability to be productive, law-abiding citizens of their classroom society by paying their bills on time and going at least a month without a discipline referral, they earned the right to apply for a classroom job, such as IT support, zoo-keeper or gardener (caring for a classroom pet or plant), or store manager for the Friday store. For these jobs they would need to fill out an application and be interviewed by the teacher. They would earn additional money for completing these jobs, and the jobs lasted for one month, at which point they could reapply for the same job or for another job, as long as they continued to be eligible. If a student holding a job became ineligible by receiving a discipline referral, they forfeited their job and it would open up, and another student could apply for it.

Individual students could earn "bonuses" for areas that were most challenging for them. For example, a student who was great at reading and struggled with math would earn bonuses for doing extra math problems, but not for extra reading. Another student who has no trouble with math might earn a bonus for doing extra reading because it is more difficult for her. Social students earn more for studiousness, and studious students earn more for engaging in appropriate social interactions. Aiden earned bonuses for coming in after lunch and either participating in class on a good day or choosing to go to the safety zone on a bad day. Everyone earned a small bonus for completing the "How are you doing?" forms.

Aiden's teacher decided to include a response cost in the form of paying "fines" for breaking classroom rules, to highlight the fact that in real life there are consequences if you break the law, including financial consequences.

Although this token economy system required a great deal of prepping on the part of the teacher and aides, and took up more of the instructional day than some systems, Aiden's teacher felt this was a worthwhile expenditure of time. They were practicing addition and subtraction when balancing their checkbooks, and gaining skills that would be of lifelong value.

Here are the steps she used when designing this token economy.

Step One: Which desirable behaviors will be targeted to be increased?

- Being on task and productive, coming in calmly after lunch or choosing the safety zone if needed.

Step Two: What tokens will be earned?

- Classroom dollars to be paid by check into their checking accounts.

Step Three: Why are they collecting tokens? What is the backup reinforcer?

- A range of goods and services may be purchased at the classroom store. In addition, by keeping their checkbooks balanced and having good behavior, students may earn the right to apply for classroom jobs.

Step Four: How Much? What is the token exchange rate?

- One-to-one: one "dollar" earned equals one "dollar" to spend.

Step Five: Where and When will the tokens be exchanged for the backup reinforcers?

- Every Friday afternoon Aiden's teacher set aside a full period devoted to paying bills, balancing checkbooks, applying for jobs, and purchasing goods and services at the store. This time is built into her schedule to ensure enough time for each student to get the tasks done and go to the classroom store to make their purchases.

Although it was time consuming, after the initial training period Aiden's teacher saw success and felt it was worth the time and work she put into it. She acknowledged that a system like this was not for everyone, but in her small special day class this was a useful strategy that she planned to continue year after year.

ACT IV, Scene Twelve Summary

In Scene Twelve we learned the five steps necessary for a successful token economy system, (which behavior, what tokens, why, how much, where and when) and how they can be useful either individually or for the whole class. We read examples of how they can help increase desired behaviors and decrease undesired behaviors in a range of settings and situations. Although a token economy system might not be for every classroom, student, or teacher, it is an effective, evidence-based strategy that many students benefit from. Still, it's not the only trick we have up our sleeves. In the Scene Thirteen we'll look at another evidence-based strategy: the behavioral contract.

 ACT IV, Scene Twelve Vocabulary

backup reinforcers   bootleg reinforcers

differential reinforcement of other behaviors (DRO)

evidence-based practice (EBP)   exchange rate

functionally equivalent replacement behavior (FERB)

response cost   socially significant

token   token board

token economy

ACT IV, Scene Twelve Discussion Topic

With your small group, list as many ideas as you can for backup reinforcers which are free, at no cost to the teacher. These may include various classroom privileges, services, activities, and opportunities.

 ACT IV, Scene Twelve Questions

1. FERB stands for:
    A. Forming evidence-related behaviors.
    B. Functionally equivalent replacement behavior.
    C. Fully equal reinforcement base.
    D. First evidence reinforced behavior.

2. EBP stands for:
    A. Emerging behavior standards.
    B. Excessive behavior stimulation.
    C. Extremely beneficial systems.
    D. Evidence-based practices.

3. DRO stands for:
    A. Differential reinforcement of other behavior.
    B. Dependent relationship occupation.
    C. Differential replacement of other behavior.
    D. Distal reinforcement out of school.

4. Your student is working for cheese puffs as a reinforcer after lunch. His mother had packed him a large bag of cheese puffs in his lunch, which he has just eaten. Now he doesn't want to work. This is an example of:
    A. Bootleg reinforcement.
    B. Satiation.
    C. Both A and B.
    D. Neither A nor B.

5. In the example above, after you find out that your student has just eaten a bag of cheese puffs, what should you do now?
    A. Nothing—keep on working using cheese puffs as a reinforcer because it is in your plan and it has been shown to be effective in the past.
    B. Immediately stop offering any reinforcement, as the use of reinforcers has been spoiled for this student.
    C. Switch from using cheese puffs as a reinforcer to using sips from a juice box instead.
    D. All of the above.

6. The following are steps in planning a token economy:
    A. Plan which behavior will be targeted for increase or decrease.
    B. Plan what tokens will be used as conditioned reinforcers.
    C. Plan what backup reinforcers the tokens will be exchanged for.
    D. All of the above.

7. The following are also steps in planning a token economy:
    A. Plan the rate of exchange of tokens for backup reinforcers.
    B. Plan where and when the tokens will be exchanged.
    C. Both A and B.
    D. Neither A nor B.

Scene Thirteen

The Behavioral Contract: Wheeling and Dealing

You may have experienced a kind of behavior contract that specifies what the student is supposed to do (or not do), as well as what will happen if the student breaks the contract; for example, being suspended or expelled from school. In some school systems, having a behavior contract in place is required before they may suspend or expel a student, especially a student with an individualized education program (IEP). An administrator in charge of discipline may write up a contract stating, "Student will refrain from hitting, hurting, or threatening others. If student engages in these behaviors, student will be suspended for five days." There is no plan to help prevent the fighting or bullying; the entire burden is placed on the student. The adults have no responsibility other than waiting to see if the student will be suspended or not. This may be fine for general education students, but it is not an effective way to work with students on the spectrum. (I'm not saying it is fine for general education students, but that's another book.) If a student with autism is fighting or bullying, the school needs to help them find better ways to communicate and meet their needs without engaging in these behaviors. We have a responsibility to teach better behavior, not just hope for it.

What Is a Behavioral Contract?

In this scene, we're talking about something different from the behavior contracts you may have seen in schools. A *behavioral contract*, based on the science of behavior analysis, is not just a threat and a promise, but a way to help students (and teachers) do what they agree to do. Also called a *contingency contract*, a behavioral contract is a formal, clearly written statement of a target behavior and consequences contingent on the occurrence or nonoccurrence of the behavior. Preferably, the consequences should reinforce appropriate behavior rather than punishing inappropriate behavior.

For example, a high school student with a history of truancy might agree to attend every class all week, with the consequence of receiving a coupon for a free slice of pizza from the cafeteria on Friday.

A sixth grader has a history of making rude noises with his mouth or armpit during group assemblies. Following an assembly with zero occurrences of this behavior, he may earn a consequence of being seated beside a peer of his choosing at the next assembly rather than sitting by a teacher or aide.

When a kindergarten student who usually wanders around the classroom sits on the carpet throughout story time, her consequence is receiving a star stamped on the back of her hand after the story.

Types of Behavioral Contracts

There are two types of behavioral contracts: one-party contracts and *two-party contracts.*

In a one-party contract, also called a *unilateral contract*, one person is working on changing a target behavior. The *contract manager* (usually the teacher) writes up the contract and implements the contingency. An example of this would be a contract wherein a student will maintain a neat and orderly assignment binder which passes daily binder inspections all week, after which the student earns a "Trade One" Homework Pass (see appendix).

In a two-party or *bilateral contract*, two people agree to change a behavior, with consequences contingent on the occurrence or nonoccurrence of the behavior. One type of two-party contract is a *parallel contract*, with separate and unrelated consequences for each. For example, a student agrees to present an "I need a break" card when he is becoming overly stressed; his consequence is being allowed to go to the break area. As a separate agreement, his teacher agrees to refrain from calling on the student to read aloud in class; as a consequence, he agrees to read an easy-reader book to a kindergarten student on Friday afternoon. Each of them have agreed to increase (or decrease) a behavior, and each receive a separate consequence contingent on engaging in (or refraining from engaging in) the specified behavior.

Another type of two-party contract is the *quid pro quo contract*, in which the behavior change of one party acts as a reinforcer for the other party. For example, one student agrees to help another student with his math homework, and the second student agrees to help the first student with her reading homework. After both students have helped one another, each of them receives a "Toss One" Homework Pass (see appendix).

Why do Behavioral Contracts Work?

Behavioral contracts are effective in changing behaviors for several reasons. One is that putting the behavior in writing brings it to everyone's attention, so the student is thinking about the behavior rather than engaging in it habitually or mindlessly.

The fact that the contract is in writing makes it a public commitment, even if only the student and contract manager see it. A public commitment is more likely to be kept than a silent promise to oneself. In addition, many ASD students value routine, order, and following rules, and so are likely to appreciate and honor a public commitment.

Planning consequences is another important part of motivating the student to comply with the contract. This is true whether it is an enjoyable consequence following the occurrence of a desired behavior, or an unwanted consequence after engaging in the problem behavior.

Behavioral contracts also work because they serve as an establishing operation (EO), making engaging in the desired behavior (or refraining from engaging in the problem behavior) more valuable and motivating.

Finally, behavioral contracts work because of the effects of *rule-governed* behavior. This means that the student's behavior is controlled by a rule (verbal or written) about a contingency between their behavior and a possible future consequence. The verbal rule is more important than the actual reinforcer.

The Six Parts of a Behavioral Contract

Here are the six components you should include in any behavioral contract:

1. **WHAT** behavior will be targeted for change? It is important to describe the behavior clearly. Is it a desirable behavior to be increased, or an undesirable behavior to be decreased? Specify this in the written contract.

2. **HOW** will the behavior be measured? If we don't keep data, we won't know how often the behavior happened, and whether or not the behavioral contract is working. Keeping data might include a physical or *permanent product*, such as a completed work paper. If "teacher observation" is to be used, be sure that your notes reflect what day and time you observed the behavior.

3. **WHEN** should the target behavior occur (in the case of a behavior to be increased)? Don't be ambiguous about the time expectation. If homework is to be turned in by 8:15 in the morning on the day it is due, say so explicitly. This can prevent arguments about whether or not the student should get credit for turning in the homework later in the day after completing it during recess, for example.

4. **WHY** should they engage (or refrain from engaging) in the behavior? What's in it for them, or what is their motivation? The consequences

must be stated clearly, and should be chosen with the student's own preferences in mind. It would be a good idea to give the student responsibility to choose the consequences (within reason), with the teacher retaining veto privileges.

5. **WHO** will deliver the contingency or consequence? Don't be ambiguous here. Everyone needs to know whether the teacher, one of the aides, or someone else will be in charge of this.

6. **WHEN** will the consequence be delivered? Make the time and write it down. At the end of a busy day it's easy to forget this important detail; make sure the consequence gets delivered on schedule.

It is vital that we respect the contract as much as we expect the student to respect and comply with it. If we get too busy and forget to provide the promised reinforcer even once, we have broken our contract with the student. This communicates rather strongly that it is not necessary to honor the contract, allowing the student to also break the contract. Trust is lost. Take the contract seriously.

Examples of Behavioral Contracts

Let's take a look at how a behavioral contract might be useful with each of our five example students, starting with Anthony.

Example One: Can a Behavioral Contract Prevent Anthony's Acting Out?

Anthony's teacher decided to use a simple two-party behavioral contract called a "Promise Page." The teacher's promise to provide the preferred reinforcer is contingent on Anthony keeping his promise to write three sentences (see appendix).

Here are the components of Anthony's behavioral contract:

1. **WHAT** behavior will be targeted for change?
   • Sentence writing, to be increased to three sentences.

2. **HOW** will it be measured?
   - Anthony's journal or Dinosaur writing pages and teacher records will serve as a permanent record.

3. **WHEN** should the target behavior occur?
   - First thing each morning during the journal-writing period.

4. **WHY** should Anthony engage in the behavior?
   - To receive a star stamp on his Steggo Star-Us chart.

5. **WHO** will deliver the contingency or consequence?
   - His teacher.

6. **WHEN** will the contingency be delivered?
   - Every school day morning at the end of the journal-writing period.

Anthony's teacher tried this behavioral contract "Promise Page" with Anthony for a week, and then found that the contract was not necessary for him. The presence of the Steggo Star-Us chart on his desk, combined with the teacher's direction to the class to write three sentences, were enough to prompt him to write the sentences. The teacher consistently remembered to give him his star after he completed the task, and the "Promise Page" was discontinued.

Example Two: Can a Behavioral Contract Reduce Destiny's Disruptions?

Destiny's teacher, hypothesizing that Destiny desired attention and recognition for her abilities, designed a unilateral one-party contract. If Destiny refrained from interrupting or calling out answers without raising her hand or waiting for her stick to be drawn during twenty group lessons, she would earn the right to read a chapter of the current literature book out loud to the rest of the class, ask three questions about the chapter, and draw sticks for three of her classmates to answer questions. At the end of each group lesson during which Destiny did not interrupt or call out an answer, her teacher put a tally on a card. If Destiny had interrupted or called out, no tally was added.

However, because she was earning the tallies cumulatively (she did not start over when she failed to earn a tally), and there was no response cost, no tallies were lost or removed. On the next Friday afternoon following the accumulation of the twenty tally marks, Destiny read the chapter instead of her teacher reading it and asked three comprehension questions. To avoid peer resentment, the teacher made a blanket offer that any student who wanted to read aloud could meet with her to develop a similar contract based on what they most needed to learn or improve.

Here are the components of Destiny's behavioral contract:

1. **WHAT** behavior will be targeted for decrease?
   - Interrupting or calling out answers during group lessons.

2. **HOW** will it be measured?
   - By tallies on a card kept by Destiny's teacher.

3. **WHEN** should the target behavior be measured?
   - During group lessons.

4. **WHY** should Destiny refrain from engaging in the behavior?
   - To earn an opportunity to act as "teacher," reading to the class, and asking three questions.

5. **WHO** will deliver the contingency or consequence?
   - Destiny's teacher will determine that Destiny has earned the right to read to the class based on the tally card.

6. **WHEN** will the contingency be delivered?
   - On the next Friday afternoon following completion of the twenty tallies.

Although it took several weeks for Destiny to reach twenty tally points and earn the reward, it seemed to become easier over time. Her teacher did not forget to show her when she earned a tally mark and remind her what she was working for every day. The first few times Destiny failed to earn a tally mark she was upset and tried to argue with the teacher about it, but her teacher pointed out that she would never lose a point or have to start over, and that there would soon be another lesson and another chance for a tally. Then the teacher stopped responding to Destiny's arguments and went on with the day. Destiny began earning the tally marks more frequently and arguing less when the teacher did not take the bait and get pulled into a discussion with her. When she finally earned the right to read a chapter to the class, she did an excellent job, asked good questions, and praised the students answering the questions. Her teacher decided to continue to contract for the rest of the year. It not only made it easier for her to teach without Destiny's interjections, but the class seemed to enjoy having Destiny read to them as an interesting change of pace.

Example Three: Can a Behavioral Contract Reduce Daniel's Defiance?

Daniel's teacher wants him to reduce incidents of work refusal, such as saying, "I won't," or "I can't," as soon as a worksheet is given to him. She wants him to try it first and then request help appropriately if needed. He has been working on using a "help" card as well as a "break" card, but he often still forgets and says "I can't" out of habit before he even looks at the page. His teacher would like for him to become more aware of this so that he can decrease his use of this negative stock phrase. She asks him to tally his use of negative phrases ("I can't") and positive phrases ("I'll try") on a two-column chart. He agrees to keep track and try to decrease his use of the phrase "I can't," substituting other self-talk phrases such as "this is hard, but I can try" and "I'll try it first, and I can get help if I need it." At the end of the week, if his data shows an increase in positive self-talk and a decrease in saying "I can't," he will earn a "Trade One" homework privilege (see appendix).

Here are the components of Daniel's behavioral contract:

1. **WHAT** problem behavior will be targeted to be decreased, and what replacement behavior is targeted for increase?
   - Decrease negative comments associated with work refusal (i.e., "I can't").
   - Increase use of positive self-talk phrases (i.e., "I'll try").

2. **HOW** will it be measured?
   - By tally marks on a two-column chart for negative and positive self-talk.

3. **WHEN** should the target behavior to be increased occur?
   - When Daniel is given a worksheet to complete independently.

4. **WHY** should Daniel engage in the behavior to be increased (positive self-talk) and refrain from the behavior to be decreased (negative self-talk)?
   - To earn a "Trade One" homework privilege.

5. **WHO** will deliver the contingency or consequence?
   - Daniel's teacher will provide him with the "Trade One" file when earned.

6. **WHEN** will the contingency be delivered?
   - Every Friday afternoon that Daniel's chart shows both an increase in positive self-talk and a decrease in negative self-talk for the week.

At first, because he was not yet self-aware of his negative phrases, his teacher silently pointed to the negative column when she heard him say "I can't," and to the other column when he made a positive comment. He was better at remembering to give himself a tally for "I'll try" because he had to put forth conscious effort to change his usual response to new work papers. During the first day he used negative phrases far more often than positive self-talk, and he noticed this on the chart. With prompts or cues from his teacher, he began to make a change, so that by Friday he had tallied one more positive comment than negative. His teacher was more directive in encouraging him to use the chart the first week because it was important for him to earn the reward the first time. She wanted him to experience success. Later, she decreased her level of prompting as he became more self-aware. She occasionally made comments about how confident or happy he looked when he used positive self-talk. Gradually, there were fewer and fewer tallies in the "I can't" column and Daniel showed a more positive outlook on trying new work pages. His teacher felt it was a success, and she continued with it because he seemed to enjoy tallying his own responses and earning the "Trade One" privilege each week.

Example Four: Can a Behavioral Contract Work for Sophia?

Because Sophia has a strong preference for any activity involving numbers and she shows no interest in letters of the alphabet, her teacher wants to increase her engagement with alphabet tasks. Sophia demonstrates little comprehension of time and contingencies, so any complex behavioral contract is unlikely to be successful. Instead, her teacher uses a very simple FIRST/THEN contract. A piece of white paper is divided by a line down the middle, with the word "FIRST" at the top of the left side and the word "THEN" at the top of the right side. It is laminated, and a hook sticker of hook-and-loop fasteners is placed in the center of each side. Two laminated cards each have a loop-sticker on the back, one with "A, B, C" printed on the front and the other with "1, 2, 3" printed on it. Sophia's teacher or aide presents the FIRST/THEN contract, and places the "A, B, C" card on the FIRST half and the "1, 2, 3" card on the THEN half of the contract, while telling Sophia, "First we do A-B-Cs, and then you can do numbers." The number activity (either a number puzzle, book, flash cards, numeral magnets, or a math work sheet) is shown to Sophia and placed at the far right side of the table, closer to the THEN side of the page. The alphabet task or activity is placed in front of Sophia. If she reaches toward the number activity before completing the letter activity, she is redirected to the task before her and the adult repeats, "First letters, then numbers." After she has completed the letter task, she is given the number activity that she has been working for.

Here are the components of Sophia's FIRST/THEN behavioral contract:

1. **WHAT** behavior will be targeted for increase?
   - Engagement with alphabet tasks and activities.

2. **HOW** will it be measured?
   - The adult will keep data on tasks completed in Sophia's data binder.

3. **WHEN** should the target behavior occur?
   - When presented with a non-preferred alphabet task during center rotation.

4. **WHY** should Sophia engage in the alphabet activity?
   - To gain access to her preferred activities involving numbers.

5. **WHO** will deliver the contingency or consequence?
   - The teacher or aide working with Sophia at the time.

6. **WHEN** will the contingency (number activity) be delivered?
   - Immediately upon completion of the alphabet task.

Although at first Sophia tried to reach for the number task several times, she complied when redirected to the alphabet task. After several days she stopped reaching for the number task first and started in on the alphabet task, finishing it as quickly as she could before reaching for the numbers. The FIRST/THEN behavioral contract was considered a success and her teacher continued using it throughout the year, later expanding it for use with other less preferred activities and using it with other students.

Example Five: Can a Behavioral Contract Prevent Aiden's aggression?

Aiden had been doing well with the classroom token economy of earning "money," paying bills, and obtaining privileges such as classroom jobs; however, the available classroom jobs were not very interesting to him. He came up with a new job he wanted his teacher to add. While walking around the perimeter of the campus, he passes by the fenced play yard of the adjacent preschool. He noticed that their tricycles were wobbly and sometimes the wheels or handlebars came loose. When this happened the trike was removed and placed in a shed, leaving fewer trikes for the children to share. Aiden has been repairing his own and his younger siblings' bicycles for years, and he wanted to help the preschool. He asked his teacher if he could have a job as "tricycle mechanic" to fix the preschool tricycles for them. She spoke to the principal and preschool director, and they came to an agreement with certain contingencies.

First, Aiden was to write up a job proposal stating what he would do for the preschool, e.g., cleaning and maintaining tricycles by tightening loose wheels, handlebars, and seats.

Second, he would obtain two letters of recommendation regarding his skills as a bicycle repairman. These letters could come from his father—a mechanic who has worked with Aiden on similar jobs at home—and a younger brother whose bike Aiden has successfully repaired.

Third, he must complete the job application form that his teacher uses in the classroom token economy.

Fourth, and most importantly, Aiden must be free from discipline referrals, including in-class aggressive incidents, for at least a month prior to being hired.

Finally, he must participate in a job interview with the principal, his teacher, and the preschool director. Aiden was highly motivated to do this job, so he worked hard to fulfill his part of the behavioral contract.

Here are the components of Aiden's behavioral contract:

1. **WHAT** behavior will be targeted for change?
   - Aggressive behaviors must be eliminated for one month.

2. **HOW** will it be measured?
   - Discipline records and classroom behavioral data.

3. **WHEN** will the target behavior, aggression, be counted?
   - Throughout the school day, in all school settings.

4. **WHY** should Aiden stop engaging in aggressive behavior?
   - To earn the right to hold the position of tricycle mechanic.

5. **WHO** will deliver the contingency or consequence?
   - Aiden's teacher will notify him and the preschool director that he has earned the job upon completion and acceptance of all contingencies noted in the contract.

Because of his strong interest in vehicles and the feeling of accomplishment he receives from successfully repairing a bike or trike, Aiden was strongly motivated to do whatever it takes to earn the position he created for himself. Once he knew he would be protected from bullying attempts, he felt safer and more confident. He completed all the tasks required to apply for the job, including having a clean discipline record with no aggressive misbehavior for one month. After a successful interview, he became the school's first tricycle mechanic. The preschool director was also grateful that tricycles could be repaired and put back to use quickly, rather than waiting for the county repair requisition process.

ACT IV, Scene Thirteen Summary

Behavioral or contingency contracts can be one-party (unilateral) contracts or two-party (bilateral) contracts. Two-party contracts may be parallel contracts or quid pro quo contracts. The six necessary parts of a behavioral contract include WHAT behavior is targeted for change, HOW the behavior will be measured, WHEN the behavior should occur, WHY the student should change the behavior (the contingency), WHO will deliver the contingency, and WHEN the contingency will be delivered. When all these parts are in place, behavioral contracts are more likely to be successful. Choosing a consequence or contingency that motivates a student is important to success. The contract itself serves as an establishing operation (EO), which increases the value of engaging in the desired behavior (or refraining from the undesired behavior). In addition, many individuals on the autism spectrum are to some extent rule-governed; a contract is a rule, and that in itself increases the likelihood that they will comply. We have seen how a range of different behavioral contracts worked for our five students. In Scene Fourteen, we will look at self-management strategies, putting students in charge of their own behavior change process.

In Their Own Words

"My kindergarten teacher really knew how to get me to do schoolwork during class. I struggled with lack of focus during the school day. Getting worksheets done seemed boring. I could get it done, but I didn't feel like it because it wasn't exciting and my mind was elsewhere. I imagine that she was frustrated because I never completed any work. My desk was set apart from others in order to limit distractions, but that didn't really stop my mind from wandering. She devised a plan where I only had to complete the most important work of the day. It may have been a math worksheet or a piece of writing that served as my primary focus. She described this to me as a 'have-to' activity. If an activity or an assignment was not a 'have-to' I could play with Tinker Toys or Lincoln Logs instead. I was always passively listening to her and learning even though I was playing while she was teaching. As the year progressed there were more and more 'have-to' tasks. By the end of the year it seemed as though I didn't need the 'have-to' system anymore. This system gave me the chance to adapt to obeying instructions from a teacher. She communicated her expectations in a way that made sense to me."

~ Elliot, high-functioning Asperger's syndrome and ADHD

What Can We Learn from Elliot's Story?

With a kindergartener like Elliot, his informal behavioral contract was as simple as being told which assignments were "have-to" tasks and which were optional. Compromising and allowing young students to have more play time, while specifying which activities are required, can help them learn to love school while getting used to the structure and expectations. Later, you can increase the amount of time spent engaged in the required tasks. And remember, your students may hear and understand every word you say even while they are playing or fidgeting with something. One more thing—separating a student by having him sit far away from his peers will not solve problems of inattention and distractibility, but it can make a student feel isolated and singled out.

ACT IV, Scene Thirteen Vocabulary

behavioral contract	bilateral contract	contingency contract
contract manager	one-party contract	parallel contract
permanent product	quid pro quo contract	rule-governed
two-party contract	unilateral contract	

 ACT IV, Scene Thirteen Discussion Topic

Discuss with your small group which kinds of behavioral contracts might be more effective with students of various ages and ability levels. Have you used a behavioral contract in your practice? Share your experience.

 ACT IV, Scene Thirteen Questions

1. A behavioral contract and a behavior contract are the same thing; they both stipulate that if a student engages in a specific misbehavior, then the student may be suspended or expelled from school. TRUE or FALSE?

2. A behavioral contract and a contingency contract are the same thing, and are based on the science of behavior analysis. TRUE or FALSE?

3. It makes no difference whether a behavioral contract is a written document or a verbal agreement. TRUE or FALSE?

4. Why do behavioral contracts work?
   A. Because of the contingent consequences.
   B. Because the student makes a public commitment.
   C. Both A and B.
   D. Neither A nor B.

5. What are some other reasons that behavioral contracts work?

    A. Because of the influence of rule-governed behavior.

    B. Because the contract itself acts as an establishing operation (EO).

    C. Both A and B.

    D. Neither A nor B.

6. The components of a good behavioral contract include:

    A. Identifying a target behavior to be increased or decreased.

    B. Stating how the target behavior will be measured.

    C. Stating when the student must engage in the behavior.

    D. All of the above.

7. Other components of a good behavioral contract include:

    A. Identifying the contingency or reinforcers.

    B. Stating who will implement the contingency.

    C. Neither of the above.

    D. Both of the above.

8. A good behavioral contract also includes:

    A. A written rationale describing why the teacher feels it is necessary.

    B. When and where the contingency will be implemented.

    C. None of the above.

    D. All of the above.

Scene Fourteen

Self-Management: Empowering the Actors

The ultimate goal of any behavior change plan is for your students to learn to manage their own behaviors, rather than becoming overly reliant on someone else. You can help them achieve this goal by teaching them the skills they need to engage in self-management. A *self-management program* is a way for someone to manipulate antecedents and consequences to change their own behaviors. Once your students are mature enough, this is a powerful tool you can place in their hands.

There are several ways that students can manage their own behaviors, including setting goals and *self-monitoring* their behavior, setting up *antecedent manipulations*, and *arranging consequences*.

Goal Setting

The first step in self-monitoring is to choose an appropriate goal with your student. It is important that the student is a collaborator in this process, so sit down together and brainstorm a target goal you can both agree on. This target must be both *achievable* and *meaningful.*

An achievable goal is one that is within the student's current *repertoire* of behaviors, that is, things that they are already able to do. Self-management is not the time to try and teach a new behavior, but choose one you know they can be successful at with room for improvement. For example, if you have a student who has never yet sat quietly during a fifteen-minute story, do not set a goal to sit for thirty minutes, or even fifteen minutes. You and the student both know they can't do it yet, so you would be setting them up for failure. Not only that, but once they fail, they won't trust any future self-management programs you may suggest. Worse, they may lose trust in you. If you know they can sit quietly for ten minutes, set the first self-monitoring goal for five minutes. Let them get the feel for successfully self-monitoring their behavior in small increments.

A second consideration when choosing a goal for self-management is that the goal must be meaningful for the student. This is not the time to push your own agenda for what you want the student to do. What behavior change would make a difference in their life? If the student feels badly about not being able to sit quietly in class when their classmates are able to, then it might be a meaningful behavior to work on. On the other hand, a student who loves getting attention by clowning around and disrupting class will not be likely to choose this as a goal for self-monitoring. Not every behavior is amenable to this strategy, and you can find another way to deal with disrupting class if the student does not want to work on it. Ask what they would like to change. Do they want to break a habit that they are embarrassed about, such as thumb-sucking? Do they want to learn a new skill that the other students already possess, such a dribbling a basketball in PE? You may not care whether or not they can dribble a basketball, but if they care, they will work on it. Starting with something they're really interested in opens the door for learning to self-monitor in other areas of their life. If they want to make a meaningful change, and you help them set up the components of the self-management program, they are much more likely to put in the work required.

You can help your student select and write down a target self-monitoring goal that is both achievable and meaningful. If their first goal is readily achievable and they succeed, they will be motivated to try more self-management programs in the future. If the goal is meaningful and important to them, not simply something their teacher wants them to work on, they are more likely to put effort into self-monitoring to reach their goal.

Antecedent Manipulations

Another way that students can self-manage their behavior is through antecedent manipulations. They can use some of the same strategies that we have previously discussed in ACT III, but in this case they will be making purposeful choices rather than having the adults make these decisions for them. Where we use language like "present the discriminative stimulus (S^d) for the desired behavior," you will want to use simpler, more direct language with your students. Here are some of the antecedent manipulations we talked about, and how they might be used in a self-management program:

Present the Discriminative Stimulus (S^d) for the Desired Behavior = Get a Cue

This might be a sticky note or something else that prompts your students to do what they're supposed to do. One student asked for a reminder card taped to his desk with a list of what he can do when he finishes his work early. This helped him make a good choice rather than trying to play with his friends who were still working.

Remove the S^d for the Problem Behavior = Get Rid of Temptation

If there is something distracting in the area that leads your student astray, let them make a change for the better, such as deciding to move their desk away from the book shelf, window, or their best friend, as these things tend to trigger misbehavior or getting off-task.

Decrease the Response Effort for the Desired Behavior = Make It Easier to Do the Right Thing

If your student wants to remember to ask for a break with a break card rather than yelling for a break, don't put the break card across the room. Put it right on their desk where they can see it and pick it up easily.

Increase the Response Effort for the Undesired Behavior = Make It Harder to Do the Wrong Thing

Maybe your student plays with gadgets, toys, and key rings hanging from their backpack straps rather than working. Maybe their parents gave them a cell phone for emergencies, but they find it almost impossible to resist taking it out and checking for texts or messages during class. Help them find a place to stash their backpack or phone where it will be safe (and safely out of reach) so it will not lead them into temptation.

Arranging Consequences

In addition to manipulating antecedents, it is important to arrange consequences. These can include the reinforcing consequences they earn for managing their own behavior, as well as unwanted consequences if they make unfortunate behavior choices. Students can be pretty good at coming up with their own consequences, which are frequently right on the mark and appropriate, but they still need some guidance. Reinforcing consequences should be something the student wants enough to work for, but not over-indulgent. A small box of raisins for a month of returning homework is unlikely to be successful, for example. On the other hand, don't give in to the student who suggests, "If I bring back my homework all week, then I should earn no homework for the rest of the year." Look for a happy medium, something they want and that you are willing to provide. As far as undesired consequences when they don't stick to the program, you can help them come up with a consequence which is neither too strict ("If I forget my homework again, you can suspend me for three days") nor too lenient ("If I get in another fight on the playground, you can reduce my computer time by one minute"). Make sure that consequences are appropriate, meaningful, and somehow related to the misbehavior. For example, picking up trash on the playground might be an appropriate consequence for dumping over a trashcan, but not for forgetting homework. Losing recess time is never an appropriate consequence for a student with autism. This is a vitally needed time to either be physically active, or to be alone and get away from demands. If your student suggests giving up recess as a consequence, please veto that idea and come up with something different. Then find out why they want to get out of recess, and see if you can solve their problem by finding them something constructive they can do during that time, such as going to the library or joining the chess club.

Other Strategies for Self-Management Programs

There are other strategies which can also be used in a self-management program with your students, including behavioral contracts, social support, and self-talk.

Behavioral Contracts

Behavioral contracts (see Scene Thirteen) can be an effective part of a self-management program. Sit down with the student and develop the contract together to make it meaningful to the student. If your student wants more control of the contract and consequences, consider offering a quid pro quo two-party contract in which you offer to do something for the student if the student successfully manages their own behavior. Specify all contingencies in the written contract so there will be no misunderstandings.

Social Support

Another important component of a self-management program is *social support*. When a student makes a behavior change that gets reinforced in other settings, it is more likely to be maintained over time.

Here's an example of using social support in a self-management program. Jacob has been working on raising his hand instead of calling answers out in his special day class (SDC). He and his teacher developed a self-management program and he self-monitored his own hand-raising behavior. He showed significant improvement, until eventually he rarely forgot to raise his hand. When he went to the general education class for social studies, he raised his hand more frequently, too. His general education teacher noticed and praised him, which was reinforcing. Because the behavior had social consequences in other settings, it was reinforced naturally, which perpetuated the behavior.

In another example, Madison is a tall seventh-grader who was clumsy and not confident in her ability to participate in sports. In her general education PE class she was picked first for basketball teams because of her height, and because the team captain did not realize Madison was afraid of the ball. After struggling with the rudiments of the game and being embarrassed when her teammates berated her, she asked her special education teacher for help. They developed a self-management program for learning to catch, dribble, and pass the ball, and to block the basket. This was practiced in isolation with an aide or volunteer, without the stress of an actual game or the presence of peers. Madison self-monitored her progress in being able to perform these skills. As she became more proficient, her teammates noticed and stopped putting her down; some even complimented her when she made a good pass or successfully guarded the basket. The social support was reinforcing to her, and she continued to improve.

Self-Talk

Self-talk, including both *self-instruction* and *self-praise*, can be an effective tool and contribute to a successful self-management program.

With self-instruction, students remind themselves of what they are supposed to do. Some already do this naturally as a memory device, but it can also be taught. It helps to suggest that the student whisper the instructions so as not to disturb peers. Older students may be able to engage in nonverbal self-instruction, going over the steps of the task silently in their mind.

When students have completed a task, it can be reinforcing to engage in self-praise, whispering or thinking to themselves, "I did it!" or "That was awesome!" You can help your students identify specific self-talk phrases that will be most helpful and meaningful to them (phrases which were "cool" for the teacher's generation may be less reinforcing for students today). Practice the phrases in advance so they will be prepared to make good use of the strategy.

Steps to Take for a Successful Self-Management Plan

Miltenberger (2012) identifies nine basic steps that a self-management plan should have in order to be successful.

Decide
The first step is for your student to make the decision to engage in a self-management plan. This must be the child's choice, not yours. We have plenty of other strategies we can use if self-management is either inappropriate for a student, or if the student just doesn't want to do it. Don't push for self-management if your student is not on board.

Define
The second step is to clearly define the behavior that needs to be changed. Determine whether it is a positive, useful behavior that needs to be increased, or a problematic behavior that needs to be decreased. What does the behavior look like? Use student-friendly language and define it clearly enough that there's no "wiggle room."

Set Goals

The third step is to set goals. Remember to make the goals achievable and meaningful. Again, describe the goals as clearly as you defined the behavior. How often, when, and where is the behavior to be performed? Be clear.

Self-Monitor

The fourth step is your student's opportunity to be in charge of their own behavior in a meaningful way. They, not you, will be counting or measuring the behavior to determine whether or not a goal has been met. You can monitor the self-monitoring if you suspect that a student will falsify their data; however, if this is something you strongly suspect will happen, maybe this student is not yet ready to engage in a self-management plan. You might be better off choosing a different behavior change strategy.

What's the Function?

The fifth step is to come up with hypotheses about the function of the behavior. Conducting an informal functional assessment gives us valuable information about the reason why the student engages in a certain behavior. What function does the behavior serve, or what need is fulfilled by engaging in the behavior? Without a working hypothesis of the function of the behavior and a plan to allow the student to meet the same need in a better way, our efforts to change the behavior may go nowhere.

Strategize

The sixth step is to choose which strategies to use to support the self-management program. There are a wide range of strategies that can be used either to increase a desired behavior where there is a behavioral deficit, or to decrease a problem behavior in the case of a behavioral excess. This book has many examples, as do the books in the recommended reading list. Be purposeful in selecting strategies with your student that you both agree are the right fit for the situation.

Evaluate Change

The seventh step, after the program has been going on for a time, is to evaluate the behavior change (if any). How is your student doing with the self-management plan? Are they on track? Has the behavior been changing in a significant way? Keeping data on the behavior is the only way to know for sure if there has been change, and if so, how much. Data is knowledge, and knowledge is power.

Reevaluate Strategies

The eighth step, after evaluating the change that has (or has not) occurred, is to reevaluate the strategies your student is using. Did you see good progress when you evaluated change? If so, great, just keep on doing what works. If you did not see significant change in the targeted behavior, then it is time to re-evaluate the strategies. First, take a look at whether everything in the program has been implemented with *fidelity* or *procedural fidelity*—that is, according to plan. If not, you may not see the success you expected. For example, if a student is gaining access to the reinforcer without fulfilling his part of the bargain (bootleg reinforcement), then he won't be likely to work to get the reinforcer. You need to sew up that loophole. If you've given it a fair chance and you've determined the plan is being implemented with fidelity, but still your strategies don't result in improvement, it's time to go back to the drawing board. Look at other strategies and choose one or more with student input. If the student is not on board with any of the chosen strategies, don't go forward with them. The result could be sabotage, either intentional or subconscious. Communicate with your student at every step of the way. If you find that it is still not working, then maybe self-management is not for this student at this time. Use one of the many other strategies for behavior change instead.

Maintain

Success at last! At the ninth step, your student has demonstrated their ability to change their own behavior using the selected self-management strategies. This is no time to rest on your laurels, though. Don't forget to keep monitoring for maintenance to ensure that the behavior will continue after the self-management program has ended. You'll want to reevaluate the behavior at regular intervals to make sure that entropy is not bringing about the return of the problem behavior, or a decline in the desired behavior. However, there is reason to celebrate and commend your student for taking control of their own behavior.

Examples of Self-Management Programs

Let's take a look at how each of our five students might benefit from a self-management program. We'll start again with Anthony and his acting out behavior.

Example One: Can Anthony Use Self-Management to Stop Acting Out?

Although Anthony is not yet old enough or sufficiently mature to fully engage in a self-management program, his teacher wanted to begin to work in that direction. She taught him to use self-talk as a means of self-regulating when feeling overly-stressed by saying to himself, "I'm okay," and "I can try." This was meaningful to Anthony, because he did not like the feeling of being overwhelmed and out of control due to stress. This gave him some control. Self-talk was considered achievable because occasionally his teacher noticed him spontaneously using self-talk; for example, saying to himself, "That's loud," or "This is easy." She introduced self-talk as a self-management strategy with this brief Social Story™:

> Dinosaurs lived long ago. Many dinosaurs were big and strong. They could do hard things, like stepping over a tree or walking through a lake. That's hard work! Even when it was hard, dinosaurs stayed strong. If they needed a break, they rested under a giant tree. After a break they were okay. If things are hard for me, I can say, "I'm okay, I can try." If I need a break, I can ask for one. After my break, I can say, "I'm ready, I can try." Dinosaurs were strong. They worked and rested and worked. I'm strong, too, like a dinosaur.

Anthony's teacher read him this story several times, and had him read some of the words with her, as he was able. She also placed a picture of a dinosaur on his desk with a word balloon saying, "I'm okay, I can try!" Self-talk was Anthony's first step toward one day being able to participate in a full self-management program.

Example Two: Can Destiny Use Self-Management to Stop Disrupting?

Destiny's teacher talked with her about how Destiny felt when she got in trouble for talking out, and learned that even though she liked answering questions, she really didn't like getting in trouble when it got out of control. Her teacher agreed to call on her a fair number of times by using the name sticks. Using this system helped Destiny realize that the teacher was not being mean or unfair when she didn't call on her. The teacher asked Destiny to answer only when her name stick was drawn, and at other times if she had a question, to raise her hand and wait to be called on. Destiny said she would, and together they agreed that this goal was both meaningful and achievable for her.

Destiny liked to be in charge of her own record keeping. Her teacher gave her a 3x5" card and asked her to make a star on the card every time she raised her hand without calling out. At the end of the day her teacher made a note of how many stars she had, wrote an encouraging note on the back, and let her take the card home. This simple self-monitoring strategy seemed to help Destiny focus on remembering to raise her hand quietly without blurting out answers. It also provided positive reinforcement, and she enjoyed the praise she received from her parents and grandparents when she brought home a card full of stars and a good note from her teacher.

Example Three: Can Daniel Use Self-Management to Stop Being Defiant?

Daniel's teacher asked him how he felt about using the "break" card instead of defiantly saying, "I won't," or "I can't." He told her he liked the break idea, so she believed this would be meaningful for him. She had already introduced the concept of self-talk with Daniel, encouraging him to substitute "I'll try" or "I need help" instead of his negative phrases. Because he responded well to this, she felt a self-monitoring goal would be achievable for him. She asked him to self-monitor his change in self-talk by tallying on a card each time he used the new, positive phrase instead of the negative phrases. Later, she told him she was proud of how well he had done at requesting a break when he needed it. She also wondered how many minutes per day he was on a break instead of working. Daniel agreed to start keeping track of how many minutes he spent on break. She did not discourage him from taking breaks when needed, but she wanted him to be aware of how much time he was missing. After the first week of counting minutes on break, his teacher told him that if the next week showed a decrease of five minutes, he would earn a "Trade One/Toss One" homework privilege (see appendix). Now, whenever he asked for a break, he wrote down what time it started on his chart, and when he returned to his desk he wrote down the time again. He did the math to figure out how many minutes he had spent on the break. Using a timer could help make this process easier, but Daniel had a math goal about telling time, so his teacher wanted him to work with the clock. At the end of the week, Daniel created a bar graph showing how many minutes he spent on break for each day of the week. Graphing was included in the math standards for his grade level, so this was productive. The bar graph provided a clear, visual way of tracking his progress; as the bars got shorter, it meant he was spending less and less time on breaks.

Putting these self-management tools in his hands, rather than having the teacher keep the data for him and show it to him at the end of the week, made the process much more meaningful to Daniel, and ultimately much more successful.

Example Four: How Can Sophia Use Self-Management?

Sophia did not yet have the ability to engage in a self-management program. However, to increase her participation in her own reinforcement, she was the one to put the tokens on her token board. When she refrained from self-injurious behavior (SIB) for the specified amount of time according to the behavior plan, the aide or teacher working with her gave her specific praise while handing her a token and telling her to "token up." Since the goal was for her to be engaged in her task instead of engaging in SIB, the specific praise related to her attention to task, not to her lack of SIB. For example, she was told, "I saw you working hard on that puzzle," rather than, "Good job not biting your hand." The latter statement would call attention to the SIB that they wanted to reduce, so staff refrained from mentioning it while working with Sophia.

Sophia responded well to being prompted to put her own number tokens on the board. Her teacher felt that this was meaningful to her because of her love of numbers. In addition, going from being handed a token and gently guided to put it on the token board, to putting it on the board herself once it was offered to her was an achievable goal. Sophia's success with this plan supported that it was both meaningful and achievable.

Example Five: Can Aiden Use Self-Management to Reach His Goal?

Aiden's teacher felt he had the maturity, motivation and self-awareness to engage in a self-monitoring program, and she believed doing so would increase his feelings of capability and self-esteem.

Here are the nine steps they went through on this journey:

1. Decide

First, Aiden's teacher scheduled some time to sit down with him and explain the self-management process. He asked a few questions, and then decided that he wanted to participate in it. Together they went through the remaining steps.

2. Define

Next, they chose and defined a target behavior. His teacher thought he might choose a behavior that had gotten him into trouble in the past, such as his name-calling and negative remarks that sometimes preceded aggressive behavior, but Aiden had a different idea. He wanted to become a better reader. Aiden noticed that most of the others in his class were better readers than he was. As a teenager, he was embarrassed when his younger brother enjoyed reading chapter books that he was unable to read. His primary goal was to be able to read and understand the articles in his father's *Popular Mechanics* and *Car and Driver* magazines, rather than just looking at the pictures.

3. Set Goals

Currently, Aiden's reading level was at the middle third-grade level according to standardized tests. Most newspapers and magazines are written at the fifth-grade level, so Aiden needed to achieve two years' growth in reading comprehension to reach his goal. His teacher gave him a bonus assignment to look up how to be a better reader on the internet, and he learned that he needed to start at a comfortable reading level and read every day, during his free time as well as during his reading lessons and assignments. He chose as his goal to read for forty-five minutes every day: fifteen minutes before school, fifteen minutes after school, and fifteen minutes before bedtime. The school librarian recommended some books about cars and other vehicles which were at the third-grade reading level. She quickly learned that he refused to even look at a book with a cartoon-character vehicle, as he stated that those were for "babies." She found a number of books which were at his reading level and also at a high school interest level. The goal was meaningful to Aiden, as it supported his interest in vehicles, and especially because he chose it entirely himself without being guided or pressured by his teacher. Aiden's teacher had experience with other highly motivated students showing similarly impressive reading growth when they significantly increased their daily reading, so she believed it was an achievable goal for Aiden.

4. Self-Monitor

Aiden's teacher made a chart for him to track his daily reading by minutes using a bar graph, where he colored in a bar for each five-minute interval he read daily. At the end of the week he had a visual representation of how much he had read each day, and he could see his progress.

As part of his math standards, each week he transcribed this data from the bar graph to a cumulative line graph as another way to visualize how much he was reading.

At the end of the month, he took all the data and divided it into two categories: how many days he met his reading goal of at least forty-five minutes, and how many days he did not meet that goal. He showed this in a pie chart. He appeared to enjoy these visual representations.

5. What's the Function?

Aiden and his teacher skipped the functional assessment step. Because he had chosen a behavior deficit to strengthen rather than a behavior excess to reduce or eliminate, they did not need to conduct a functional assessment to determine the function of the behavior. This would have been an important step if he were working on reducing name-calling, for instance, to determine the function of the name-calling behavior. In fact, his teacher hypothesized that one function of his name-calling might have been to deter attention away from his own lack of reading skills. She felt that as he became a more confident reader, he might be less inclined to call his classmates names. This was a possible side effect, but was not monitored because it was not a meaningful goal for Aiden.

6. Strategize

Aiden and his teacher came up with several strategies to help him stick to his plan of reading at least forty-five extra minutes every day. Because he enjoyed the charts and graphs, self-monitoring was itself a supporting strategy. In addition, his teacher allowed him to go to the school library and check out a new book as soon as he finished one, rather than waiting until their classroom's regularly-scheduled library day. The school librarian was happy to be on Aiden's team and always had several books set aside that she thought he might enjoy. He also started carrying a book with him everywhere he went, so he could read in the waiting room while his mother took his brother to speech therapy, or in the food court while his mother shopped at the mall.

7. Evaluate Change

Every week Aiden met with his teacher to go over his weekly data chart. The first week he often forgot to do the extra reading, and his bar graphs did not reach the forty-five-minute line. The second and third weeks showed some improvement, but many days he still fell short of his goal. At the end of the first month, the pie graph showed that he was usually not meeting his goal.

8. Reevaluate Strategies

At the one-month check, Aiden and his teacher realized they needed better strategies. Aiden was carrying a book with him in his backpack, but he was often reluctant to bring it out and read it in front of others, even at home. His teacher scheduled a parent conference to tell his parents about the goal he was working on, and why he wanted to improve his reading. His father was surprised to learn that Aiden wanted to become a better reader so he could share his own love of cars. After the parent conference he started praising his son when he saw him reading. He also sat with him for an hour every Saturday morning and read magazines with him, helping him with words he didn't know, instead of watching television or playing video games all morning. Getting his father on board with the plan was one of the most important pieces supporting Aiden's success. His reading confidence and skill grew as he spent more and more time reading outside of school. The more he read magazines with his father, the less his father had to help him. Aiden had achieved his goal of being able to read *Popular Mechanics* and *Car and Driver* and to understand what he was reading.

9. Maintain

Even though he had reached his personal goal, Aiden's teacher knew that if he stopped reading he might lose ground. They continued to meet monthly to go over his pie charts and to discuss the books and magazines he had read during the previous month. His father continued to share his magazines with Aiden, and even when they didn't read them together, they would discuss the articles they had both read. For his birthday his parents gave him a *Total Bicycle Repair and Maintenance* magazine subscription, and he eagerly read each issue from cover to cover. Aiden had established a reading habit which would help him continue to increase his reading comprehension skills beyond his immediate goal.

ACT IV, Scene Fourteen Summary

In Scene Fourteen we've explored ways to put the power of behavior change solutions into your students' hands with self-management programs. The goals your students choose need to be both achievable and meaningful. Self-monitoring, manipulating antecedents, and arranging consequences can be used with other strategies to promote success. The steps in developing a self-management program include (1) deciding to engage in self-management, (2) defining the target behavior to be increased or decreased, (3) setting goals, (4) self-monitoring progress toward those goals, (5) hypothesizing the function of the problem behavior through functional assessment if needed, (6) implementing strategies, (7) evaluating behavior change, (8) reevaluating strategies if needed, and (9) maintaining the improved behavior. We read examples of how our five students might use some or all of these components to help them take charge of their own behaviors at whatever level was achievable for each of them.

In ACT V we'll look at ways to generalize behaviors to different settings and with different people and new materials, as well as how to maintain the improved behavior over time.

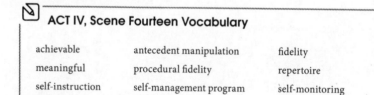

ACT IV, Scene Fourteen Vocabulary

achievable	antecedent manipulation	fidelity
meaningful	procedural fidelity	repertoire
self-instruction	self-management program	self-monitoring
self-praise	self-talk	social support

ACT IV, Scene Fourteen Discussion Topic

In your discussion group, share examples of self-talk, including both self-instruction and self-praise. Have you used these strategies yourself? Have your students used them? What results have you noticed? Discuss what makes for successful use of this strategy, and when it may become counter-productive (as with an internal self-critic). How can you change negative or toxic self-talk into constructive, supportive self-talk?

ACT IV, Scene Fourteen Questions

1. A successful self-management goal
    A. must be achievable.
    B. must always include punishment when goals are not met.
    C. must be meaningful to the student.
    D. Both A and C.
    E. All of the above.

2. Strategies which can support a successful self-management program include:
    A. Antecedent manipulation to support the program.
    B. Arranging consequences.
    C. Both A and B.
    D. Neither A nor B.

3. Scene Fourteen discusses how the following strategy or strategies support self-management programs:
    A. Social networking.
    B. Social support.
    C. Both A and B.
    D. Neither A nor B.

4. Self-talk is an effective strategy for self-management programs.
    TRUE or FALSE?

5. Self-instruction and self-praise are two ways of saying the same thing.
    TRUE or FALSE?

6. Teachers should always select the goals for students' self-management programs because they have better perspective. TRUE or FALSE?

7. Self-management goals do not always need to be relevant to students' preference if they strongly reflect and support the teacher's need for a well-managed classroom. TRUE or FALSE?

8. It is important for all self-management goals to be achievable. TRUE or FALSE?

9. Steps for a self-management program include:
    A. Deciding to engage in self-management.
    B. Defining the target behavior for self-management.
    C. Setting goals which are both meaningful and achievable.
    D. All of the above.

10. Additional steps for a self-management program include:
    A. Self-monitoring.
    B. Conducting a functional assessment if needed.
    C. Choosing appropriate strategies.
    D. All of the above.

11. More steps for a self-management program include:
    A. Conduct an ecological assessment.
    B. Evaluate change in behavior.
    C. Evaluate peers' response to student's changed behavior.
    D. All of the above.

12. Still more steps for a self-management program:
    A. Reevaluate strategies if needed after evaluating behavior change.
    B. Implement maintenance strategies.
    C. Both A and B.
    D. Neither A nor B.

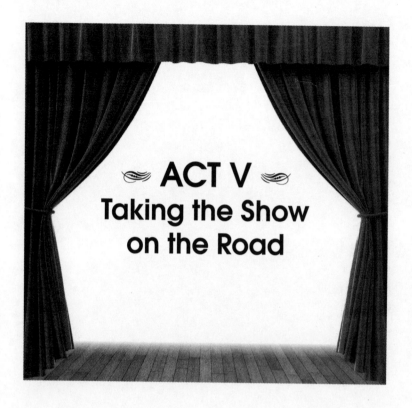

~ ACT V ~
Taking the Show
on the Road

The greatest sign of success for a teacher ... is to be able to say, "The children are now working as if I did not exist."

~ Maria Montessori

Let us remember: One book, one pen, one child, and one teacher can change the world.

~ Malala Yousafzai

Scene Fifteen

Generalization: Different Stages, New Audiences

By now you may be pleased with the success your students are showing in their classroom with you. But what happens when there is a substitute teacher? Or when they go to another classroom? Or when something else is changed about the environment they are used to? For many students on the spectrum, changes like these lead to a return to behaviors you thought had already been managed. It's time to talk about *generalization*.

Generalization is described by Miltenberger as "a process in which the behavior occurs in the presence of antecedent stimuli that are similar in some way to the discriminative stimulus present when the behavior was reinforced" (Miltenberger, 2012). This means that your students who learned behavior in one place, with certain people and materials present, can demonstrate the same behavior in a new place with different people and materials. Teaching them to do this is sometimes called *transfer training* (Kearney 2015).

Three Ways to Generalize

There are three ways that our students need to generalize their learning. Generalization across materials means learning to work and maintain the good behavior they have learned with different props or learning tools. Generalization across people means keeping up the same good behavior with a new teacher or aide or a substitute teacher. Finally, generalization across places means carrying over what they have learned and their new behaviors into different classrooms, other places on campus, at home, and in the community.

Generalization across Materials

Most of us like to work with the tools we're most familiar with. Give us a new smart phone or computer operating system and we are thrown for a loop until we figure it out. Our ASD students are even more attached to the familiar than we are; dealing with something as simple as the difference between a photocopied page and a page in a workbook may make a huge difference to them. If they have always figured out simple addition and subtraction problems using small, plastic counting bears and a teacher asks them to count with plastic cubes, they may become unable to answer 2 + 2. When confronted with the unfamiliar, responses may range from confusion and a "slow down" of work while they process the change, all the way up to a full-blown "fight, flight or freeze" reaction.

In order to help your students become comfortable with many different materials, include *programming common stimuli* (planning familiar materials). This just means purposefully using similar, but not identical, materials when planning your lessons. If you have a math learning center with small plastic manipulatives for counting, be sure to change them often, rotating through counting bears, blocks, beans or any other small objects. If you notice that a child always reaches for the green crayon at every coloring opportunity, one day give him a box with no green to encourage him to get used to using another color. If you usually present a lecture while writing key points on the white board, try using an overhead projector sometimes, or make a slideshow presentation on the computer instead. Look for ways to change the materials your students use so that they may become familiar with a wide range of learning tools.

Planning for change by programming common stimuli will help your students feel safe and comfortable, and they will behave accordingly when they leave your classroom and encounter different learning materials.

Generalization across People

"Generalization across people" simply means becoming accustomed to working with different people instead of only performing well with you and you alone. If you are fortunate enough to have classroom aides, volunteers, interns, or student teachers, the presence of other adults in the room will help your students with this. Even if you do not have these luxuries, you can find ways to allow your students to interact with other adults.

If your young students have learned to look at you and say, "Good morning," "Hello," or "Good-bye," they can learn to greet other adults at school in the same way. Plan to take them on a tour of the office, school library, and/or cafeteria (but not during the lunch rush). First practice greetings in the classroom with you and with each other, playing various roles. After they're comfortable in the familiar setting they will be ready to go on the road, greeting others the same way they learned to greet their teacher and classmates.

With older students, provide opportunities to send them on errands to other classrooms or to the office, library, or cafeteria. (Plan this in advance to make sure they will be welcomed.) Invite the principal or other school personnel into your classroom for an interview or short presentation on what their job is, so your students can get used to seeing and talking with them. In the future, if they get sent to the office for any reason, it will be less frightening or stressful if they have already met these new adults in the safety of their own classroom.

Many students with autism have their most difficult days when there is a substitute teacher. Of course, when you know in advance that you must be absent you have time to prepare them, but that is not always possible.

For younger children, having a Social Story™ that you read aloud periodically through the year can be very helpful. Here is an example:

> In room thirty-two, our teacher is Ms. Brown. Most days Ms. Brown is here when we come to school in the morning. She does not live at the school, she works here. After school when she finishes her work, Ms. Brown goes to her home. Sometimes, Ms. Brown can't come to school. Maybe she is sick, or maybe she has to go to a meeting. If she cannot be here, another teacher will come instead. This is our substitute teacher. Having a substitute teacher is different, but that's okay. The rules are the same, and we try to work just like we do with Ms. Brown. We can learn and have a good day with a substitute teacher. When Ms. Brown comes back, she will be happy we did good work with the substitute teacher.

Social Stories™ such as this may be personalized for your classroom (Gray, 2015).

For older students, a social article or narrative may be more appropriate. Here is an example of a *social narrative* for older students:

> Usually Mr. Green is at school on weekdays. Occasionally he may be absent due to illness, meetings, or other unavoidable reasons. When this happens we will have a substitute teacher, also called a "sub." When we have a sub, the rules and expectations remain the same. The sub will write a note to Mr. Green at the end of the day, letting him know how the day went. It will be helpful if we all try to do our best work and treat the sub and other students with respect. When Mr. Green comes back to school, he will be pleased to learn that we have been respectful, worked hard, and followed the rules in his absence.

Generalization across Settings

One of the biggest challenges to generalization comes when our students must leave the familiar classroom and go into other settings. They may be meeting all of their behavior goals until the day comes that they are invited to story time in the school library, or to join another history class to watch a video about your topic of study. Suddenly, it seems all the work you have done was for nothing. The little angel who sits "crisscross applesauce" on your carpet is crawling around under the library tables. Your star pupil is rocking back and forth, hands over his ears, and humming loudly throughout the history video.

So what happened?

These students had not generalized their behaviors to different settings. There are a number of ways a teacher can prepare students for success outside of the classroom.

In the case of the first student, the teacher could take her class on a visit to the school library before the story time and have them practice sitting on the carpet. In this setting she could re-read a Social Story™ she used when they were first learning to sit quietly on the carpet in her classroom. In addition, if students sit on individual carpet squares on the rug in her room, they could bring the familiar squares with them to the new carpet. The teacher, story, and carpet squares would be the same; only the room itself would change. This makes it easier for her students to remember their best story time behavior. Another time their teacher might take them to the library again, read one story, and then invite the librarian to read another story. The change is gradual, and eventually sitting "crisscross applesauce" on the library rug while the librarian reads will be just as natural as sitting in their own classroom.

The second student may have been reacting to sensory stimulation overload in a noisy mainstream classroom. Visit the room in advance and determine if the room is particularly loud as compared to the classroom he's familiar with. Is there a fan, a buzzing fluorescent light, or a higher level of classroom noise such as shuffling feet and papers and side conversations among students? How high will the volume be set on the video? Your student might do better seated at the back. Wearing ear buds (not plugged in to a device) may partially block out extraneous noise without interfering with his ability to hear the video. A short visit to the mainstream classroom prior to the date of the video will help the student, and you may be able to tell what could potentially bother him in the new setting. Preparing in advance for the differences of a new learning environment will help your students with autism be more comfortable and show off their best behavior.

Seven Ways You Can Promote Generalization

There are a number of things teachers can do to help students generalize their newly-learned behaviors when using new materials, working with new people, and going out to new places. Here are some ideas based on Miltenberger's seven strategies (Miltenberger 2012).

1. Applause, Applause – Reinforce it When You See it

I am sure you have often heard the expression "catch them being good." It may be a cliché, but it's a good one. Science shows that reinforcing a behavior results in an increase of the behavior. Any time you see your student engaging in the new, improved behavior—especially when the behavior occurs in different settings and with different people—be sure to reinforce it with praise and with tokens if you are using a token economy. Reinforcing the behavior you want is the best way to see that behavior repeated.

2. Rehearse – Train the Skills They Need to Succeed

Practice, practice, practice. You need to give them opportunities to experience success time and time again, with unfamiliar materials, new people, and in different places.

3. Advertise – Make Sure the Improvement gets Noticed

We want our students to contact reinforcement wherever they go, so their desired behaviors will continue to increase and their undesirable behaviors to decrease. When your student has learned a new skill in your classroom, let their other teachers know to be on the lookout for it. When adults notice and praise the behavior in other settings, this promotes generalization. But don't assume the other teachers will do this automatically; they may not notice your student raising their hand in a sea of other raised hands unless you have told them this is a behavior you are trying to develop in new settings. This goes for parents, too; let them know about the new, improved behavior you see at school, and ask them to praise it when they see it at home. When all the adults in the child's life know about the behavior plan, they can all become partners in improvement.

4. Improv – Help Them Be Ready for Anything

Improvisation, or "*improv*," is a skill that actors use to be ready for anything unexpected that happens on stage. They may know their lines perfectly, but they'll be in trouble if they can't come up with something to say if someone else forgets their lines, the telephone fails to ring on cue, or a dog unexpectedly runs across the stage. In the same way, your students need to be able to improvise and "go with the flow" when something unexpected happens in the middle of their classroom performance. Practicing improvisation techniques can be helpful for our students on the spectrum who are particularly inflexible. Some teachers of young children do this by providing only part of what is needed, to encourage students to reach out to an adult for help. They may provide coloring pages at a work station with no crayons or pencils, or puzzle frames with no puzzle pieces. The students must bring the "mistake" to the adult's attention.

Other teachers play a game of "Change-It-Up" (see appendix). They give each student a toy, book, or other learning material to use, but each time the bell rings they must pass their object to the student on their left and take a new one from the student on their right. Being forced to stop doing something and switch to something else is a difficult thing for many of our students to be comfortable with, so be sure to offer frequent praise and reinforcement every time they must switch activities.

Older or more capable students may act out improv games, such as role playing and then having new information added, forcing them to adjust. ("Pretend you are a farmer feeding your chickens. Now pretend there is a dinosaur in the group of chickens, and it's trying to eat all the corn. What do you do?") Any activity you can use to help your students get more comfortable with change will support them when they must transition to something completely different.

5. Prop Box – Take the Props Along When You Go on the Road

Just as Dumbo needed his "magic" feather to feel confident in his ability to fly at first, your students may benefit from having a familiar object to take with them into new situations. The young child in a new story time setting can feel more at home if she's sitting on the same carpet square she sits on in her own classroom. An older child might prefer to bring his own favorite pencil, or a keychain that helps him focus when he holds or fidgets with it. A child who feels anxious about being away from parents may want a small picture of them in his pocket at school. As long as it is used as a helpful tool and not a distracting toy, any familiar object can help a student feel more comfortable in an unfamiliar setting.

6. Ad Lib – Help Them Learn to Communicate Flexibly

Knowing our lines—what to say in any given situation—helps us all feel confident. Practicing stock phrases such as "Hello, friends," "Help, please," and "Can I play?" can help our students when they are first learning to communicate. However, if they continue to always say the same thing in the same way, it can be off-putting. Typically, people use a variety of greetings, such as "Hi," "Good morning," "How are you?" "Hey," or "Hello." If your student learned to sing out "Hello, friends," every morning when he walked in to preschool, his teachers and parents probably thought it was adorable. If he's still saying it in second grade, the other kids might find it weird. How do they greet each other on the playground? Listen, and teach your student to use a wide range of the phrases that their typical peers use naturally.

Be sure to teach the difference between greeting a peer or an adult authority figure such as the principal. Different types of language are needed for each. The sixth-grade boy who says "Good afternoon," and offers to shake hands with his classmates every morning may find himself the object of teasing, or worse. By the same token, "Wassup?" is not usually considered an appropriate way to greet the school principal, depending on the principal. Being able to use language flexibly with different people and in different situations is a valuable skill.

7. "Break a Leg" – and Other Good Luck Charms

The phrase "break a leg" is a common show business greeting, meant to counteract a theatrical superstition that wishing someone good luck is bad luck. Your students may have a superstition or good-luck charm that can help them remember to practice their new, improved behavior. For some, it is a card with a picture of a favorite character or hero and an encouraging phrase like "Wonder Woman always tries her hardest, and I can, too," or "Albert Einstein was smart to use his words instead of fighting. I can be smart like him." Be sure the character chosen is a particular favorite of your student, and not just someone that many children admire. This should be personal and meaningful.

Examples of Generalization

Let's take a look at how our five students worked on generalizing their newly learned behavior to other settings and situations.

Example One: Can Anthony Learn Not to Act Out with Other People?

Anthony's behavior is improving, and he responds well to his teacher. Unfortunately, he has not generalized his improved behavior across people. The last time there was a substitute teacher, he had such a bad day that his mother was called to pick him up and he missed half a day of school. She has offered to keep him home next time there will be a substitute, but Anthony's teacher refused the offer. She explained that Anthony should not lose even a day of his legally-guaranteed *free and appropriate public education (FAPE)* because of his behavior. Now his teacher has started programming (or planning) for generalization across people by helping him get used to different staff members. Although he prefers to have his teacher help him when he raises his hand, she has asked her aide to get there first to help him as often as she can, and to praise and reinforce him when he works well with her. She also introduced a Social Story™ about substitute teachers and reads it to the class at least once a week. Prior to a planned absence, knowing she would be going to a teachers' conference, she began reading it daily and asking comprehension questions about the story. She also had an afternoon of pretending to be a substitute teacher, greeting her students wearing a wig and a nametag that read "MS. SUB." This was a fun activity for the class, and it gave her students a chance to rehearse how they would behave when they had a substitute teacher. Ms. Sub read the class books such as *Mishmash and the Substitute Teacher* by Molly Cone, *Pete the Cat and the Surprise Teacher* by James Dean, and *Miss Nelson is Missing!* by Harry Allard: all books about of substitute teacher experiences. These activities helped her class (and especially Anthony) rehearse how they would behave with a substitute teacher. In addition, Anthony was given a card with a picture of his favorite dinosaur, a stegosaurus, to keep with him. The card says, "Stegosaurs keep calm when things change. I can, too." He looked at it often when he started to feel stressed, and practiced taking slow breaths while counting each of the stegosaur's back plates. After Anthony's teacher came back from her absence, she was sure to praise and reinforce all the good behaviors the substitute told her about.

Example Two: Can Destiny Learn Not to Disrupt in Other Settings?

Destiny responded very well to the strategies her teacher used to decrease her talking out and disrupting the class in the small class setting. During the second half of the school year, however, the fourth grade instituted a rotational system between teachers so that all students moved to a different class and teacher for one period each morning. Unfortunately, Destiny immediately reverted to her previous practice of shouting out answers and challenging and arguing with her new teacher. She was pulled from the rotation while her teacher worked on helping Destiny generalize her newly learned appropriate behaviors to a different fourth grade classroom.

The first thing Destiny's teacher did was to share with the other teacher all the strides Destiny had made in her behavior. She had to advertise so the other teacher would know what to look for. She also had to tell the other teacher that she had learned to avoid arguing with Destiny by refusing to respond or give her an opening. Instead, she shared how she used nonverbal references to the rules without engaging her. Just as important was learning to notice and reinforce the times Destiny did raise her hand before answering a question. Finally, Destiny's teacher told her new teacher about the stick-drawing process of ensuring that everyone had an equal opportunity to answer questions without raising hands. Because the other teacher was interested in doing this in her own classroom, Destiny's teacher helped her make a stick cup and box similar to the one Destiny was used to. This would serve as a familiar prop to remind her to wait her turn. Destiny's teacher also looked around at how the other teacher's classroom was set up, and adopted a few of the other teacher's practices and cues for her own classroom. For example, the other teacher had colorful posters reminding students to raise their hands and be respectful, so Destiny's teacher copied the same posters and put them on her own walls. In these ways she programmed common stimuli, or planned for things (stimuli) to be similar between the two rooms.

Finally, Destiny was allowed to bring the small plastic hand her teacher had given to her in her pocket as a "lucky charm" to remind her to raise her hand when appropriate. As long as she did not play with the object, she could keep it in her pocket or lay it on her desk.

By making the situation in the two classrooms as similar as possible, her teacher was helping her generalize across settings. It is hoped that generalization will continue in other settings, for example, if Destiny listens quietly without engaging the speaker during an all-school assembly. It may even transfer outside of the school setting if she stops interrupting her Sunday school teacher.

Example Three: Can Daniel Use New Materials Without Becoming Defiant?

Daniel has been working on reducing his defiant behaviors, and his teacher is pleased. It helped when she realized he truly did not understand some of the problems and that he was embarrassed. He didn't want to admit that he didn't know how to do work that he saw his classmates doing with ease. Now that she has modified the grade level of his assignments to match his independent ability level, his teacher wants to introduce different ways of using new materials so he can learn to improvise without losing his cool. In the beginning, every page he was given included only problems that were presented vertically: the way he had learned to add and subtract. The next step was to present a page alternating pairs of the same problem presented vertically and horizontally. The answer would be the same, no matter how the problem was oriented on the page. After he became comfortable with this, she mixed them up so that they were not in pairs. Later, she introduced word problems in the same way: first she would present $\begin{smallmatrix}2\\+3\end{smallmatrix}$ vertically, followed by 2 + 3 = _____ presented horizontally, immediately followed by a word problem of the same sum, for example, "A computer technician repairs two laptop computers, and then repairs three electronic tablets. How many did the technician repair in all?" Again, after presenting all of the ways to show the same problem grouped together, his teacher began mixing up the problems on the page. In this way she helped him learn to improvise and adapt to new presentations, so that when he meets with different kinds of problems in the future he will be less likely to shut down or become defiant, and more likely to try the new problems.

Example Four: How Can Sophia Generalize Behavior to Other Settings?

At first, Sophia learned to hand an aide a picture icon card to request books or coloring materials (instead of biting her hand) after she had finished her task at the work centers. However, during other times of the day, such as circle time on the carpet, she still sometimes bit her hand. Because there was no other activity to request during circle time, the picture icon she used successfully in centers was not appropriate. After observations and interviews, the behavior analyst noticed that she only bit her hand during the story portion of circle time. During the music activities, Sophia took her hand out of her mouth and bounced up and down to the music. It was hypothesized that she may be biting her hand out of boredom when not engaged with the story being read. One change that was made was to move her to the front, closer to the teacher, in an effort to increase her engagement with the story by proximity. This allowed the adult to direct her gaze toward the pictures in the book when she started to put her hand to her mouth. In addition, after consulting with the occupational therapist (OT) a special fidget object was provided for Sophia to hold during stories. Its use was two-fold: first, it was intended to occupy her hands so that she would be less likely to put her hands to her mouth. In addition, it was made of non-toxic, food-grade plastic and was designed for individuals with oral sensory-seeking behaviors to chew. Each time Sophia started to bite her hand, she was prompted to bite on the object instead. Her teacher worked with the OT to find something with the correct level of hardness and shape to fit her needs. When they found one that was successful, they put it on a pendant she could wear around her neck as jewelry so that it would always be easily accessible. This helped Sophia generalize her non-SIB behavior from one setting to another.

Example Five: Can Aiden Eliminate Aggression in Other Settings?

Aiden effectively eliminated his aggressive behaviors in the classroom setting through the use of the strategies described in previous scenes. The changes his principal made on the playground helped reduce bullying on the playground, which reduced referrals based on Aiden reacting aggressively to bullying attempts. However, he was still getting in trouble on the bus before and after school. There were three students who had previously bullied him on the playground on the same bus. These students would quietly make comments intended to be threatening or demeaning, and then they would watch Aiden explode. They played innocent and denied that they had any part in his reaction, which resulted in Aiden getting blamed for "blowing up for no reason," while the instigators went unpunished.

Aiden eventually felt comfortable telling an adult what was going on. His teacher obtained permission for a staff member to ride the bus with Aiden for a week, for the purpose of documenting what was happening. The first two days, no incidents occurred, but after the presence of the observer had become normalized the students began behaving as usual again. She noticed the quiet comments they made to Aiden, as well as noting where the students sat and at what point during the ride the bullying behavior occurred. This gave Aiden's teacher and behavior specialist the information they needed to come up with a plan for the bus.

The first part of the plan involved preferential seating, allowing Aiden to sit at the front of the bus near the driver. This was not to punish him but to allow the driver to hear if anyone threatened or belittled him. It reduced the instances of Aiden getting in trouble for outbursts without the others involved being implicated. Although Aiden could not escape the consequences of his aggressive outbursts, it was fair to also provide consequences to students who targeted him and planned to trigger his outbursts. In the meantime, Aiden was taught some stock phrases to use when responding to bullies. During sessions with his behavior specialist or teacher he practiced holding his head high and looking as if he were unaffected by their words, then delivering a neutral response such as, "So?" before turning his back on them. If they persisted and he felt that he needed assistance, he learned to say, "Please stop saying those things," in a loud, firm voice, but not a shout. The driver was alerted that if he heard Aiden say this, he knew the other boys were bothering him and he could instruct them to be quiet, or move them to a different seat farther from Aiden. Aiden rehearsed different ways of saying these things in one-on-one sessions first until he was comfortable enough to ad lib responses in his own words. These strategies helped Aiden to generalize his improved behavior from the classroom and playground to the bus.

ACT V, Scene Fifteen Summary

In Scene Fifteen we learned how to help students generalize their newly established, desirable behaviors with new people, in different places, and using unfamiliar materials. The seven ways you can promote generalization include:

1. Applause, Applause – Reinforce it When You See It
2. Rehearse – Train the Skills They Need to Succeed
3. Advertise – Make Sure the Improvement Gets Noticed
4. Improv – Help Them Be Ready for Anything
5. Prop Box – Take the Props Along When You Go on the Road
6. Ad Lib – Help Them Learn to be Flexible when Needed

In Scene Sixteen we'll look at maintenance, or how to maintain the desired behavior over time.

 ACT V, Scene Fifteen Vocabulary

ad lib	generalization
improv / improvisation	program common stimuli
social narrative	transfer training

 ACT V, Scene Fifteen Discussion Topic

In pairs, brainstorm various ways to program common stimuli for students who will be moving from one learning environment to another. Share your top three ideas with the rest of the group.

▣ ACT V, Scene Fifteen Questions

1. How can you ensure that your special education student's newly learned desirable behavior will contact reinforcement in the general education classroom?
   - A. Let other adults who work with the student know about the new, improved behavior the student has learned (or let them know that they are working hard to decrease the problem behavior).
   - B. Ask the general education teacher to be on the lookout for the new behavior and to praise the student when they see it in their room.
   - C. Both A and B.
   - D. Neither A nor B. This is a trick question, because behaviors do not contact reinforcement in general education settings, only in special education settings.

2. What are some strategies for supporting generalization?
   - A. Reinforce the desired behavior.
   - B. Practice the desired behavior.
   - C. Tell others who work with the student about the new behavior.
   - D. All of the above.

3. What are some other strategies for supporting generalization?
   - A. Practice flexibility.
   - B. Punish inflexibility.
   - C. Use objects as physical reminders for the new behavior.
   - D. Both A and C.

4. Which of these may be useful when helping students generalize behaviors?
   - A. Having a card with the student's favorite cartoon character and an encouraging phrase to take to the new classroom.
   - B. Using similar materials in the special education classroom that are used in the general education classroom.
   - C. Teaching a child how to ask for help in many different ways, so they can be flexible in their new classroom.
   - D. All of the above.

Scene Sixteen

Maintenance: Keeping It Fresh, Show After Show

Once we've succeeded in changing a behavior, we need a plan to help the new, improved behavior continue over time, even after we gradually phase out the supports we put in place to establish the behavior. You and your student have worked hard to make these behavior changes, and the last thing you want to do is to just drop everything that got you here without a plan.

This is where *maintenance* comes in: maintaining the student's new behavior into the future. *Response maintenance* occurs when the student continues to respond in the desired way after the intervention has been withdrawn. Maybe you don't want to keep using a time-consuming token economy with lots of reinforcers once your student is performing successfully in all arenas. You're understandably tired, and you wish you had a "break" card you could play.

But be careful. If you suddenly drop all reinforcers, your students may rebel and revert to previous behaviors. If you want to maintain the progress you have made, you need to carefully plan how you will reduce or withdraw the interventions.

Fading

We can reduce interventions while continuing to promote maintenance of behavior over time through *fading*. Fading is the gradual removal of interventions as the behavior continues to occur in the presence of the discriminative stimulus (S^d). It may be in the form of *prompt fading* or *stimulus fading* or *reinforcement fading*.

Prompt Fading

Prompt fading occurs when the teacher gradually decreases the intensity, frequency, or completeness of a prompt which guided a student to make the correct response.

For example, when teaching a student to touch a picture card when the teacher says the name of the object pictured, the first time she physically guides the student's hand to the correct picture. Then she touches the student's hand to get the motion started, but doesn't guide the hand all the way to the correct picture. Later, she just barely touches the student's elbow with the verbal prompt. Finally, she will not need to touch the student at all when she asks him to touch a picture; the verbal prompt has become sufficient.

Another example is a teacher who engages in a "group write" activity when she first introduces paragraph writing. She presents the writing prompt, and the class comes up with ideas as a group under her guidance. She points out the types of sentences needed to answer the writing prompt question and elicits ideas from the class, writing them on the board. The students need only copy the paragraph that they wrote together on to their paper. Later, she discusses the ideas needed to respond to the writing prompt and writes the first topic sentence together as a group activity, after which each student finishes writing the paragraph independently.

Finally, she needs only provide a writing prompt and her students write their own paragraphs.

In each of the examples above, the teacher has faded the prompt, initially giving a lot of support so that their students experienced success, and gradually pulling back the level of support until their students performed the tasks independently.

Stimulus Fading

Stimulus fading is when a physical stimulus which has been used to support the correct behavior is gradually made smaller or less intrusive.

One example is in the case of a young child who frequently wandered out of the classroom during free choice time. At first, her teacher placed a traffic cone in front of the door with a large STOP sign on top of it at approximately the child's eye level. This stimulus was fairly intrusive, but the teacher felt that it was necessary because of the potential danger of elopement (wandering out of the classroom). The class had been studying the word "stop" and practicing stopping when the teacher held up the sign, so the girl understood the concept. Blocking the door with the cone and STOP sign effectively stopped her from wandering out of the classroom. Later, the teacher made the STOP sign smaller, and it continued to be effective. Finally, the traffic cone was removed and the smaller STOP sign placed directly on the door. The teacher felt it was appropriate to remain at this level without removing the sign altogether, because having the stop sign permanently on the door was effective and not intrusive. It also reminded other students that when they line up to go to recess, they must stop there until the teacher opens the door to dismiss them.

A teacher who was teaching her young students how to print the letters of the alphabet first gave them pages where the letters were written in bold print and asked them to trace over the letters. Later, the letters were written in different colors of highlighter starting from the darkest color, blue, to the palest, yellow, and her students traced the letters even as they became lighter and lighter. Then the letters were presented in dashed lines to trace, followed by dots to connect to form the letters. The final step was to simply place a dot at the point on the page where each letter was to start (top, middle, or bottom line depending on the letter) and the students wrote the letters independently. Eventually, no dots at all were needed and they wrote their letters independently. Their teacher had systematically faded the prompts until they were successful without them.

Another example is a resource teacher who wanted her students to answer comprehension questions after reading a chapter in their social studies textbook. At first, she gave them photocopies of the text material and highlighted each question and the sentence in the text that answered the question. Later, she only made a small mark beside the paragraph that included the answer to the question in the corresponding color. Next, instead of highlighted photocopies, she had them read the text out of the book and gave them a notes sheet that listed the paragraph number where the answer could be found next to each question. As they continued to be successful, she reduced the physical prompts until she had only to tell them the section to read and give them the questions, and her students were able to find the answers for themselves.

Reinforcement Fading

When teachers engage in reinforcement fading, they are decreasing the amount or frequency of reinforcement. When you first begin a new behavior change program, it is good to start with a *rich schedule of reinforcement*. This means reinforcing often and immediately.

Sometimes, with severe behaviors, a schedule of *continuous reinforcement* is recommended. This means providing reinforcement every single time the student engages in the behavior. Although it can be quick and effective in changing behavior, keeping up continuous reinforcement indefinitely is neither practical nor advisable.

Once the desired behavior is established it is time to start *thinning* the reinforcement schedule, or moving from continuous reinforcement to *partial reinforcement* or *intermittent reinforcement*. This means providing the reinforcement sometimes, but not always.

Schedules of Reinforcement

There are several types of reinforcement schedules, and whichever one you use may be thinned (reduced) once the behavior has been established. These include fixed ratio (FR), variable ratio (VR), fixed interval (FI), and variable interval (VI) reinforcement schedules.

Fixed Ratio

Intermittent reinforcement may be based on a *ratio schedule* of how often the student engages in a desired behavior, such as how many math problems are completed or how many pages are read. When it is always the same it is a *fixed ratio (FR)*, such as providing reinforcement after every fifth math problem (FR 5) or every third page read (FR 3). This is the simplest ratio to use, but that does not mean it is necessarily the most effective. When students know they will be reinforced after they complete exactly five math problems, they may rush through the first four without giving them much thought. They know that as soon as they reach five, they will get their reward and they can take a break. Fixed ratio reinforcement schedules can result in fast but sloppy work, followed by a slowdown after reinforcement.

Variable Ratio

A highly effective schedule is the *variable ratio (VR)* in which reinforcement is provided after an average number of occurrences within a range, but not always the same number. For instance, a "VR 5" schedule means a variable ratio with an average of five, which could be every second to eighth math problem completed, or after reading between three and seven pages. This schedule is very effective in maintaining behavior. It works for casinos: gamblers keep playing in hopes that their next push of a button could mean a big payoff, but they never know when it will be. A VR schedule provides high, steady response without a lag or slowdown after reinforcement. Students tend to keep working (and gamblers to keep playing) because they are looking forward to eventual reinforcement, but they don't know when it will come.

Fixed Interval

Reinforcement schedules are not always based on the number of behaviors but may be based on the amount of time a student spends in a desired behavior (such as working on an assignment or sitting quietly during a lecture) or not engaging in a problem behavior (such as throwing work materials, self-injuring, or whispering during a lecture). This kind of schedule is called an *interval schedule*. In an interval schedule you are measuring the amount of time, not the number of behaviors. A *fixed interval (FI)* schedule means the reinforcement is provided on a set time schedule, provided the student is engaging in the desired behavior (or not engaging in the problem behavior) at the moment when the time is up. With fixed interval, the teacher always provides reinforcement, if earned, after the same amount of time. For instance, every fifteen minutes a teacher might check the classroom, and if everyone is on task she gives the class a token toward their group reward goal. The downside of this happens when the students figure out her timetable. If they know she will give points every fifteen minutes they feel free to goof off for twelve or thirteen minutes, and then suddenly shape up and start working right before her regularly-scheduled check-in. FI is easier for a teacher to manage, but it is not effective if the students figure out the fixed interval ratio.

Variable Interval

An effective alternative to the fixed interval is a *variable interval (VI)* schedule. Reinforcement is provided somewhere within the timeframe, but not after the same number of minutes each time. A "VI 10" means the teacher will check the classroom and give a token on an average of every ten minutes, which could range from every five minutes to every fifteen minutes. The students never know exactly when the reinforcement will be available, so they need to keep working continuously until they get the token. Right after a token is given there is usually a slump when students know that it will be a while before the teacher will give them another token. The slump doesn't last too long, though, when students are unsure of when the reinforcement is coming.

Examples of Maintenance Strategies

Let's look at how our five students respond to maintenance strategies to keep up their new behavior patterns over time.

Example One: How Can Anthony Maintain His Good Behavior?

Anthony's teacher was happy that he had improved his behavior significantly, with no more "acting out" incidents. In addition, he was behaving well for substitute teachers and in other classrooms and situations. Now she wanted to start decreasing the amount of time she was spending on his reinforcement system.

Anthony worked well using the "Steggo Star-Us" token economy chart to earn stars on the stegosaur's back plates, resulting in the privilege of washing the classroom's toy dinosaurs. At first his teacher went to his desk frequently to give him stars, and she found that he was earning the privilege to wash the dinosaurs every day. She felt the amount of time he spent at the sink could be spent more productively, once his acting-out behaviors were under control. She wanted to reduce his time away from work through reinforcement fading.

First, she found a new picture of a stegosaurus that had more plates on its back, so that it would take longer to fill in the plates with stars. The new picture was less "cartoon-like" and more realistic, which Anthony appreciated.

At the same time, she decreased the frequency of checking on him and giving him stars using "VI 10," a variable interval with an average of ten minutes between check-ins. She continued to offer praise along with the stars. This was an effective first step in thinning his reinforcement schedule. He was no longer washing the dinosaurs every day, which meant more time on task. Still, his teacher felt reinforcement could be further reduced without sacrificing progress.

Toward that end, she added a new step to earning the privilege. She cut a picture of a dinosaur into three large puzzle pieces. Each time Anthony finished a "Steggo Star-Us" page, he got one of the puzzle pieces to glue onto a paper. When he had all three pieces, he earned the privilege of washing the dinosaurs.

Over time, she cut the dinosaur pictures into more, smaller pieces so that it took even longer for him to earn the privilege. She also offered other privileges he might choose instead of washing the dinosaurs, such as being first in line for recess, which did not impinge on his instructional minutes.

Anthony's teacher knew it was worth giving up some time away from academics at first to address the behavior concern; the outbursts, if ignored, could become worse and lead to much more instructional time lost. Once the behavior was under control, however, she wanted to gradually get back to a reinforcement plan that would not take him out of class.

The variable interval (VI) reinforcement schedule was effective for Anthony, because it continued to feature his favorite dinosaur. Even though he had to earn more stars to fill in the many plates on the new picture, he was happy to have a novel and more realistic dinosaur picture to work with. Also, even though the addition of the puzzle pieces meant a longer time before he earned the dinosaur-washing privilege, he loved puzzles and was happy to accept this intermediate step.

All these changes were introduced gradually, one change at a time, so that he had an easy time adjusting to each transition and his good behavior was maintained throughout the year. At the end of the year, his teacher met with Anthony's new teacher to share with him the techniques and strategies that had been effective in first grade so that there could be a smooth transition with carry-over of familiar pictures and puzzles. The next teacher did not have toy dinosaurs in his classroom that Anthony could wash; however, his current teacher suggested that if Anthony showed exemplary behavior throughout a month or grading period, they could arrange for him to visit her classroom during recess to wash the dinosaurs for her as a rare and special reward.

Example Two: How Can Destiny Maintain Her Non-Disruptive Behavior?

When she first started working with Destiny on remembering not to interrupt, Destiny's teacher gave frequent prompts. Later, she wanted to fade the prompts so that they would become subtler and less intrusive.

Here is the hierarchy of prompts that Destiny's teacher used, from most to least prompts.

Prompt-Fading Hierarchy:

First (maximum prompt)

1. Point to the chart on the wall with the classroom rules.
2. Say, "You are interrupting. Rule four says, 'No interrupting.' Please wait your turn to talk."

Second (fading prompt)

1. Point to the rules chart.
2. Say, "Rule four, no interrupting," while holding up four fingers and giving no eye contact to Destiny.

Third (minimal prompt)

1. Point to the rules chart.
2. Hold up four fingers, no verbalization, no eye contact, ignore Destiny's interruption.

Destiny's teacher also wanted to use stimulus fading with Destiny. At first, she gave Destiny a large sticky note with a reminder, "Raise your hand," written on the note. She also gave her a plastic hand toy that she could hold to remind her to raise her hand. These things were somewhat intrusive, so she decided to use stimulus fading.

Here is how she did it, from most intrusive to least intrusive stimuli.

Stimulus Fading Hierarchy:

First (most intrusive stimulus):

1. 3"x5" sticky note with "Remember to raise your hand."
2. Plastic toy hand to hold during group lessons when she was most likely to interrupt.

Second (fading stimulus):

1. 2"x2" sticky note with "Raise your hand," when the first note fell off.
2. Plastic toy hand only available if she asked for it and she did not use it as a toy.

Third (least intrusive stimulus, to be faded completely eventually):

1. Tiny sticky flag with the word "hand," which was not replaced when it finally fell off her desk.
2. Plastic toy hand only used when transitioning to a different classroom.

By using both prompt fading and stimulus fading, Destiny's teacher helped her maintain her improved behavior over time. Her teacher continued drawing name sticks to determine who would answer a question, as this was beneficial to the entire class and was neither time consuming nor effortful.

Example Three: How Can Daniel Maintain His Non-Defiant Behavior?

Daniel has shown great improvement in reducing his defiant outbursts and work refusal. Now his teacher would like to spend less time on the token economy system, but she still wants to reward him for completing his work. She decides on two things: fading the token economy and at the same time reinforcing work completion using a variable ratio (VR) schedule of reinforcement.

Here are her plans for fading out the token economy.

Token Economy-Fading Hierarchy

1. Daniel's teacher switched from providing tokens for requesting help appropriately to reinforcing problems completed. He could still ask for help when needed, but did not receive a paper clip on his folder unless he had completed a set number of problems.
2. Daniel's teacher began increasing the number of problems that he needed to complete to earn a paper clip. She made this a challenge, asking him, "How many problems do you think you can finish before I come back to check on you?" Based on his response, she praised him for his positive attitude, for his hard work, and for his finished problems.

3. Daniel's teacher had told the class at the start that the items and privileges available for exchange, as well as the prices, would change periodically. This way Daniel would not be surprised by the changes when she began thinning the reinforcement. She separated the "Trade One/Toss One" privilege (see appendix) into two separate items to be purchased, "Trade One" and "Toss One," and raised the price on popular items and anything that took time away from class.

In addition, Daniel's teacher wanted to reinforce his work completion using a variable ratio reinforcement schedule, where she would give him a paper clip after every eight to twelve problems that he completed—an average of every ten problems (VR 10).

Even though the token economy system was faded so that it required less of the teacher's time and less class time, the "VR 10" reinforcement schedule helped Daniel maintain his improved work habits and attitude through the year.

Example Four: How Can Sophia Maintain Behaviors Replacing SIB?

At first, Sophia required significant physical prompting to engage in the behavior of handing an icon card to an adult to request a desired item instead of biting her hand. She generally made no attempt until the aide placed the card in her hand and physically guided her hand for her. Her teacher wanted to reduce her prompt dependency and fade the hand-over-hand guidance that the aides had been providing. Sophia's teacher scheduled a training session with her classroom aides to go over the prompt fading schedule. Using full physical prompting or *"motoring"* Sophia through the task was quicker and easier for the aides. However, the teacher wanted her staff to understand that while it might feel helpful and practical to do it for her, Sophia needed to learn to communicate on her own without an adult prompting her to request what she needed.

The teacher presented the prompt-fading steps in a staff meeting, she modeled how to do the steps, and finally had her staff practice with her or each other before they used the prompt-fading hierarchy with Sophia. She also requested formal training for her staff in the picture exchange communication system (PECS).

Here is the hierarchy they used, starting with full physical guidance (hand-over-hand motoring) and gradually reducing the physical prompts so that Sophia was doing more on her own.

Prompt-Fading Hierarchy

First (full physical guidance):

Staff had already been using a full, physical motoring assist: placing their hand on Sophia's hand, helping her hold the icon in her limp fingers, and moving her hand with the icon to the aide who would receive it. This was often the same aide who was prompting her unless they had two staff members at her center. The aide would then give Sophia the item pictured on the icon. During this exchange Sophia did not look at the aide or at the icon, and did not appear to notice that her hand was being moved with an icon in it. This was not helping her learn to make an exchange independently.

Second (fading physical prompt):

Staff began using the steps they had learned in their picture exchange communication system (PECS) training for phase one. The objective is, "Upon seeing a 'highly preferred' item, the student will pick up a picture of the item, reach toward the trainer, and release the picture into the trainer's hand," (PECS Manual). Rather than just placing the icon in her hand and then giving her whatever free choice item was available at that center, they put one of her favorite objects, a number puzzle, near her and waited for her to notice it and reach for it. They went through the PECS procedures of the fully assisted exchange, then faded physical assistance while still providing an outstretched hand to receive the icon, and eventually fading the open hand cue.

By fading the physical prompting they had been using with Sophia systematically following the guidelines provided in their PECS training, Sophia's teacher and aides helped her learn to initiate a request on her own using picture icons. Communicating with picture icons was an important, *pivotal* skill that would carry over to many situations. Sophia maintained her ability to communicate in this way without engaging in self-injurious behaviors.

Example Five: How Can Aiden Maintain His Non-Aggressive Behavior?

Aiden had been successfully keeping out of trouble for several months, and his teacher wanted to fade some of the interventions without losing the progress he had made. She decided to continue the behavioral contract and keep the job of tricycle mechanic because it was socially reinforcing for him and benefited the preschool. His aggression had become a thing of the past, because the bullying problem had been addressed schoolwide and because of his strong desire to maintain his job as tricycle mechanic.

His teacher also wanted to continue the class-wide token economy, which has been successful for everyone and also supported math, economic, life skills, goals, and standards. Each week the store items were somewhat different, so her students were not surprised by changes. However, she had been spending her own money on items for the classroom store, and she wanted to fade this kind of reinforcement. First, she significantly raised the price on each item she had paid for with her own money. She rotated them each week so that some items were unavailable one week but were back the following week. She also included more and more privileges that the students enjoyed but that cost her nothing, such as being able to move their desk to a better spot, empty the trash can, help set up and clean up playground materials or PE equipment, "Toss One" or "Trade One" homework privileges (see appendix), or to choose which game the class would play on Friday afternoon (if earned).

She found that the students worked harder to earn the privileges, and the items she had purchased became less popular. She was able to effectively fade the costly reinforcement items in favor of the privileges.

Aiden's self-management program to increase his reading had maintenance built in. Initially, his teacher checked on his progress daily to make sure he knew how to record the data of how much he had read. Then, they only met once a week. As he became more and more proficient at keeping his own data and charts, and as she noticed his motivation to read material related to his interest in cars and bikes, they switched to monthly meetings to share his progress. In each case it was a fixed interval (FI) schedule, fading from a fixed one time per day, to one time per week, to one time per month. When he was able to comfortably read his father's *Car and Driver* and *Popular Mechanics* magazines and understand what he was reading, Aiden eventually told his teacher he had met his goal and didn't need to continue with the charts. His improved reading accuracy and comprehension were reflected in his end-of-the-year academic testing.

ACT V, Scene Sixteen Summary

In Scene Sixteen, we learned a number of ways to maintain behavior over time while decreasing the intensity of the interventions which brought about the improved behavior. Maintenance strategies include fading, such as prompt fading (reducing prompts from most to least), stimulus fading (making stimuli less intrusive), and reinforcement fading (thinning the schedule of reinforcement). There are four reinforcement schedules we can use, which may then be thinned or ultimately eliminated. Fixed ratio (FR) means providing reinforcement after the behavior has occurred a specific number of times. With FR, students may work fast but not very accurately and produce sloppy work, followed by a work slowdown immediately after reinforcement. Variable ratio (VR) means providing reinforcement after an average number of times the behavior occurs, but not at the same time. With VR, students tend to work steadily and there is rarely a slowdown after reinforcement since they aren't sure how much they need to do be reinforced again. Fixed Interval (FI) means reinforcing after the same amount of time, and variable interval (VI) means after an average number of minutes, which varies. FI is easier for teachers, but students can figure out when they need to be good, be off task for most of the interval, and suddenly shape up right before the interval is up. With VI, students don't know when the teacher will provide reinforcement, so they tend to be on their best behavior throughout the period. Any or all of these strategies may be part of a successful behavior maintenance plan.

In Their Own Words

"Knowing that I have a learning disorder hasn't really affected me. I live a normal life and do normal things. One benefit of having Asperger's is that I'm very creative. Ever since I was a little kid, I loved building things with wood. Because my grandpa also loved to build things, he and I would do little projects about whatever my mind was thinking.

"When I was nine, I joined 4-H. Of course, because I loved being creative and building things, I signed up for the woodworking project. Being in woodworking was amazing. I loved building the little things like bird houses, foot stools, a microscope box, and a little book case.

"My dream when I started was to eventually build a desk, and during my fourth year of woodworking, I decided to take a huge risk and go for it. Now this desk was a dream, and I wanted to enter it in the county fair. When I told my woodworking teacher, Mr. Mahacek, about my idea, he and I were ready to tackle the project. We thought it was going to be a short job, but it wasn't finished until a week before the fair. We planned the desk for a week before we started to buy wood and supplies for this big project. We started cutting wood, measuring, and seeing what would look good. Halfway into building the desk, we had finished the two sides that would house my printer, laptop, and other stuff. By late May, we were staining and finishing the desk. I stained the desk, drilled the holes for my cords, and did final touches to it. Eight long months later, my desk was finished. We brought it to the Merced County fairgrounds.

"The first night of the fair, we decided to go see how I did. My thought was that I was going to get second place. When we walked into the building, my desk was sitting in front of everyone else's projects. On the desk, I had three ribbons and one plaque. I had gotten Best in Show, Best in 4-H, First Place, and Best in Division. I never thought that I could have won that many ribbons. While I was taking pictures, people came up and asked me if I built it. They were amazed that a twelve-year-old built a humongous oak desk. The supervisor of the building came up to me and asked me if I was the one who made this desk. When I told her yes, she was amazed and congratulated me on my accomplishment.

"Building things is really fun. The year after I built the desk, I built a hutch for my desk, and that turned out amazing also. My woodworking teacher is really supportive of my ideas. He has done woodworking for many years and he told me that when he was my age, he had built a desk just like mine. Overall, this is a memory I will never forget!"

~ Aidan, Asperger's, identified in preschool

What Can We Learn from Aidan's Story?

Mentorship is an important aspect of success. One teacher, or one adult mentor, has the power to encourage and support students on the spectrum to follow their dreams. There is no limit to what they may accomplish. Believing in them, and helping them believe in themselves, is one of the most powerful things you can do as a teacher.

ACT V, Scene Sixteen Vocabulary

continuous reinforcement	fading
fixed interval (FI)	fixed ratio (FR)
intermittent reinforcement	interval schedule
maintenance	motoring
partial reinforcement	pivotal
prompt fading	ratio schedule
reinforcement fading	response maintenance
rich schedule of reinforcement	stimulus fading
thinning	variable interval (VI)
variable ratio (VR)	

ACT V, Scene Sixteen Discussion Topic

With a partner, choose one type of fading to discuss: prompt fading, stimulus fading, or reinforcement fading. Brainstorm ways it could be useful in your practice. Share your ideas with the rest of the group.

 ## ACT V, Scene Sixteen Questions

1. A teacher shows a preschooler how to wash her hands by (1) helping her turn on the water faucet hand-over-hand, (2) holding her hands under the water, (3) helping her squirt on the soap hand-over-hand, (4) co-washing and rinsing their hands together, (5) helping her get a paper towel hand-over-hand, and (6) co-drying hands together. Later, she goes through the first five steps and prompts the student to get the towel and dry her hands independently. Then, she goes through the first four steps and lets the student do the final two steps. The teacher continues to drop out later steps in the process until eventually the student is washing her hands independently. What is this an example of?

   A. Prompt fading.

   B. Reinforcement fading.

   C. Stimulus fading.

   D. None of the above.

2. A teacher reads a story with predictable, repeated phrases to her class. The first few times she comes to the repeated phrase she reads it all. Later, she says the first word or two of the repeated phrase and pauses to allow her students to fill in the rest. Later, she says the first sound of the first word. Then she stops each time she comes to that phrase and her students say the phrase independently. What is this an example of?

   A. Prompt fading.

   B. Reinforcement fading.

   C. Stimulus fading.

   D. None of the above.

3. A teacher gives her class points when she sees a few students working quietly and continues giving points as she sees other students start working, too. By the time the whole class is working quietly, she has added ten points to the group total. Later, she reduces the number of points she gives while they are getting down to work. Finally, she gives one point when she sees the first student working, and then stands at the board holding her marker ready while watching the class. She gives one more point when about half the class is working, then waits and watches again, marker in hand. When the entire class is working quietly, she adds one more point. She has reduced the number of points given from ten to three. What is this an example of?

   A. Prompt fading.

   B. Stimulus fading.

   C. Reinforcement fading.

   D. None of the above.

4. A teacher puts a star on a card for every fifth problem her student completes during math time. This is an example of which kind of reinforcement schedule?

   A. Fixed interval (FI).

   B. Fixed ratio (FR).

   C. Variable interval (VI).

   D. Variable ratio (VR).

5. A teacher gives points to his class approximately every fifteen minutes that they have been working quietly. Sometimes it is after around five minutes of work, sometimes around twenty minutes, and sometimes another length of time within that window. His students cannot predict when he will be checking and giving points, so they work steadily. What kind of reinforcement schedule is this an example of?

   A. Fixed interval (FI).

   B. Fixed ratio (FR).

   C. Variable interval (VI).

   D. Variable ratio (VR).

6. A teacher checks how well his students are working every ten minutes and puts a kernel of popcorn in a jar when the class is working quietly at the moment his alarm buzzes at ten-minute intervals. They often goof off for the first eight or nine minutes and then get busy. This is an example of which kind of reinforcement schedule?

   A. Fixed interval (FI).

   B. Fixed ratio (FR).

   C. Variable interval (VI).

   D. Variable ratio (VR).

7. A teacher walks around the room checking on her students as they work independently. When she passes by each student, she sometimes adds a tally to their point card for working independently. This might be after completing five problems, fifteen problems, or anything in between—but usually around ten problems. The number of problems varies on how quickly the students work and on how long it takes her to make her rounds and get back to a student again. This is an example of which kind of reinforcement schedule?

   A. Fixed interval (FI).

   B. Fixed ratio (FR).

   C. Variable interval (VI).

   D. Variable ratio (VR).

Epilogue

Summing it All Up

We've been through a lot with Anthony, Destiny, Daniel, Sophia and Aiden, haven't we?

We started out in ACT I learning the basics about autism, behavior, and the vocabulary we use in behavioral science.

In ACT II we learned about the behavioral A-B-Cs: antecedents, behaviors, and consequences. Antecedents, what happened before the behavior of concern, tell us a lot about the function of the behavior or the reasons behind it. We learned to look at and define behaviors clearly so that everyone is on the same page. We also learned how consequences, everything that happened right after the behavior, can make a difference in whether or not the behavior is likely to be repeated again in the future. Finally, we looked at some immediate interventions, or what we can do when the behavior happens again while we're still trying to get a plan in place.

In ACT III we learned how to set the stage for success through antecedent control procedures, or changing what happens beforehand to try to keep the behavior from occurring. We looked at ecological assessment, with our classroom and learning materials as the set and props for our students' performance. Staff training is vital to the success of any behavior change program; our students and aides are our cast and crew, and we need to be their director. Finally, we learned effective ways to provide cues, as a prompter feeds lines to an actor who forgets what to say or do.

In ACT IV, we went into detail about three evidence-based strategies that work to help us stage a smash hit rather than a flop. We learned how to pay the players with a token economy, how to make a deal with a behavioral contract, and how to empower our actors by teaching them self-management strategies.

Finally, in ACT V we learned how to generalize students' behaviors to take their show on the road into other classrooms and environments, and how to help our students maintain their improved behavior over time.

As you meet your own students and learn more about them and their unique behaviors and needs, think about which of these techniques, tips, and strategies might be most useful for each of them. I encourage you to follow your instincts and your knowledge of your students to develop a plan that will benefit them and help them meet their needs in an appropriate way.

Charles Dickens' Scrooge said of his old employer, Fezziwig: "He has the power to render us happy or unhappy; to make our service light or burdensome; a pleasure or a toil ... his power lies in words and looks; in things so slight and insignificant that it is impossible to add and count up ... The happiness he gives, is quite as great as if it cost a fortune." You have that same power in your own classroom, by your words and looks, by your positive attitude, and by understanding your students and their behavior. Use that awesome power with wisdom and with kindness.

Glossary

ABLESPLAIN when a non-disabled person explains a disability to the person who actually has the disability; while well-meant, it usually is perceived as patronizing, condescending, and unwelcome.

ABOLISHING OPERATION (AO) a type of *motivating operation (MO)* which makes the reinforcer less valuable, so students are not motivated to work for it. One example is *satiation*.

ACHIEVABLE within reach, possible.

AD LIB in show business, actors ad lib when they speak extemporaneously, without a script. When students learn to ad lib, they can communicate flexibly.

ANTECEDENT what happened before the behavior.

ANTECEDENT CONTROL PROCEDURES also called *antecedent manipulation*, things teachers can put into place in advance for the purpose of setting their students up for success.

ANTECEDENT MANIPULATION see *antecedent control procedures.*

AO see *abolishing operation.*

ASD see *autism spectrum disorder.*

ASPERGER'S DISORDER often used to describe an individual on the autism spectrum who has no deficits in cognition or language. Asperger's disorder was not included as a separate disability in the DSM-5; however, the term is still used informally in the United States, and in formal diagnoses in other countries such as the United Kingdom.

ASPERGER'S SYNDROME see *Asperger's disorder.* The preferred label for many who do not consider Asperger's to be a disorder.

AUDITORY information brought in via the ears, including speech and other sounds.

AUTISM SPECTRUM DISORDER (ASD) a disability characterized by deficits in social communication and interaction and restricted, repetitive patterns of behavior, interests, or activities.

AVERSIVE unpleasant, to be avoided.

BACKUP REINFORCERS *primary reinforcers*: things your students want which they can purchase by trading in the conditioned reinforcers (tokens) they earned in a token economy.

BCBA® see *Board Certified Behavior Analyst®.*

BSP see *behavior support plan.*

B. F. SKINNER Burrhus Frederic Skinner (1904-1990) was an American behaviorist and psychologist who is considered by many to be the father of modern behaviorism. Skinner created the operant conditioning theory, the idea that behavior could be determined by consequences which could make it more or less likely that the behavior would occur again.

BEHAVIOR human behavior is how people act in response to a stimulus or situation. It's what we do. (Note: If a rock can do it, it's not a behavior.)

BEHAVIORAL CONTRACT also called a *contingency contract*, a written statement of agreement to engage in a desired behavior or to refrain from engaging in an unwanted behavior, with contingencies stipulated as a consequence.

BEHAVIORAL DEFICIT a behavior that would be desirable to establish, or to increase in frequency, duration, or intensity.

BEHAVIORAL EXCESS a behavior that would be desirable to abolish, or to decrease in frequency, duration, or intensity.

BEHAVIOR SUPPORT PLAN (BSP) a plan developed by a student's IEP team after a behavioral assessment, designed to help increase positive behaviors and reduce or eliminate problematic behaviors.

BILATERAL CONTRACT also called a *two-party contract*, a behavioral contract between two people in which each person agrees to do something.

BOARD CERTIFIED BEHAVIOR ANALYST® (BCBA) a professional who has been certified by the Behavior Analysts Certification Board (BACB) to provide and supervise behavior analysis services.

BOOTLEG REINFORCERS reinforcers which students access without earning them.

CFR see *Code of Federal Regulations*.

CHOICE BOARD a way of visually presenting a student's choices, such as the reinforcer they will work for or what they can choose to do during recess/free time.

CODE OF FEDERAL REGULATIONS (CFR) the set of rules and regulations issued by the United States related to education.

COMMUNICATIVE INTENT the meaning behind the behavior, or what the student is trying to communicate through behavior.

CONDITIONED REINFORCER see *secondary reinforcer*; not valuable or desirable in and of itself, but it can be exchanged for *primary reinforcers*.

CONSEQUENCE what happens after a behavior.

CONTINGENCY CONTRACT see *behavioral contract*.

CONTINUOUS REINFORCEMENT a schedule of reinforcement in which the student is reinforced every time they engage in the target desirable behavior.

CONTRACT MANAGER the person who develops and oversees a behavioral or contingency contract.

COVERT BEHAVIOR see *private events*, not observable to other people.

DENSE SCHEDULE OF REINFORCEMENT see *rich schedule of reinforcement*.

DEPRIVATION the absence or lack of something, such as being deprived of a reinforcer.

DEVELOPMENTAL relating to development or growth, or occurring during the childhood years.

DIAGNOSTIC AND STATISTICAL MANUAL OF MENTAL DISORDERS, FIFTH EDITION (DSM-5) used by psychological and medical professionals to clinically diagnose conditions such as autism spectrum disorder.

DIFFERENTIAL REINFORCEMENT OF OTHER BEHAVIORS (DRO) a procedure whereby we reinforce a student for refraining from engaging in a problem behavior by reinforcing any other behavior.

DISCRIMINATIVE STIMULUS (S^D) a stimulus which is present when a particular behavior is likely to be reinforced. It is a cue or prompt that reinforcement is available.

DRO see *differential reinforcement of other behavior.*

DSM-5 see *Diagnostic and Statistical Manual of Mental Disorders, Fifth Edition (DSM-5)*

DURATION the length of time a behavior continues.

EBP see *evidence-based practice.*

ECOLOGICAL ASSESSMENT evaluating how a student functions in different settings.

ECOLOGY also called the classroom *environment*; includes the physical set up as well as a positive environment with supportive accommodations in place.

EF see *executive function.*

ELOPEMENT educationally, a student leaving the classroom or assigned area without permission.

ENVIRONMENT see *ecology.*

EO see *establishing operation.*

ESCALATE to increase rapidly, such as when a mild behavior escalates into a major meltdown.

ESTABLISHING OPERATION (EO) a type of *motivating operation (MO)* which makes a reinforcer more potent or valuable so that the student is more likely to work for it.

EVIDENCE-BASED PRACTICE (EBP) the practice of making decisions and choosing strategies and interventions based on real evidence, not just on our best guess.

EVOKE to call forth; a behavior or response can be evoked by stimuli.

EXCHANGE RATE in a token economy system, the exchange rate indicates how many conditioned reinforcers (tokens) are needed to earn each backup reinforcer (privilege or item for sale).

EXECUTIVE FUNCTION (EF) the set of mental skills needed for such tasks as organization, time management, and attending.

EXPRESSIVE conveying thoughts, ideas, or feelings. Expressive verbal language is speaking and expressive written language is writing.

EXTINCTION the process of reducing or eliminating a behavior by removing reinforcement.

EXTINCTION BURST when a behavior is no longer reinforced, it temporarily increases in frequency, duration, or intensity before it decreases. New behaviors and emotional reactions may also occur during an extinction burst.

EXTINGUISH when a behavior stops occurring after being put on extinction by withdrawing reinforcement, the behavior has been extinguished.

FA see *functional analysis.*

FBA see *functional behavioral assessment.*

FADING the process of gradually removing the interventions which had been effective in establishing a new behavior or eliminating a problem behavior.

FAPE see *free and appropriate public education.*

FERB see *functionally equivalent replacement behavior.*

FIDELITY refers to how faithfully the strategies or interventions are provided as planned; also called *procedural fidelity.*

FIDGET BASKET a basket, box, or tub filled with small items that students may fidget with if they need to keep their hands busy in order to pay attention.

FIGHT, FLIGHT, OR FREEZE to escape stress, students with autism may *fight* or have a meltdown, take *flight* by running away, or *freeze* and become unable to talk or even move.

FIXED INTERVAL (FI) reinforcement is provided for the first occurrence of the behavior after a set amount of time (*interval*), which is always the same (*fixed*). Characterized by slow responding, followed by a rush right before the interval and a slowdown after reinforcement.

FIXED RATIO (FR) reinforcement is provided after a set number of responses or a specific number of times the student engages in the desired behavior (*ratio*) and the number of responses needed does not change (*fixed*). Characterized by students rushing through and completing problems carelessly, perhaps incorrectly, so they can get their reinforcement.

FREE AND APPROPRIATE PUBLIC EDUCATION (FAPE) Section 504 of the Rehabilitation Act of 1973 provides rights to disabled individuals, including education. An appropriate public education means education services designed to meet the individual education needs of the qualifying disabled student, provided with nondisabled students to the maximum extent appropriate to the needs of the student with a disability.

FREQUENCY see *count*, the number of times the student engages in the behavior.

FUNCTION see *communicative intent*, the purpose or the reason behind the behavior.

FUNCTIONAL ANALYSIS (FA) usually conducted by a Board Certified Behavior Analyst® (BCBA), antecedents and consequences are systematically manipulated and data analyzed to determine a functional relationship between the environmental events and the behavior.

FUNCTIONAL BEHAVIORAL ASSESSMENT (FBA) often conducted by a school psychologist, examines the relationship between a behavior and the environment, antecedents, and consequences to determine the function of the behavior.

FUNCTIONALLY EQUIVALENT REPLACEMENT BEHAVIOR (FERB) a more acceptable behavior to replace the problem behavior which serves the same function for the student.

GENERALIZATION expanding the use of a newly learned behavior or transferring it to other, similar situations, also called *transfer training*.

GUSTATORY referring to the sense of taste.

HAND-OVER-HAND see *motoring*; a full physical prompt, guiding the child to engage in a behavior by placing the adult's hands over the child's hand and doing the task for/with the child.

ICON a small card with a picture on it often used on choice boards, visual schedules, or to communicate using a system such as the *picture exchange communication system (PECS)*. Note: the small picture card used in PECS is not called a "pec." It is an icon.

ID see *intellectual disability*.

IDEA see *Individuals with Disabilities Education Act*.

IGNORE to remove attention or fail to give attention, especially when a student is engaging in a behavior you don't want to encourage.

IMPROV (IMPROVISATION) in show business, an improv (short for improvisation) is when actors are given a situation to perform but no script to follow. In the classroom, students need to be flexible and improvise when they are faced with something new.

INCIDENTAL LEARNING opportunities to learn that come up naturally in the environment rather than in a planned lesson.

INDIVIDUALIZED EDUCATION PROGRAM (IEP) a legal document for students with disabilities who receive special education services. It includes present levels of performance, goals, and services provided by the school to help meet those goals.

INDIVIDUALS WITH DISABILITIES EDUCATION ACT (IDEA) legislation ensuring that students with disabilities are provided with *free appropriate public education (FAPE)* designed to meet their individual needs.

INTELLECTUAL DISABILITY (ID) formally mental retardation, a disability defined by significant deficits in cognitive ability and adaptive behavior or self-help skills.

INTENSITY magnitude or physical force of a behavior.

INTERMITTENT REINFORCEMENT also called *partial reinforcement*; a behavior is reinforced sometimes, but not every instance of the behavior will be reinforced.

INTERVAL SCHEDULE REINFORCEMENT is provided based on the amount of time which has passed; it may be a *fixed interval* schedule (after the same amount of time) or a *variable interval* schedule (varying around an average length of time but not always the same amount of time).

INTERVENTION an action, strategy, or technique employed which is intended to improve a situation, reduce a problem behavior, or establish a desirable behavior.

JOINT ATTENTION also called *shared attention*; occurs when two people are looking at, thinking about, or talking about the same thing, especially when one person nonverbally draws the other's attention to something by looking at it or pointing toward it.

LATENCY the amount of time between the stimulus and the response, or between the antecedent and the behavior.

MAINTENANCE continuation of a behavior over time, especially after the reinforcement has been faded.

MANIPULATIVES small objects that students use for hands-on learning.

MANNERISMS unusual body movements. Also called *stereotyped*, restricted, repetitive behaviors, or self-stimulatory behaviors (*stims* or *stimming*), often used to help the student relieve stress or self-regulate emotions.

MOTIVATING OPERATION (MO) changes the value of the reinforcer, making it either more or less reinforcing, see also *establishing operations (EO)* and *abolishing operations (AO)*.

MOTORING see *hand-over-hand*.

NEUROBIOLOGICAL related to the science of the living organism including function and growth, specific to the nervous system (which includes the brain). Autism spectrum disorder is considered a neurobiological disorder.

NEUROTYPICAL (NT) this is the way many people on the spectrum refer to those who do not have autism.

NT see *neurotypical*.

OBSERVABLE able to be seen, see also *overt*.

OCCUPATIONAL THERAPY / OCCUPATIONAL THERAPIST (OT) to help people develop, regain, or maintain meaningful activities or occupations. In the schools, an occupational therapist may help students perform tasks necessary for learning, such as holding a pencil to write, or cope with sensory integration challenges.

OLFACTORY related to the sense of smell.

ONE-PARTY CONTRACT also called a *unilateral behavioral contract*, this written agreement specifies only what the student will do and the consequences for engaging in the desired behavior or refraining from the problem behavior.

OT see *occupational therapy/occupational therapist*.

OVERT see *observable*.

PARALLEL CONTRACT a type of *bilateral* or *two-party behavioral contract* in which each party agrees to do something which is not necessarily related to or reinforced by the other party's agreement.

PARTIAL REINFORCEMENT see *intermittent reinforcement.*

PECS see *picture exchange communication system.*

VARIABLE RATIO (VR) a schedule of intermittent or partial reinforcement in which the reinforcement is delivered after an average number of times the behavior occurs, which varies. Characterized by a high level of responding with no significant slowdown after reinforcement.

PERMANENT PRODUCT a way to record behavior in which there is a durable product of the behavior, such as homework papers.

PICTURE EXCHANGE COMMUNICATION SYSTEM (PECS) an evidence-based, functional system of communication developed by Andy Bondy and Lori Frost which uses picture icons to help pre-verbal students communicate by exchanging an icon for the item or activity pictured on it. Learn more at www.pecsusa.com.

PIVOTAL behaviors which can open doors to successful functioning in many areas. Self-help skills, self-managing of behaviors, and functional communication are all pivotal behaviors. Once students are able to do these things, they will be better able to learn other related skills.

PLAN B when your daily schedule (Plan A) falls through, always have a Plan B ready.

PRIMARY REINFORCER something which is reinforcing in itself.

PROCEDURAL FIDELITY see *fidelity.*

PROGRAM COMMON STIMULI a strategy for helping students generalize behaviors across settings by programming or planning to use similar learning materials in both the familiar setting and the new setting.

PROMPT FADING the gradual removal of prompts after your student has started engaging in the behavior in response to the discriminative stimulus (S^d) or cue.

PROPRIOCEPTIVE one of the senses having to do with feelings of deep pressure in the muscles and joints.

PUNISHMENT behaviorally, the process in which a behavior is followed by a consequence that results in a decrease in the future probability of the behavior.

QUANTIFY to count or measure the quantity of something. We quantify observable behaviors by measuring the dimensions of *frequency, duration, intensity,* and *latency.*

QUID PRO QUO CONTRACT this is a two-party or bilateral behavioral contract in which both parties identify a target behavior to change and the behavior of each serves as reinforcement for the other.

QUIET ZONE a designated place where a student who is overwhelmed by stress or sensory overload may go to calm down and self-regulate.

RATIO SCHEDULE reinforcement is provided based on the number of responses, or how many times the student engages in the desired behavior.

RECEPTIVE receiving information. Receptive verbal language is listening, and receptive written language is reading.

REINFORCEMENT the process in which a behavior is followed by a consequence that results in an increase in the future probability of the behavior.

REINFORCEMENT FADING the gradual thinning or reducing of reinforcement after your student has started engaging in the behavior in response to the discriminative stimulus (S^d) or cue.

REINFORCER this is a stimulus, event, token, or reward that increases the future probability of the behavior following presentation of the reinforcer.

REINFORCING resulting in an increase in the behavior in the future.

REPERTOIRE the collection of behaviors that a person is able to do.

RESPONSE one occurrence of a behavior.

RESPONSE COST in a token economy, taking away tokens which have been earned due to engaging in problem behaviors. Not recommended.

RESPONSE EFFORT the degree of difficulty involved in a task or activity.

RESPONSE MAINTENANCE continuing to respond or behave as desired over time, rather than reverting to previous problem behaviors or responses.

RESTRICTED behaviors or interests which are repetitive, ritualized, circumscribed, or limited in range.

RICH SCHEDULE OF REINFORCEMENT also called a *dense schedule of reinforcement*, a schedule in which reinforcement is easy to obtain and is earned frequently.

ROCK TEST the author uses this to help determine whether something is a behavior. Can a rock do it? Then it's not a behavior. Being quiet is not a behavior because it fails the rock test; a rock can do it. Raising a hand before talking is a behavior because a rock can't do it. Many behaviorists use the "dead man's test" in the same way, that is, if a dead man can do it then it is not a behavior. The author prefers rocks.

RULE-GOVERNED behavior which is controlled by a verbal or written statement or rule.

SATIATION occurs when a student receives so much of a reinforcer that it is no longer reinforcing.

SDC see *special day class*.

SECONDARY REINFORCER see *conditioned reinforcer*.

SELF-INJURIOUS BEHAVIOR (SIB) purposeful self-harm such as biting, hitting, or scratching oneself. It does not include getting hurt accidentally.

SELF-INSTRUCTION a form of *self-talk* in which students repeat to themselves, either mentally or in a whisper, what it is that they are supposed to do.

SELF-MANAGEMENT PROGRAM a program designed to support students in changing their own behavior.

SELF-MONITORING the student keeps track of their own data, counting their own behaviors.

SELF-PRAISE a kind of *self-talk* in which students give themselves praise, such as whispering quietly, "That's good, I did it," or "That looks awesome."

SELF-TALK students talk to themselves, usually to give themselves feedback, instructions, or praise either by whispering or by mentally thinking the positive phrases.

SENSORY-AVOIDING BEHAVIORS behaviors that students engage in to avoid painful, uncomfortable, or stressful sensory experiences.

SENSORY CENTER a place dedicated to allowing students to relieve stress through sensory experiences.

SENSORY INTEGRATION describes how your students organize and process sensations from their environment or their own bodies. Many students with autism have unusual responses to typical sensory experiences.

SENSORY PROCESSING see *sensory integration.*

SENSORY-SEEKING BEHAVIORS behaviors used to arouse the nervous system by seeking out certain sensory experiences.

SETTING EVENT a kind of antecedent that is not controlled by others; it describes a state of being rather than an object or action, such as the state of being hungry, tired, sick, in pain, or afraid.

SHARED ENJOYMENT desire to interact with others just for the sake of making a connection and sharing an enjoyable experience with another person.

SIB see *self-injurious behavior.*

SLD see *specific learning disability.*

SLP see *speech and language pathologist.*

SOCIAL-EMOTIONAL RECIPROCITY a back-and-forth flow of social interaction.

SOCIAL ARTICLE a longer form of a Social Story™ better suited to older students.

SOCIAL NARRATIVE see *social article.*

SOCIAL STORY™ a concept devised by Carol Gray to model appropriate social interactions by describing situations, including others' perspectives, and suggesting appropriate responses to the situation in story form. Learn more at www.carolgraysocialstories.com

SOCIAL SUPPORT other people who are significant to the student provide praise and recognition when the student engages in the desired behavior.

SOCIALLY SIGNIFICANT behaviors that have immediate and long-term benefits for the student, not just for the teacher.

SPECIAL DAY CLASS Also called *SDC,* a special education setting where disabled students with an IEP may receive services for more than 50% of their school day.

SPECIFIC LEARNING DISABILITY Also called *SLD,* a disorder in one or more of the basic psychological processes (i.e., attention, auditory, cognitive, sensory-motor, or visual) adversely affecting a student's ability to listen, think, speak, read, write, spell, or do mathematical calculations.

SPECTRUM a range of different colors, as seen in a rainbow. Autism spectrum disorder (ASD) includes a range of many different behaviors.

SPEECH-LANGUAGE PATHOLOGIST (SLP) also called a speech and language therapist, a professional trained in communication including speech (how to make sounds) and language (how to put sounds together to communicate meaningfully).

STIMULUS (PLURAL STIMULI) an environmental event which can be detected through the senses; it stimulates or provokes a reaction or response of some kind.

STIMULUS FADING the gradual reduction of stimuli used to encourage a behavior after the student has started engaging in the behavior in response to the discriminative stimulus (S^d) or cue.

TACTILE sensory information provided by touch.

TARGET BEHAVIOR the behavior we want to change; either a desirable behavior to establish or increase, or a problematic behavior to reduce or eliminate.

THEORY OF MIND (TOM) described by Simon Baron-Cohen with Alan M. Leslie and Uta Frith, this refers to the ability to think about thinking, and to think about what other people might be thinking.

TOKEN is a *conditioned reinforcer* or *secondary reinforcer* used in a token economy which may be exchanged for a primary reinforcer such as privileges or items that the student values.

TOKEN BOARD a place where students can "token up" by putting a token on the board. When a given number of tokens have been placed on the board, students earn their reinforcement.

TOKEN ECONOMY a system of reinforcement in which students earn tokens (conditioned or secondary reinforcers) for engaging in the desired target behavior, or for refraining from a problem behavior. The tokens are later exchanged for primary reinforcers.

TOM see *theory of mind.*

TRANSFER TRAINING see *generalization*.

TRIGGER an informal term for stimuli or events that provoke or set off certain behaviors, see also *triggering event*.

TRIGGERING EVENT an event or stimulus that sets off a particular response or reaction.

TWO-PARTY CONTRACT see *bilateral contract*.

UNILATERAL CONTRACT see *one-party behavioral contract*.

VARIABLE INTERVAL (VI) reinforcement is provided after an average length of time, characterized by a steady, moderate rate of responding with no slowdown.

VARIABLE RATIO (VR) reinforcement is provided after an average number of responses, but not always the same number, characterized by a high steady rate of responding with no pause after reinforcement.

VERBAL BEHAVIOR communication which involves a receiver or listener, as well as a communicator. It includes talking, signing, gesturing, writing, exchanging picture icons, or pointing.

VESTIBULAR relating to the sense of balance.

VISUAL related to sight.

WEAK CENTRAL COHERENCE (WCC) a theory proposed by Francesca Happe and Uta Frith, suggesting that students with autism are often unable to see the "big picture" and focus on small, often unimportant details instead.

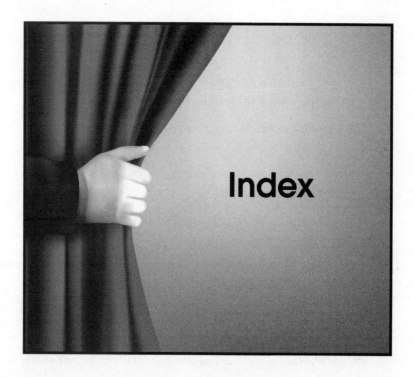

Index

Allard, H. G. (1977). *Miss Nelson is Missing!* New York, NY: Houghton Mifflin Company.

American Psychiatric Association. (2013). *Diagnostic and Statistical Manual of Mental Disorders (5th ed.).*

Attwood, T. (2007). *The Complete Guide to Asperger's Syndrome.* London: Jessica Kingsley Publishers.

Baer, D. M., M.M, Wolf, and T.R. Risley. (1968). "Some Current Dimensions of Applied Behavior Analysis." *Journal of Applied Behavior Analysis,* v1(1): 91-97.

Bailey, J. and M. Burch. (2006). *How to Think Like a Behavior Analyst: Understanding the Science That Can Change Your Life.* New York, NY: Routledge.

Baron-Cohen, S., A.M. Leslie, and U. Frith. (1985). "Does the Autistic Child Have a 'Theory of Mind'?" *Cognition,* 21: 37-46.

Bondy, A. and L. Frost. (2011). *A Picture's Worth: PECS and Other Visual Strategies in Autism*. Bethesda, MD: Woodbine House

Bossenmeyer, M. (2016). *Peaceful Playgrounds: Designed for Learning*. https://peacefulplaygrounds.com/peaceful-playgrounds-designed-for-learning/ .

Cone, M. (1963, 1991). *Mishmash and the Substitute Teacher*. New York, NY: Houghton Mifflin Company.

Cooper, J. O., T.E. Heron, and W.L. Heward. (2007). *Applied Behavior Analysis, Second Edition*. London: Pearson.

Dean, J. (2017). *Pete the Cat and the Surprise Teacher*. New York, NY: HarperCollins Children's Books, a division of HarperCollins Publishers.

Dickens, C. (1843). *A Christmas Carol in Prose, Being a Ghost-Story of Christmas*. London: Chapman & Hall.

Fouse, B. and M. Wheeler. (1997). *A Treasure Chest of Behavioral Strategies for Individuals with Autism*. Arlington, TX: Future Horizons, Inc.

Frost, L. and A. Bondy. (2002). *The Picture Exchange Communication System Training Manual, Second Edition*. New Castle, DE: Pyramid Educational Consultants, Inc.

Grandin, T. and S. Barron. (2005). *Unwritten Rules of Social Relationships: Decoding Social Mysteries Through the Unique Perspectives of Autism*. Arlington, TX: Future Horizons, Inc.

Gray, C. (2015). *The New Social Story™ Book, Revised and Expanded*. Arlington, TX: Future Horizons, Inc.

Happe, F. and U. Frith. (2006). "The Weak Central Coherence Account: Detail-Focused Cognitive Style in Autism Spectrum Disorders." *The Journal of Autism and Developmental Disorders*, 36 (1): 5-25.

Kearney, A. J. (2015). *Understanding Applied Behavior Analysis: An Introduction to ABA for Parents, Teachers, and Other Professionals, Second Edition.* London: Jessica Kingsley Publishers.

McAfee, J. L. (2002). *Navigating the Social World: A Curriculum for Individuals with Asperger's Syndrome, High Functioning Autism and Related Disorders.* Arlington, TX: Future Horizons, Inc.

Miltenberger, R. G. (2012). *Behavior Modification: Principles and Procedures, Fifth Edition,* Belmont, CA: Wadsworth Cengage Learning.

Notbohm, E. (2012). *Ten Things Every Child with Autism Wishes You Knew.* Arlington, TX: Future Horizons, Inc.

Notbohm, E. with V. Zysk. (2006). *Ten Things Your Student with Autism Wishes You Knew.* Arlington, TX: Future Horizons, Inc.

Shakespeare, W. (1603). *Hamlet, Prince of Denmark: A Tragedy in Five Acts.* First Quarto, London: Nicholas Ling and John Trundell.

Shore, S. (ed.). (2004). *Ask and Tell: Self-Advocacy and Disclosure for People on the Autism Spectrum.* Shawnee Mission, KS: Autism Asperger Publishing Co.

Skinner, B. F. (1971, 2002). *Beyond Freedom and Dignity.* Indianapolis, IN: Hackett Publishing Company, Inc.

Yacio, J. G. (2015) *Temple Did It, and I Can, Too! Seven Simple Life Rules.* Arlington, TX: Future Horizons, Inc.

Ylvisaker, M. with M. Hibbard and T. Feeney. (2006). *Transfer of Training or Generalization.* http://www.projectlearnet.org/tutorials/transfer_of_training_or_generalization.html

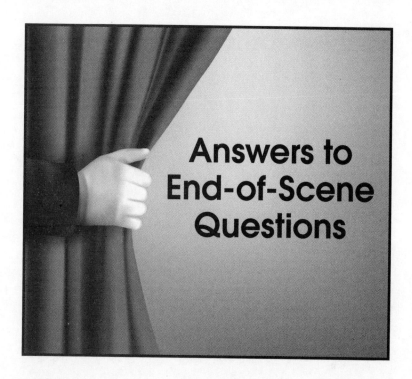

Answers to End-of-Scene Questions

Scene One

1. B
2. C
3. D
4. E
5. FALSE

Scene Two

1. A
2. B
3. latency
4. frequency
5. intensity
6. duration
7. excess
8. deficit
9. covert
10. overt

Scene Three

1. B
2. C
3. B
4. D

Scene Four

1. C
2. C
3. B
4. A
5. FALSE

Scene Five

1. D
2. NO
3. TRUE
4. setting event
5. antecedent
6. antecedent
7. setting events

Scene Six

1. B
2. NO ("Rudeness" is not defined.)
3. YES
4. NO (Neither the self-harm nor the stress are described.)
5. FALSE (The term *elopement* is a behavioral term to describe leaving an assigned area without permission, wandering off, or running away.)

Scene Seven

1. D
2. decreased (This surprised his teacher; however, because the student hates going out to recess, the consequence she hoped would increase his homework completion rate has had the opposite effect.)
3. increased
4. decreased
5. FALSE

Scene Eight

1. BAD IDEA
2. BAD IDEA
3. GOOD IDEA
4. BAD IDEA
5. GOOD IDEA

Scene Nine

1. FALSE
2. TRUE
3. TRUE
4. FALSE

Scene Ten

1. BAD IDEA
2. BAD IDEA
3. BAD IDEA
4. BAD IDEA
5. GOOD IDEA
6. GOOD IDEA

Scene Eleven

1. BAD IDEA (The teacher has made the desired behavior, presenting a break card, much more difficult than the student's current behavior of poking his eyes. She needs to reduce the response effort for the desirable behavior, not increase it.)
2. BAD IDEA (His students are satiated on candy, cookies and chips, so a box of raisins is not valuable or worth working for.)
3. TRUE
4. FALSE
5. TRUE

Scene Twelve

1. B
2. D
3. A
4. C
5. C

Scene Thirteen

1. FALSE
2. TRUE
3. FALSE
4. C
5. C
6. D
7. D
8. B

Scene Fourteen

1. D
2. C
3. B
4. TRUE
5. FALSE
6. FALSE
7. FALSE
8. TRUE
9. D
10. D
11. B
12. C

Scene Fifteen

1. C
2. D
3. C
4. D
5. D

Scene Sixteen

1. A
2. C
3. C
4. B
5. C
6. A
7. D

Hot Lava Balloon Toss Game

This game is not educational in any way, but may be used as a reward to be earned. It should be played in the last few minutes of the school day, because students will not calm down enough to get back to work after playing. Only play this if student desks are sturdy enough for students to safely sit on them.

Students sit (never stand!) on their desks, because the floor has become hot lava. The teacher blows up a balloon and tosses it out. Students must keep it in the air by hitting it upwards. If a balloon touches the floor, the teacher retrieves it to be launched again. If a student touches the floor, or stands on their desk or chair, they must sit on their chair rather than on their desk for the remainder of the game, although they can still hit a balloon if it comes to them. For larger classes or just for added excitement, the teacher might use multiple balloons.

Materials: round balloons, not too small. Other shapes of balloons do not lend themselves to being hit up into the air.

Change-It-Up!

This is a game to increase ability to transition flexibly from one task to another. Students are seated in a circle, or small squares of four students each. Each student is handed something to look at or use; it may be a book or a toy or some other object. Students play with or look at what they have been given until a signal lets them know it is time to "Change-It-Up!" Then each one hands their toy or book to the person on their left and gets a new one from the person on their right. Now they have a short time to look at the new object, until the next signal to switch.

This will be difficult for many students on the spectrum. It is hard to shift gears and transition to the next thing. That is why we are helping them strengthen that muscle by exercising it with this game. It may be a bit easier because they know a change is coming, so it is not unexpected. To make it even easier at first, consider using books or objects which are not too interesting, and don't make the time too short. Keep an eye on their engagement level. Also, choose a signal which is not too jarring. If you have several options, give them input on what signal they'd like to hear: a bell, a buzzer, a barking dog, etc. Gradually, you can increase the interest level of the items and decrease the amount of time they get to use each item. The ultimate goal is for them to be able to leave something they really like, such as the computer, and more easily move on to the next task or activity.

Materials: books, toys, or items of interest for students to look at.

Trade One / Toss One Homework Pass

This is a privilege which may be earned by students for engaging in appropriate behavior. It may be used as two separate rewards, "Trade One" or "Toss One," or it may be combined for a more valuable reward, "Trade One/Toss One."

"Trade One" means the student may choose one page from their homework packet for that week and trade it for an easier review page from the teacher's "Trade One" file.

"Toss One" means the student may choose one page from their homework packet and "toss" it (return it to the teacher). The teacher keeps the tossed and traded pages and re-introduces them into a future homework packet. It may be useful to put a dot on the corner of the page each time it is tossed. If the same page is tossed three times, re-evaluate it. Is it at the appropriate level for the student to successfully complete it independently? Is it longer than average, or is the font smaller than other pages? Why does it keep getting tossed?

Materials: a file of easy, review work that students may choose to trade a page for. Also keep tossed pages on file to return them to a future homework packet.

Promise Page

Here is an example of a blank Promise Page, and one filled in for Anthony:

PROMISE PAGE

1. I promise to _____

   _____

   _____

   signed: _____

2. I promise to _____

   _____

   _____

   signed: _____

PROMISE PAGE

1. I promise to write three sentences during Journal Writing every morning.

   signed: *Anthony*

2. I promise to stamp a star on Steggo Star-Us after Anthony writes three sentences every morning.

   signed: *Anthony's Teacher*

About the Author

Dr. Wendela Whitcomb Marsh, MA, BCBA, RSD, has been a special education teacher, school psychologist, autism specialist, speaker, writer, counselor, university instructor, and Board Certified Behavior Analyst®. She is the mother of two awesome individuals with autism, and was married for twenty-seven years to an amazing man with Asperger's syndrome. People on the spectrum, and the dedicated teachers who work with them, are among her favorite people in the world. Dr. Marsh lives in Salem, Oregon with her three children.

DID YOU LIKE THE BOOK?

Rate it and share your opinion.

amazon.com

BARNES & NOBLE
BOOKSELLERS
www.bn.com

Not what you expected? Tell us!

Most negative reviews occur when the book did not reach expectation. Did the description build any expectations that were not met? Let us know how we can do better.

Please drop us a line at *info@fhautism.com*.
Thank you so much for your support!

FUTURE HORIZONS INC.